SOUNDSCAPES FROM THE AMERICAS

In memoriam
Dr. Gerard Henri Béhague
(1937–2005)

Soundscapes from the Americas
Ethnomusicological Essays on the Power, Poetics, and Ontology of Performance

Edited by
DONNA A. BUCHANAN
University of Illinois, USA

LONDON AND NEW YORK

First published 2014 by Ashgate Publishing

Published 2016 by Routledge
2 Park Square, Milton Park, Abingdon, Oxon OX14 4RN
711 Third Avenue, New York, NY 10017, USA

First issued in paperback 2017

Routledge is an imprint of the Taylor & Francis Group, an informa business

Copyright © 2014 Donna A. Buchanan

Donna A. Buchanan has asserted her right under the Copyright, Designs and Patents Act, 1988, to be identified as the editor of this work.

Bach musicological font © Yo Tomita

All rights reserved. No part of this book may be reprinted or reproduced or utilised in any form or by any electronic, mechanical, or other means, now known or hereafter invented, including photocopying and recording, or in any information storage or retrieval system, without permission in writing from the publishers.

Notice:
Product or corporate names may be trademarks or registered trademarks, and are used only for identification and explanation without intent to infringe.

British Library Cataloguing in Publication Data
A catalogue record for this book is available from the British Library

The Library of Congress has cataloged the printed edition as follows:
Soundscapes from the Americas : ethnomusicological essays on the power, poetics, and ontology of performance / edited by Donna A. Buchanan.
    pages cm. — (SOAS musicology series)
  Includes bibliographical references and index.
  ISBN 978-1-4724-1583-7 (hardcover)
  1. Music—Social aspects—Latin America.
  2. Music—Latin America—History and criticism. I. Buchanan, Donna Anne.

  ML3917.L27S68 2014
  780.97—dc23

2013051046

ISBN 13: 978-1-138-06254-2 (pbk)
ISBN 13: 978-1-4724-1583-7 (hbk)

Contents

List of Figures	*vii*
List of Music Examples	*ix*
Notes on Contributors	*xi*
Foreword by Richard Bauman	*xiii*
Acknowledgments	*xv*

Introduction: Doing Ethnomusicology "Texas-Style": A
Musical (Re)Turn to Performance   1
Donna A. Buchanan

PART I: GENRES, HISTORIES, AND DISCOURSES OF POWER PERFORMED

1   The *Teatro Bufo*: Cuban Blackface Theater of the
Nineteenth Century   25
Robin Moore

2   *La Música Nacional*: A Metaphor for Contrasting Views of
Ecuadorian National Identity   43
Ketty Wong

3   Conserve, Adapt, and Reconverge: Rationalizing a Template in
Hawai'i Puerto Rican Musical Performance   61
Ted Solís

PART II: PERFORMING PRACTICE: STYLE AND THE POLITICS OF SUBJECTIVITY

4   Transformation in Communion: Toward an Aesthetic
of Improvisation   89
Tim Brace

5   Feminine Flowers among the Thistles: Gendered Boundaries of
Performance in Chilean *Canto a lo poeta*   101
Emily Pinkerton

PART III: SITUATED EVENTS AND PERFORMANCE POLITICS: FIESTA, FESTIVAL, STAGE, AND STREET

6   The Way of Sorrows: Performance, Experience, and the Moral
    Society in Northern Ecuador   127
    Michelle Wibbelsman

7   Performing Indigeneity: Poetics and Politics of Music Festivals in
    Highland Bolivia   143
    Thomas Solomon

References   *165*
Index   *185*

List of Figures

1.1   Víctor Patricio Landaluze, *The Kiss*, oil on canvas, ca. 1880.
Photo used by permission of the Museo Nacional de Bellas Artes,
Havana, Cuba.   30

2.1   Disc rack of *música nacional* in Almacenes Feraud Guzmán,
Guayaquil. Photo by Ketty Wong.   47

2.2   Los Conquistadores performing "El conejito" in the Coliseo Julio
César Hidalgo, 2002. Photo by Ketty Wong.   58

3.1   Charlie Vegas, plucked lead "violin-shape" modern *cuatro;* August
Rodrigues, strummed Spanish guitar; Ted Solís, *güiro.* Lawai
Valley, Kauai, Hawai'i, June 1990. Photo by Virginia Rodrigues.   70

3.2   Miguel Rodrigues, holding an ornate "old *cuatro,*" standing with
musician Tanilau Dias (1908–c.1994). Hilo, Hawai'i, July 1990.
Photo by Ted Solís.   71

3.3   Boy and His Family Troubadours, 1947. Joseph "Boy" Sedeño and
his brothers-in-law. Honolulu, Hawai'i. Photo gift of Joseph and
Maria Sedeño.   77

5.1   *Guitarrón* of Fidel Améstica made in the mid twentieth century.
Photo by Emily Pinkerton.   105

6.1   Presentation of the Stations of the Cross in Cotacachi by a troupe
of *mestizo* actors. Photo by Michelle Wibbelsman, 2001.   133

6.2   Indigenous catechists perform the Living Portraits of Christ in
Arrayanes. Photo by Michelle Wibbelsman, 2001.   135

7.1   Performers from the community of Jant'a Pallqa at a music festival
in the community of Irupata, June 1993. Photo by Thomas Solomon.   153

List of Music Examples

2.1 Typical triple-meter *pasillo* rhythmic accompaniment derived from the waltz. 50

2.2 "Manabí," composed in 1933 by Francisco Paredes Herrera; lyrics by Elías Cedeño. 51

2.3 "Pobre corazón" [Poor heart], composed in the late 1910s by Guillermo Garzón. 55

5.1 Standard *guitarrón* tuning in A. 106

5.2 *Entonación la común* in A, played by Alfonso Rubio. 106

5.3 *Entonación la común* in D, played by Myriam Arancibia (original key: C). 107

5.4 Standard male and female vocal ranges (left) compared with the melodic range of *la común* in D, C, A, and G (right). 109

Notes on Contributors

Tim Brace received his Ph.D. in Ethnomusicology from the University of Texas at Austin in 1992 with a dissertation on the modernization of music in contemporary China. A highly trained classical guitarist and composer with expertise in early music, rock music, and sacred music performance, Brace has written or arranged more than fifty works for classical guitar, and arranged or composed more than thirty choral anthems. His scholarly publications have appeared in *Asian Music* and the *Journal of Popular Music Studies*. He is employed by the University of Texas as Senior IT Manager for the Office of Admissions and remains active as an independent scholar.

Donna A. Buchanan is Associate Professor of Musicology and Anthropology at the University of Illinois, Urbana-Champaign. A specialist in the musical styles of Bulgaria, the Balkans, and the NIS (especially Russia, Armenia, and Georgia), Buchanan's scholarly interests include the implication of music in cosmology, acoustic ecologies, and relations of social power and identity. She is the author of *Performing Democracy: Bulgarian Music and Musicians in Transition* (University of Chicago Press, 2006) and an edited collection, *Balkan Popular Music and the Ottoman Ecumene: Music, Image, and Regional Political Discourse* (Scarecrow Press, 2007).

Robin Moore, Professor of Ethnomusicology at the University of Texas at Austin and editor of the *Latin American Music Review* (since 2005), is the author of *Nationalizing Blackness: Afrocubanismo and Artistic Revolution in Havana, 1920–1940* (University of Pittsburgh Press, 1998), *Music and Revolution: Cultural Change in Socialist Cuba* (University of California Press, 2006), and *Music of the Hispanic Caribbean* (Oxford University Press, 2009). The recipient of fellowships from the Rockefeller Foundation, the MacArthur Foundation, and the National Humanities Center, Moore's research interests include music and nationalism, music and race relations, popular music, and the aesthetics of socialist art.

Emily Pinkerton, a guitarist, banjoist, and singer-songwriter, is currently an ethnomusicology instructor at the University of Pittsburgh, as well as a touring artist. The recipient of a Fulbright grant and an award from the Organization of American States for her dissertation research on the 25-string Chilean *guitarrón*, Pinkerton has resided in South America for extended periods during the past fifteen years. A student of master Chilean musicians Alfonso Rubio and Osvaldo Ulloa, Dr. Pinkerton recently released her third album of original music blending North American folk song with South American *canto*.

Ted Solís, Professor of Ethnomusicology at Arizona State University, has conducted fieldwork in north India, Mexico, Hawai'i, and Puerto Rico. His research interests are equally eclectic, embracing the Hispanic Caribbean, dance, diasporic musics, improvisation, Javanese *gamelan*, the construction of ethnomusicological careers, and the pedagogy of ethnomusicology. He is the editor of *Performing Ethnomusicology: Teaching and Representation in World Musics* (University of California Press, 2004).

Thomas Solomon is Professor of Music at the Grieg Academy-Department of Music of the University of Bergen, Norway. The editor of two recent collections, *Music and Identity in Norway and Beyond: Essays Commemorating Edvard Grieg the Humanist* (Fagbokforlaget, 2011) and *Ethnomusicology in East Africa: Perspectives from Uganda and Beyond* (co-edited with Sylvia Nannyonga-Tamusuza; Fountain Publishers, 2012), Solomon's numerous scholarly publications focus on the acoustic ecology of the Andean highlands and Turkish popular music, his two primary areas of specialization.

Michelle Wibbelsman is Assistant Professor specializing in Latin American indigenous cultures, ethnographic studies, and ethnomusicology in the Department of Spanish and Portuguese at Ohio State University. She has also taught at St. Edward's University (Austin) and the University of Texas at Austin. She received her Ph.D. in Cultural Anthropology from the University of Illinois at Urbana-Champaign in 2004. She has conducted fieldwork in the Imbabura, Pichincha, and Cotopaxi provinces of Ecuador since 1995. Her first book, *Ritual Encounters: Otavalan Modern and Mythic Community* (University of Illinois Press, 2009), presents an ethnographic study of public festivals, history, myth, memory, and the aesthetics and politics of ritual performance. Her current research centers on indigenous transnational migration, diaspora, and cosmopolitanism.

Ketty Wong, a native of Ecuador, is Associate Professor of Ethnomusicology at the University of Kansas, where she has taught since 2006. The author of *Luis Humberto Salgado: Un Quijote de la Música* (2004) and co-author of *Corsino Durán: Un trabajador del pentagrama musical* (1993), her most recent book, *Whose National Music?: Identity, Mestizaje, and Migration in Ecuador* (Temple University Press, 2012), won the 2013 Latin American Studies Association Ecuadorian Studies Section book award. The Spanish version of the book received the Casa de las Americas Musicology Award in 2010.

Foreword

I'm pleased and honored to have been invited to contribute a few words to this Festschrift in memory of my late colleague, Gerard Béhague. Recalling Gerard also calls back fond memories of our time together at the University of Texas, that heady period from 1974 to 1986 (the year I left Austin for Bloomington) when we were engaged in creating what came to be recognized as a distinctively "Texas School" of performance-oriented research. As a student of verbal performance, I have always valued working in close proximity to ethnomusicologists, who keep us language-oriented folks open to other semiotic systems and enliven the aesthetic ambience of whatever spaces they inhabit.

In my memory of those effervescent days when the Texas School took shape, the fertile ground on which ethnomusicology and folklore came together was cultivated by stages. While all of the founding members of the folklore program were sometime musicians (Américo Paredes was a professional singer and guitarist from his young days on the Border and Roger Abrahams and I were '50s folkies), we didn't incorporate ethnomusicology into the mix until Marcia Herndon arrived in 1971 and persuaded us to change the name of our center from the Center for Intercultural Studies in Folklore and Oral History to the Center for Intercultural Studies in Folklore and Ethnomusicology. Still, it wasn't until Gerard joined the faculty of the School of Music in 1974 and established a formal program in ethnomusicology that things really took off. Now, for the first time, there were graduate students in ethnomusicology, an organized program of coursework, and a developing faculty, and the crossovers began to flourish. We hosted annual meetings, organized pathbreaking conferences, formed ensembles, maintained editorial offices for the flagship journals; we had parties (I have especially vivid memories of Marcia and Norma's luaus next door, with the aroma of roast pig wafting through the neighborhood), romances, even marriages that bound the programs together.

The affinities and convergences were powerful. Ideologically, we were all committed to a vision of our disciplines as fundamentally about the politics of culture, intellectual and academic bases for the cultivation of critical vantage points on social inequality and for the development of critical correctives to social and political problems. Intellectually, we were all principled transgressors of disciplinary boundaries, resistant to entrenched divisions of intellectual labor. Our common goal was to move our fields of study beyond the hegemony of high culture, elite connoisseurship, and the autonomy of the textual object. We viewed vernacular musical and verbal art forms and other symbolic enactments as resources for the accomplishment of social life and the intensification of experience, modes of display that linked the formal and the significant in crafted expressions and that were memorable, repeatable, durable, and reflexive. The whole project came together conceptually under the rubric of performance, the situated expressive practices that were constitutive of musical or verbal or ritual enactments; and methodologically under the aegis of ethnography, the empirical discovery and interpretation of the form, function, and meaning of expressive practice in the conduct of social life. Our primary unit of description and analysis was the performance event. What were its occasioning principles? Sites of occurrence? Forms of social organization? Communicative means? Orienting frameworks for the production and interpretation of expressive forms? At the same time, however, we were attuned to broader horizons beyond the temporal and spatial boundaries of the performance event: the role of vernacular culture in the cultivation of nationalism, the dynamics and generative force of political boundaries, social diversity, and differential identity.

Synthetic summaries like this one, though, are retrospective, maybe even tinged a bit with nostalgia. They iron out the dynamics of discovery that drove our work and energized our conversations. Gerard, in his Introduction to *Performance Practice*, generously acknowledged a debt to my ideas of performance, but the process of exploration was very much a two-way street. It was Gerard, for example, who introduced me to the notion of performance practice in historical musicology. He was rightly critical of the spurious quest for authenticity and the fetishization of period instruments that marks much of the musicological literature on performance practice, but together with those caveats, what I took away from our conversations and the readings to which they led me was the importance of attending to the material and embodied aspects of musical performance in relation to time and place, the radical interrelationship of technique and style. By the same token, it was Norma McLeod—my next-door neighbor for a time, as well as my colleague—who directed me to Milton Singer's writings on cultural performances, which have been of lasting usefulness to me in comprehending the social organization and reflexive complexity of such heightened display events.

In the end, though, the only basis on which it might matter even a little bit what we were up to in Austin thirty or forty years ago is whether the foundations we strove to construct were useful to our students and colleagues in carrying the dialogue forward. On this ground, there can be no disputing that Gerard Béhague's teaching, research, and administrative labors mattered a great deal. Evidence of his legacy and his influence lies in the moving tributes that marked his passing, the classrooms and writings of his students and colleagues in ethnomusicology, and, not least, in the pages that follow—all testimonials to an inspiring teacher, a valued mentor, a foundational scholar, and a great friend.

Richard Bauman
Bloomington, Indiana
June 18, 2013

Acknowledgments

I wish to express my most sincere gratitude to the volume's contributors for their unflagging enthusiasm for this project throughout its lengthy genesis and preparation. Their encouragement, congenial assistance, and endless patience with a flood of questions, correspondence, and drafts were essential to the book's completion. I am particularly grateful to Richard Bauman for agreeing to write the Foreword, to Cecilia Pareja Béhague for supplying the cover photograph, to Thomas Turino for his contribution to the volume's conceptualization in its earlier stages and collegial support throughout the writing process, to Emily Wuchner for her skillful preparation of the index, and to my spring 2013 graduate ethnomusicology seminar class (Performance & Performativity in Practice: Ethnomusicological Perspectives) for their animated, helpful commentary on an earlier draft of the manuscript and so many of the concepts it addresses. Very special thanks to Robin Moore for his assistance with various technical issues, to Laura Macy, Ashgate's Senior Commissioning Editor in Music Studies, for her expert advice, to Ashgate Senior Editor Pam Bertram, for her infinite patience and kind help with a multitude of typesetting queries, and to Ashgate's anonymous reader and the SOAS Musicology Series Board and its editor, Keith Howard, for their constructive criticism. Finally, I would like to acknowledge the cheerful support and caring concern of family and friends, especially Christina Bashford, Dana Haviland, Thomas Turino, my mother, Elizabeth Buchanan, and husband, Stuart Folse, which I deeply appreciate.

Introduction
Doing Ethnomusicology "Texas-Style": A Musical (Re)Turn to Performance

Donna A. Buchanan

... performance is a mode of language use, a way of speaking. The implication of such a concept for a theory of verbal art is this: it is no longer necessary to begin with artful texts, identified on independent formal grounds and then reinjected into situations of use, in order to conceptualize verbal art in communicative terms. Rather, in terms of the approach being developed here, performance becomes constitutive of the domain of verbal art as spoken communication.

Richard Bauman 1977:11

The ethnography of musical performance should bring to light the ways non-musical elements in a performance occasion or event influence the musical outcome of a performance. Practices of performance result from the relationship of content and context. To isolate the sound contents of a performance and call such an operation "Performance Practice" is no longer justifiable.

Gerard Béhague 1984a:7

... the basic stuff of social life is performance ...

Victor Turner 1987:81

Performance is a paradigm of process.

Richard Schechner 1987:8

[Performance:] A mode of communicative behavior and a type of communicative event. While the term may be employed in an aesthetically neutral sense to designate the actual conduct of communication (as opposed to the potential for communicative action), performance usually suggests an aesthetically marked and heightened mode of communication, framed in a special way and put on display for an audience. The analysis of performance—indeed, the very conduct of performance—highlights the social, cultural, and aesthetic dimensions of the communicative process.

Richard Bauman 1992:41

[Music] performance must be viewed as the occasion and event that fosters through social interaction and participation the collective consciousness and affirmation of group identity or ethnicity as well as significant differences in musical styles and contents of songs that may exist within the stratified structure of the social group. It functions as a driving, crystallizing force in the enacting display of a given social group's aesthetics, that is, the value systems that validate the group's ethos. In addition music performance partakes of the system of symbols that is at the basis of cultural expression and appears fully integrated within that expression. In sum the process of performance is a central facet of musical communication. It brings together the historical and ethnographic concern with music as the enactment of prescriptions, plans, scores by specific social actors, and the sociological and psychological concern with modes of social participation that validate, reflect upon, and animate the interpretation of musical texts, styles, and genres.

Gerard Béhague 1992:177

Performances are aesthetic practices—patterns of behavior, ways of speaking, manners of bodily comportment—whose repetitions situate actors in time and space, structuring individual and group identities. Insofar as performances are based upon repetitions, ... they are the generic means of tradition making ... play[ing] an essential (and often essentializing) role in the mediation and creation of social communities, whether organized around bonds of nationalism, ethnicity, class status, or gender .... To perform is to carry something into effect .... To study the performative dimensions of experience, then, is to interrogate the processes whereby different phenomena are enacted.

Deborah Kapchan 1995:479

Performance is an act of intervention, a method of resistance, a form of criticism, a way of revealing agency. Performance becomes public pedagogy when it uses the aesthetic, the performative, to foreground the intersection of politics, institutional sites, and embodied experience. In this way, performance is a form of agency, a way of bringing culture and the person into play.

Norman Denzin 2003:9, after Bryant K. Alexander

History and Homage

Readers familiar with the performance studies literature will recognize the title of this Introduction as an ethnomusicological spin on that of an earlier study: Richard Bauman and Roger D. Abrahams's introduction to their 1981 anthology, *"And Other Neighborly Names": Social Process and Cultural Image in Texas Folklore.*[1]

---

[1] My sincere gratitude to Richard Bauman, Thomas Solomon, Thomas Turino, and members of my 2013 graduate ethnomusicology seminar class at the University of Illinois for their helpful commentary on an earlier draft of this chapter. Heartfelt thanks also to Richard Bauman for allowing me to adapt his and Abrahams's essay title.

That book, like this one, pays tribute to the scholarly legacy of a particular mentor who, together with an eminent constellation of colleagues working with folklore, oral literature, and music in and around the state of Texas and its flagship university campus, helped catapult an ethnographically situated, socially engaged, interdisciplinary approach to performance to national prominence in the late twentieth century.[2]

And Other Neighborly Names (Bauman and Abrahams 2011) borrows its title from a landmark study by folklorist and distinguished University of Texas professor Américo Paredes, the volume's dedicatee, about the socio-political ramifications of names exchanged between Anglos and Mexicans across U.S.–Mexican cultural boundaries. In their prefatory statement, "Doing Folklore Texas-Style," Bauman and Abrahams acknowledge the contributions of their scholarly progenitors—the Lomax family (John, Alan, and Bess), Dorothy Scarborough, J. Frank Dobie, and especially, Paredes himself—to a folkloristics concerned ultimately with community power relations and social difference, particularly as evidenced in border or contact zones such as Texas, and communicating about

---

[2] For a particular time in the 1970s and early 1980s, the very distinguished scholarly pantheon at the University of Texas included Américo Paredes and Roger Abrahams, who held joint appointments in English and anthropology; folklorist Richard Bauman, linguistic anthropologist Joel Sherzer, anthropologist and Mexican-American studies expert José E. Limón, and anthropologist and Native American specialist Barbara Babcock in anthropology; anthropologist Beverly Stoeltje, whose work has focused on gender, nationalism, and ritual studies in western Africa and the American West, in English; and ethnomusicologist Norma McLeod in comparative studies, in addition to Marcia Herndon (on faculty from 1971 to 1978) and Béhague in ethnomusicology (1974–2005) (see Sawin 1984). Bauman and Sherzer were classmates at the University of Pennsylvania, where they studied with another important contributor to the genesis of performance ethnography, Dell Hymes. Linguistic anthropologist Greg Urban, whose scholarly interests include ritual wailing, ceremonial dialogues, and social discourse, also taught at Texas until 1994, when he moved to Pennsylvania. McLeod was Herndon's mentor at Tulane University, where Béhague also received his doctorate. Kristina Nelson joined the Texas ethnomusicology faculty in 1980 and taught there until 1983. Prior to arriving at Texas, Béhague taught at the University of Illinois, Urbana-Champaign (1966–74), my own current place of employment as well as that of Béhague's advisee (and my former classmate), Thomas Turino (now Emeritus). Volume contributor Ted Solís worked with Béhague during his Illinois years; all of the other contributors studied with him at Texas.

Paredes strongly encouraged the establishment of the Center for Intercultural Studies in Folklore and Ethnomusicology at Texas in 1967 (Hinojosa and Rodríguez n.d.); recently renamed the Américo Paredes Center for Cultural Studies, it now offers a graduate concentration in "Cultural Forms" under the auspices of anthropology. The program's curriculum is instructive in its performance ethnography focus, entailing "ethnographic approaches to performance, representation, visual culture, aesthetics, affect, space, and publics," particularly targeting "how people perform, produce, and project cultural forms through verbal, visual, musical, kinesthetic, material, and dramatic means" (see www. utexas.edu/cola/centers/culturalstudies).

these phenomena in a manner accessible to readers beyond the academy.[3] By observing lore performance "in its living place" (and as a living entity), the authors argue, and attending to "the interactional setting of display behavior" and "situated meaning of performance forms," social inequities and tensions are revealed and illuminated (1981:3, 6). Such a critical perspective targets performance occasions as potential dramatizations of difference and social dialectics, performers as creative agents in (and embodiments of) their enactment, and expressive media as embedding and articulating "real social questions" and power asymmetries (6–7).

The intellectual tail of this approach within and beyond performance studies has been formidable, prompting advancements in Mexican-American, Chicano/a, and Latin American studies; native ethnography and postcolonial anthropology; problematizations of border zones and boundaries, communities in contact and conflict, migration, and hybridity and subalterity; studies of ethnicity, nationalism, and gender; and eventually, in its attention to contextual factors, the anthropology of space and place.[4] Its insistence on identity as intrinsically pluralistic, transient, and performative, together with its attention to issues of ethnographic representation, responsibility, and authority, also lent crucial impetus to the postmodern crisis in anthropology that facilitated the dismantling of positivistic constructions of Culture and the classic norms of ethnography in the 1980s (see Rosaldo 1993:25–45).

The present essay collection represents a similar collaborative bow to a musical colleague of the Texas cohort, ethnomusicologist Gerard Henri Béhague (1937–2005), whose pioneering work in Latin American music, popular culture, nationalism, ritual, and performance studies at the University of Texas at Austin during the mid-1970s–early 2000s contributed extensively to his discipline's development. Associate Editor of the *Yearbook for Inter-American Musical Research* from 1969 to 1977; President of the Society for Ethnomusicology from 1979 to 1981; editor of its journal, *Ethnomusicology*, from 1974 to 1978; and founder and editor of the tri-lingual *Latin American Music Review* from 1980 until his death, Béhague established the ethnomusicology graduate program at Texas in 1974, thereby influencing the training and thinking of dozens of the field's practitioners, virtually all of whom remain active as well-respected educators, scholars, and musicians.[5] As John Schechter observes, beyond applauding his students' efforts to establish and direct nonwestern music ensembles, including

---

[3] The classic exemplar of this approach is Paredes 1971; for a more recent ethnomusicological illustration see Fox 2004.

[4] Representative literature includes, but is in no way limited to Bartra 1992; Guss 2000; Hellier-Tinoco 2011; Limón 1991, 1994; Madrid 2011; Peña 1983, 1985; Rosaldo 1993; and Turino 1993.

[5] For additional information on Béhague's biography and scholarly achievements, see Buchanan 2006a; Moore 2006; Schechter 2005; Slawek, Antokoletz, and March 2006; Turino 2005; and volumes 26, no. 2 and 27, no. 1 of the *Latin American Music Review*, special memorial issues dedicated to Béhague and his scholarship.

a *mariachi*, a Brazilian ensemble, and an Andean ensemble, he "inspired them to delve deeply into musics that had often, theretofore, been unknown, marginalized, or disparaged" as lacking scholarly or artistic legitimacy (2005:144–5). He developed undergraduate courses surveying Latin America's regional musical traditions (the Andean countries, Mexico and the Caribbean, and Brazil and Argentina, including urban popular musics as well as indigenous genres) and those of sub-Saharan Africa, but also the works of twentieth-century Latin American composers, effectively incorporating all of South America and its transatlantic African and Hispanic musical links within his pedagogical compass. Graduate seminars addressed ethnomusicological theory and methods, fieldwork, and music and religion, through which Béhague introduced students to his own research on Afro-Brazilian *candomblé*, grounded in the ethnography of performance.

For younger ethnomusicologists today the "turn to performance" (Bauman 2002:92) as methodological paradigm likely seems a theoretical stance so basic as to represent the glaringly obvious entry point to musical analysis, rather than its ultimate objective. Significantly, however, the analytical embrace of performance was actually a deliberate attempt, in ethnomusicology as in folklore, to move away from the hegemony of the Textual Object (whether score, poem, or linguistic or musical transcription) and its formal constituents, so often stripped of the natural context in which they signified and then historicized. As Béhague notes in the Introduction to his *Performance Practice: Ethnomusicological Perspectives* (1984a), musicological studies of performance practice once denoted something quite different: attempts to "reconstruct the original sound of early European music of various periods through the study of a variety of literary and historical (including iconographic) sources" (1984a:3).[6] Even when the analytical subject lay outside the sphere of Western art music, he observes, ethnomusicologists confined their study to "the idiosyncratic qualities of vocal and instrumental sound production in a given culture, generally applying Western concepts of sound" (3). Because ethnomusicologists often dealt with unnotated musics, they recognized that performance was "actually their primary source of study," thus developing "an all-inclusive approach to the study of performance" (3). But few, he argues, approached music performance as both "an event and process," or music making as a true synthesis of performance *and* practice, sound *and* social context (3–4).

Bauman's groundbreaking theorization of oral literature as verbal art (1975, 1977) exposed the interface between social discourse and cultural texts (whether literary, musical, or otherwise), drawing upon and helping to shape, under the initial influence of Dell Hymes (1964), a new appreciation of performance as

---

[6] At the time that Béhague was drafting these remarks the debate over authenticity in historical performance practice was just beginning to gather momentum; he may well have had this movement in mind. Contemporaneous studies include Dreyfus 1983 and Cohen and Snitzer 1985; a representative sampler of later publications includes Kenyon 1988; Lockwood 1991; and Taruskin 1992.

6 *Soundscapes from the Americas*

communicative practice that refused the abstract formalism of structuralist paradigms (see Bauman 2002:93; Ben-Amos and Goldstein 1975). The ethnography of speaking, as academic subfield and scholarly paradigm, emerged from this effort as part of a broader engagement with an ethnography of communication situated in synergistic interchange between sociolinguists, linguistic anthropologists, and folklorists.[7] Bauman's attention to the semiotic, metacommunicative, metacultural, and poetic dimensions of performance-in-practice, which have been of particular interest to ethnomusicologists, drew inspiration from J. L. Austin's *How to Do Things with Words* (1962); the Prague School of Linguistics, particularly the writings of Roman Jakobson and Jan Mukařovský; Gregory Bateson's (1972) and Erving Goffman's (1974) problematization of the interpretive framing and cueing of communicative acts; and later, anthropologist Victor Turner's conceptualization of ritual (sacred and secular), and eventually theater and spectacle, as reflexive cultural commentary—in other words, as "cultural performances," a term originating with anthropologist Milton Singer (1955, 1972) to designate, in ethnomusicologist Marcia Herndon's words, "isolatable segments of activity considered by a group of people to be encapsulations of their culture which they can exhibit to visitors and themselves" (1971:340). They are, as Bauman elucidates, scheduled, temporally and spatially bounded, heightened and "coordinated public occasions" in which performance of some kind is typically a "criterial attribute" (1992:46).[8] Bauman (2002:94) writes that it was Barbara Babcock, his colleague at Texas at the time, who introduced him to Turner's "developing approach to cultural performances as metacultural enactments—cultural forms about culture, social forms about society—an important complement to the linguistic reflexivity with which [he was then] most centrally concerned."[9] The notion that individuals, nations, states, and other social formations wield performativity through a roster of constructed displays that highlight, reinforce, comment on, and push the boundaries of their identities remains a central premise of the anthropology of expressive culture, prompting a veritable legion of ethnographic monographs concerned with performance, poetics, politics, and power.[10]

Ethnomusicological contributions to the ethnography of performance in its formative period dovetail those in folklore and anthropology closely. "Form in

---

[7] On the ethnography of speaking see, for example, Hymes 1962 and Bauman and Sherzer 1974, 1975.

[8] In today's world, the notion of "cultural performance" might be extended to mediated genres (such as music videos) as (often) conscious, constructed displays of social identity and difference, but for performance studies scholars, the analytical emphasis remains "liveness" (see Schechner 2006:2, 7).

[9] For more on cultural performance and its analytical legacy in ritual, theater, and festival studies, see Bauman 1977:27–8; MacAloon 1984; Moore and Myerhoff 1977; and Turner 1982a, 1982b, and 1987.

[10] See, for example, Askew 2002; Buchanan 2006b; Guss 2000; Kligman 1988; Peacock 1968; and Turino 2000, among many others.

Performance: Hard-Core Ethnography" was an interdisciplinary symposium held on the Texas campus in April 1975 (see Herndon and Brunyate 1975). Spearheaded by Marcia Herndon and Norma McLeod together with their junior colleague Béhague, this event represented, as Charlotte Frisbie (1976:142) explains, "the first time a group of scholars in ethnomusicology and related disciplines ... held an organized dialogue on form in performance." Klaus Wachsmann (then at Northwestern University) participated, as did Bauman and Abrahams, with Bauman presenting a version of his "Verbal Art as Performance" (see Frisbie 1976). In her keynote address, McLeod pointed to her concept of "musical occasion," an ethnomusicological adaptation of Singer's "cultural performance" that she began to develop in conjunction with her 1957 MA thesis under the supervision of Raymond Firth at the London School of Economics, and then used, but does not really problematize, in her 1964 study of the social status of Madagascaran musicians.[11] A round table called "The Musical Occasion," moderated by Béhague on the symposium's second day, allowed McLeod to further elaborate on this important notion (Frisbie 1976:142; Herndon and Brunyate 1975:164–93), which, in her pioneering analysis of the Cherokee ballgame cycle, Herndon (1971:340) had earlier defined as

> an encapsulated expression of the shared cognitive forms and values of a society, which includes not only the music itself, but also the totality of associated behavior and underlying concepts. It is usually a named event with a beginning and an end, varying degrees of organization of activity, audience, performances, and location.

Shortly after this pivotal conference Herndon and McLeod published two volumes in quick succession that further explicated and refined emerging ethnomusicological approaches to performance: their methodological text *Music as Culture* (1979) and edited anthology *The Ethnography of Musical Performance* (McLeod and Herndon 1980). Arguing that Singer's cultural performance did not account for the many more informal or loosely organized instances of music-making of interest to ethnomusicologists, they continued to promote the musical occasion as a more inclusive, methodological (rather than theoretical) concept that

---

[11] I am deeply grateful to Thomas Solomon for identifying and correcting an unfortunate error, first appearing in Herndon 1971 and repeated in Béhague 1984a (p. 6) and elsewhere, which suggests that McLeod initially theorized "musical occasion" in her 1966 doctoral dissertation. This is not true; neither Solomon nor I can find any mention of the term "occasion" in this study, whose focus is the application of linguistic techniques to the analysis of songs from the African continent, Madagascar, and North America. Rather, in her keynote address for the 1975 symposium, McLeod describes how her understanding of occasion evolved from her comparative analysis of Firth's Tikopia data, at his request (13–17, but esp. 13–14; see also Merriam 1964:251–2, who cites McLeod's thesis apropos her "analysis of the relationship between music and occasion structure").

understood musical performance as "more usually not a conscious exhibition, but a nonverbalized expression of cognitive forms and values" (Herndon 1971:340; Herndon and McLeod 1979:21, 26).[12] The occasion, they asserted, was "the point of focus encompassing the perception, performance or creation of music" (1979:21). Frisbie (1980:75–81) likewise called for a more flexible definition of audience than that indicative of the public cultural performance, while Ruth Stone (1982:2, 20–34), cautioning against a sound-behavior split implicit in descriptions of "musical occasion," introduced the term "music event" and, like Frisbie (1980), encouraged that performance analysis be rooted in local, host-culture conceptualizations of such experiences and their boundaries.[13]

Béhague's 1984 collection tracks many of these developments in his introductory essay, laying out the basic ingredients of an ethnography of musical performance that, while taking McLeod-Herndon's musical occasion as a point of departure, tests the analytical purchase of Bauman's and Abrahams's theories for ethnomusicological research.[14] These studies were enormously important in their emphasis on performance as an organizing principle of social life, their advocation of an ethnomethodological analytical stance that took into account the evaluations and commentary of performers and audience members themselves (Béhague 1984a:8), their contribution to a cognitive ethnomusicology paralleling similar tendencies in anthropology,[15] and their promotion of participation in performance as ethnomusicological field technique (Béhague 1984a:9), a development galvanized contemporaneously by the fundamental monographs of Paul Berliner (1978) and John Miller Chernoff (1979). As Steven Feld (who came to Texas in 1985, bringing with him a whole host of new theoretical tools) remarks in his review of *Music as Culture*, the works of Herndon, McLeod, and their colleagues also pointed ethnomusicologists toward the critical realization "that humans organize sound through social means for social ends, [and] that we hear the way we do because culture constructs patterns of contextual predisposition so that we are prepared to

---

[12] See also Bauman 1977:28, who remarks that, "As interesting as cultural performances are, performance occurs outside of them as well." An important analytical task is to establish "the continuity between the noticeable and public performance of cultural performances, and the spontaneous, unscheduled, optional performance contexts of everyday life."

[13] See also Qureshi 1987a:69–70 for further discussion of event versus occasion and their cognitive and behavioral dimensions.

[14] A slightly revised and updated version of this article, written in 1997, was reprinted in 2006. See Béhague 1992 for a related essay.

[15] Indeed, by 1971 Herndon had already concluded that the musical occasion, as a frequent component of rites of passage, might yield "information about basic functions of music in human cognitive systems," and "provide both the key to and confirmation of basic values and beliefs in a given society, since it tends to be an encapsulation of these cognitive items, presented in skeletal form in the structure of the music itself as well as in surrounding ritual activities" (1971:351).

hear things as socially meaningful or not" (Feld 1980:93). In their precursory grasp of "sound structure as social structure," elaborated later in the classic studies of Feld (1984) and Marina Roseman (1984), these efforts correspondingly propelled Anthony Seeger's conception of a "musical anthropology" for which performance is "as much a part of the creation of social life as any other part of life," and that "establish[es] aspects of social life as musical and as created and re-created through performance" (2004:xiv, 83).[16]

Such was the genesis of performance theory in ethnomusicology, and with it came a new vocabulary that refocused the analytical lens from (musical/ literary) text to process, and object to enactment (see Abrahams 1977). Festivals, fiestas, rites, spectacles, and other displays or musical occasions were conceived as reflexive performances, "keyed" (Bauman 1977; Goffman 1974) by specific behavioral or verbal codes, and "framed" (Bateson 1972; Bauman 1977; Goffman 1974) in accordance with particular parameters and conventions of interpretation that demarcate them within the prosaic flow of the everyday. They were "emergent" (Bauman 1977) from and contingent upon the "symbolic interactionism" (Blumer 1969) of participants and consumers in circumscribed but mutable contexts (where, to quote Feld [1980:91–2], "context" is understood as "not merely a 'boundary' but a set of constraints upon knowing in a situated frame"), and exemplary of local-specific semiotic codes of "communicative competence" (after Chomsky 1965; refined in the scholarship of Bauman 1977; Briggs 1988; and Hymes 1971, 1972). That scholars could learn from participating themselves in the music making and/ or staging of such events, attaining aptitude (competence) approaching bi- or even multi-musicality over the course of their careers—all of these things that have become the lifeblood of our discipline and, indeed, the study of expressive culture in general were stoked by, if not fired in, the ethnography of performance forge.

Terrains of Performance

In the thirty years since the publication of Béhague's anthology, ethnomusicology's intellectual terrain has morphed in tandem with changing perspectives on performance. A brief summation might proceed something like this. Precursory studies, dating at least to 1960, placed the object performed front and center: songs, tales, epics, and their formulaic analysis prompted new theories of oral composition, the collapse of singer-poet-composer roles, and gave impetus to early studies of music and language and music and orality, paving the way for more recent treatments of musical improvisation in myriad cultural contexts.[17]

---

[16] Seeger's "Sing for Your Sister: The Structure and Performance of Suyá Akia," which was an important stepping stone to his book, appeared in McLeod and Herndon 1980.

[17] The literature on tale-singers and minstrelsy, especially in Balkan, Eurasian, and Russian studies, is too large and rich to cover comprehensively here. But for their

That tale-singers, like all musicians, shape their musical offerings to accommodate contextual factors and diverse clienteles begged the question of extra-musical influences on the performance process—the audience, mediation, reception, and their impact on communicative interchange. In his review of *The Ethnography of Musical Performance*, Michael Asch (1982:317), in keeping with the quixotic quest for a unitary field theory so indicative of the era, called for a "blueprint or set of principles upon which those ... interested in a science of culturally derived musical analysis might base a discipline." Although not a direct response to his plea, models for context-sensitive, interactional approaches to performance analysis appeared in the writings of Charlotte Frisbie (1980, in the very volume in question), Kristina Nelson (1982, 2001),[18] Regula Qureshi (1987a, 1987b, 1995), and Ruth Stone (1982); Miller 1984 and Titon 1988 represent additional exemplary studies that also nudged the discussion in the direction of ethnopoetics.

Rethinking performance as practice also raised the issue of performers themselves—what they were doing, how they were doing it, how they conceptualized their activities, and what they had to say about it all. For ethnomusicologists, artist biographies became one point of entrée,[19] while performance itself remained, and continues to remain, not just an activity to be documented, but an ethnographic immersion technique with which to actively engage. Attending to the tools of performance, such as instruments, pieces, and techniques, was still important, but the conceptual apparatus now considered musical practice as a locus of social process, one revealing of social relations and the fabric of social life, and the performing ethnographer as part of that fabric. Such participant performance is by now an ubiquitous component of the ethnomusicological trade, spawning the establishment of numerous ethnomusicologist-directed collegiate ensembles whose objectives are primarily pedagogical, or where the teaching of a particular performance practice is in the employ of applied ethnomusicology (see Solís 2004).

In its intention to build understanding through intercultural music-making, performance in ethnomusicology-related ensembles in some ways approaches, but does not emulate, performance ethnography as conceived by Victor Turner (1987:139–55), theater director Richard Schechner (1985, 2006), sociologist and communications scholar Norman Denzin (2003), and the interdisciplinary field of

---

methodological import see, especially, Azadovskii 1926; Lord 1960; Propp 1968; and more recently, Foley 2002. Early ethnomusicological studies targeting the similar physical properties of music and language include Bright 1963 and List 1963; see also Herndon 1992 for a discussion of song and verbal performance. For a comprehensive overview of the literature on music and language through ca. 1990, see Feld and Fox 1994.

[18] Nelson was my first own first mentor at Texas when I began my MM studies in ethnomusicology in autumn 1982.

[19] See, among others, Danielson 1997; Mitchell 1978; Rice 1994, 1995; and Vander 1996; for a more recent consideration of the place of the individual musician in ethnographic research, see Ruskin and Rice 2012.

Doing Ethnomusicology "Texas-Style" 11

performance studies, born of a rapprochement between theater and anthropology in the 1980s with Schechner at its helm. As Turner (1987:140–41, 145) describes it, performance ethnography embraces the ethnographic as performative medium, a form of "instructional theater" invoking a dramatic "play frame" (after Bateson) through which students, informed by pertinent literature and consultations with anthropological experts or cultural insiders, reenact rites and customs to gain a more experiential sense of their dynamics and meaning, causing them to reflect critically on how such displays have been represented in scholarly literature. For Turner, such "play ethnography" should not reinforce the "otherness of the Other," but rather target the social drama mechanism shared by all peoples and how it "subtly stylize[s] the contours of social interaction in everyday life" through cultural performances (1987:152).

As realized in the work of Denzin (in sociology) and Schechner and other practitioners of performance studies, however, performing ethnography can be a critical act intended to expose social injustices and effect positive social change through evocative, reflexive, interpersonal narratives,[20] carefully crafted exhibits,[21] and dramatic productions. Such an approach in effect argues for a performative (or enacted) ethnographic art, what Michelle Kisliuk (1998:12–13) terms "socioesthetics," which is conversant in the politics of globalization processes, rooted in social theory (poststructuralism, postcolonialism, feminist and gender studies, cultural studies, media theory, and more), and frequently dedicated to giving voice to the subaltern.[22] The stance is interventionist and, often, autoethnographic, favoring the production of performance pieces drawn from ethnography over the ethnographic analysis of performance itself,[23] but risking simultaneously (no matter how well-intentioned or artistic the goals) the narcissistic collapse of the social world, in all of its staggering complexity, with the personal lifeworld of the ethnographer (see Atkinson 2004:110–11). Although

---

[20] That such (authoethnographic) narratives are also performative is one of the premises of Denzin's theory of performance ethnography and critical pedagogy (2003), but see also Kapchan 2007:250n.16; Kisliuk 1998:12–13; Phelan 1993; and Wong 2008.

[21] The scholarship and activities of folklorist and performance studies professor Barbara Kirshenblatt-Gimblett, for instance, have encouraged attention to cultural monuments and display strategies, museum practices, tourist productions, and heritage studies and management. The University of Illinois's collaborative program in this area is currently headed by anthropologist Helaine Silverman, a 1986 University of Texas graduate.

[22] Underscoring this stance, Dwight Conquergood identifies the "three A's of performance studies" as "artistry, analysis, [and] activism" (quoted in Schechner 2006:24).

[23] Denzin, for example, advocates the creation of "a critical performative cultural politics," where "the dividing line between performativity and performance disappears," and in which "interpretive ethnographers" mount "reflexive ethnographic performances" with a moral orientation, preferably in collaboration with co-performing audiences, thereby "performing culture as [they] write it" in the service of enabling a more equitable society (2003:ix–x). He calls for "a critical performative pedagogy that turns the ethnographic into the performative and the performative into the political" (xiii).

I am personally discomfited by the ethical dilemmas and representational politics inherent in more radical enactments of performance ethnography, when just who is speaking for and assuming/rendering authoritative knowledge about whom may be riddled with power imbalances that privilege the outside "specialist," there is little question that the discipline of performance studies overlaps extensively with ethnomusicology (especially in its anthropological orientation). Recent literature in both fields[24] brings to the table an emphasis on gesture, posture, and the behavioral unspoken of metacommunicative discourse; the experientiality of sensory modalities and their narration; the convergence of ethics and aesthetics; emergent subjectivities and their embodiment; and a continued engagement with poesis and power that espouses an innovative, agency-informed understanding of performativity, particularly as theorized by Judith Butler (1993, 1997, 1999, 2004) and many subsequent interpreters of her ideas.

The shift from performance to performativity marks a critical conceptual watershed in the ethnography of performance, disclosing the related but divergent ways in which both terms have been invoked by different scholarly camps. For those oriented toward the Texas approach, performance is an acknowledged mode of communicative behavior—a discursive and reflexive mode—whose emergence and enactment unfold within a marked event, and whose investigation, as Bauman reminds us, has always been directed at "mak[ing] sense of social life more generally" (2002:97). Thus, even Bauman's more recent scholarship, such as that with Charles Briggs (1990, 2003), concerns, in his words, "how to relate the exercise of interactional power within the bounded speech or performance event to larger social formations that organize institutional power in terms consistent with the understanding—foundational to the ethnography of speaking—that society is discursively constituted" (Bauman 2002:97). Certainly, Goffman's 1959 assertion that human beings accommodate their presentations of self in everyday social interactions through (often non-verbal) behavior expressed and interpreted within semiotic communicative interchanges reliant on shared knowledge is among the most foundational to qualitative social science inquiry. Deciphering human expressive behavior is also the cornerstone of performance studies; Schechner pronounces behavior the discipline's "object of study" (2006:1).

But not all behavior can be construed as performance; if all behavior is deemed performative, then "performance" loses its analytical utility. Indeed, there are some metacommunicative behavioral devices that, while contributory (even fundamentally so) to social interaction and the constitution of social relations, are also so generic or habitual (perhaps even arising from the interface of pre-conscious biological hardwiring with enculturative processes), so low in one's focal awareness, as to resist characterization as performance.[25] Rather, "Performances are actions," writes Schechner: "any action that is framed, presented, highlighted,

---

[24] See Askew 2002; Friedson 2009; Kapchan 2007; and Sugarman 1997.
[25] My thanks to Thomas Turino for a helpful discussion of this point.

or displayed is a performance" (2006:2). Performance, in this view, is the result of enacted intent, and herein lies the move to performativity.

Butler's performativity takes its initial cue from Austin's "performative utterance" (1962), a way of speaking or proclaiming the social world into being via the commanding, often ritualistic language of authority.[26] ("I now pronounce you man and wife.") However, whereas Austin is concerned with a particular kind of illocutionary speech act, in which "the very act of speech constitutes the deed" (Sullivan 1986:9), Butler's adoption of the term seems in part an attempt to untether "performance" from bounded event, preferring a more open but transitive concept that targets how discourses fundamental to one's sense of self, such as those pertaining to gender subjectivity, adhere in (or constitute) and are simultaneously articulated by certain expressive, performative behaviors.[27] For both Schechner and Butler, performative behavior has agency; it represents an activated aesthetics—a strategic signification—with transformative potential.[28] As such, performativity's temporality is always oriented toward the future, but its successful deployment depends on the discursive—and recursive—dialectical interplay between present enactments and the prior conventions and practices from which they spring.[29]

---

[26] See Wong 2001 for an ethnomusicological extension of Austin's notion of the performative to musical and ritual behavior.

[27] In *Gender Trouble,* for example, Butler advocates that gender pertains only in its enactment, "performatively constituted by the very 'expressions' that are said to be its results" (1999:25; quoted in Allen 1998:459).

[28] See Butler 2004:204–231; Denzin 2003:7–10; and Wong 2008:5, 16. Schechner observes that "the global forces of capital" perhaps understand even better than scholars the potentialities of performance in all its transformative implications. He writes, "The interplay of efficiency, productivity, activity, and entertainment—in a word, performance—informs and drives countless operations. In many key areas of human activity 'performance' is crucial to success … . Performance has become a major site of knowledge and power" (2006:23, 26). Beyond allowing us to explore alternative ways of being, doing, and interacting— to galvanize or operationalize transformed social worlds—performance is therefore also vulnerable to manipulation and abuse, particularly as the advancing technology of digital communications masquerades the fictional ever more persuasively as the real, and fixes any captured remark or gesture as a performance susceptible to permanent display and accountability.

[29] Kelly Askew (2002) clearly demonstrates how established power structures require redundant, reiterative, stylized performative displays to materialize and sustain a particular version of social reality, but that this reality can also be upended or countermanded, even momentarily, by similar performative means. That performativity requires reiteration to accomplish its ideological work is also central to Butler's argument (see Butler 1999:140–41; also discussed in Sawin 2002:45, and Butler 1993 and 1999). Here she draws upon Derrida's notion of citationality, wherein performative gestures, whether utterances or otherwise, gain efficacy and legitimacy through redundancy, such that each pronouncement is a citation of those previous. (See Allen 1998 for a helpful overview and critique of this [pp. 462–63] and other aspects of Butler's ideas as they developed through 1997.) In her "Preface" to the 1999 edition of *Gender Trouble*, Butler writes that "The iterability of

For performance studies scholar Deborah Kapchan, attending to performativity, which she defines as "the enactment of publicly recognized (and discursively constituted) meanings," reinstates the body, its dispositions, and comportment as important to sociocultural analysis[30] and illuminates "how aesthetic practices create their object in performance" (2007:259n.16). Approached in this manner, performance, in the words of anthropologist Edward Schieffelin, "embodies the *expressive dimension of the strategic articulation of practice*" (1998:199, also quoted in Askew 2002:291; emphasis in the original).

At issue is an ontology or even phenomenology of performance that enfolds concurrently the "performative dimensions of experience" and the experiential, embodied, and inherently subjunctive (tenuous, contingent, emergent) qualities of the performative (see also Kapchan 1995:479, 481). Performativity's subjunctive modality is the locus of its transformative potential and intrinsic to its capacity for exercising political (subversive, redressive, or otherwise) and creative action. In other words, scrutinizing the performative aspects of behavior lays bare the political and poietic facilities of power discourses performed and their contribution to the articulation and experience of subjectivity. In this way, approaches sensitive to performativity continue to interrogate the power asymmetries and inequalities, the social differences and disjunctures, germane to Texas folkloristics and the recipients of its teachings, as instantiated through enactments that both express and persuade.

Legacies and Trajectories

As Robin Moore (2006:2) has observed, the breadth of Gerard Béhague's scholarship was impressively eclectic and cosmopolitan, embracing Latin American music in all its historical, topical, and regional diversity. He possessed an extraordinary ability

> to combine and synthesize this information, to move seamlessly between analyses of classical, popular, or traditional music, to discuss religious rites of indigenous Mexico one moment and Andean art song the next, *música tejana*

---

performativity is a theory of agency, one that cannot disavow power as the condition of its own possibility" (13). In other words, the very normalcy of social norms is afforded agency—afforded the *power* of normalcy—through the iterable—and sustained, habituated, and citational—quality of performativity in practice.

[30] Ethnomusicologist John Blacking played an earlier, important role in drawing attention to the body, movement, and corporeal experience in ethnomusicological and ethnochoreological scholarship of the 1970s (see, for example, Blacking 1977; Blacking and Kealiinohomoku 1979). Here the ethnography of performance intersects with contemporaneous developments in the evolution of dance ethnography, particularly in regard to the groundbreaking studies of Judith Lynne Hanna (1979, 1983).

and the compositions of Villa-Lobos, *candomblé* drumming and sixteenth-century *villancicos*, all the while linking the focus of his interests to broader conceptual concerns.

Such concerns include the social organization and patterning of performance events, the significance of physical movement and dance, the power dynamics suffusing ethnicity and nationalism as social forces, and ritual, whether public or sacred, as cultural performance.[31] The articles in this anthology reflect the heritage but also contemporary trajectories of these issues in a similar geographic framework. Mirroring Béhague's own graduate training with Americanist Gilbert Chase at Tulane University's Inter-American Institute for Musical Research in the 1960s and his lifelong engagement with Brazilian music, Andean music, and the impact of west African styles on South American and Caribbean popular musics, each chapter portrays a snapshot (or perhaps better, "soundshot") of musical life in representative communities of the Americas, including the southwestern and Pacific U.S., Puerto Rico, Bolivia, Chile, Cuba, and Ecuador. Five chapters treat popular genres; four are situated in Andean locales; and three take an overtly historical approach—considerations also key to Béhague's scholarship and teaching throughout his career.

The volume's contents are organized in three parts that demonstrate important dimensions of how the ethnography of performance, as paradigm and analytical approach, have evolved in the work of contemporary music scholars. Part I, "Genres, Histories, and Discourses of Power Performed," explores how the histories and stylistic shifts manifested by Cuban *teatro bufo*, the Ecuadorian *pasillo* and *sanjuanito* (both types of Ecuadorian *música nacional*), and the Jíbaro repertory of Puerto Ricans in Hawai'i and Puerto Rico itself are implicated in discourses of social power that pertain to the politics of identity (apropos race, ethnicity, class, nationalism, and migration) and play out through musical performance.

In the opening chapter, Robin Moore considers how the changing manner in which Euro-descendant Cuban authors depicted Afro-Cuban slaves and free blacks in Cuban *teatro bufo*, or blackface comic theater, mirrored shifting nineteenth-century socio-political contexts and racial ideologies. Predating U.S. minstrelsy by about 15 years, *teatro bufo* was the most popular form of Cuban musical and stage entertainment in the 1800s. It also represents a unique development in Latin American performance; no other Spanish- or Portuguese-speaking country developed anything similar. Moore's analysis recognizes three phases into which portrayals of black characters fall. During the initial stage (1812–67), playwrights tended to depict blacks through song and dance as ridiculous and clown-like, yet cheerful and content. Portrayals such as these encouraged an ideology effected by

---

[31] While some have distinguished between sacred and secular or civic rites, in his keynote study of *candomblé*, Béhague describes "public musical occasions" as "open to all, including outsiders such as tourists" (1984b:237).

those anxious to justify slavery. During the second period (1868–80), the genre gained national prominence as the Cuban insurrection against Spain began in earnest. The appeal of *teatro bufo* at this time apparently resulted from the fact that sketches took on a local hue, thus distinguishing the genre as Cuban rather than Spanish. As Moore explains, "blackface characters continued to be buffoons, but many audience members also read them positively as symbolic representations of the Cuban nation." Many sketches of the 1870s also made veiled references to politics, thereby supplying contemporary social commentary while avoiding Spanish censorship. The final period of the genre's development (1880–95), Moore observes, is differentiated by

> a diversification of racialized characters to include white and mixed-race protagonists as well as a wider range of blackface types. Representations of blacks at this time, which corresponded to abolition (1886), began to include drunks, hustlers, and razor-wielding thieves, depicting a more dangerous and angry black persona and reflecting white unease about the presence of free black citizens in the insurgent nation.

Ketty Wong contributes a complementary inquiry into Latin American nationalism, ethnicity, and class structures from the standpoint of contemporary Ecuador. Her study, the volume's second chapter, teases out changing perceptions of the Ecuadorian *mestizo* nation as engendered in changing interpretations of the rubric *música nacional*. Wong explores how this phrase, which must be understood as both metaphor and genre, embraces the elite construction of a hegemonic national music vis-à-vis the popular expressions of indigenous persons and the *mestizo* working class. By carefully considering which forms of Ecuadorian music were ascribed to this general category by different populations at different moments, Wong locates two major discourses of Ecuadorian nationalism whose class-, racially, and ethnically inflected premises are also exemplified by two emblematic genres of Ecuadorian music: the *pasillo* and *sanjuanito*. While the *pasillo*'s "refined poetry, waltz-derived rhythm, and elaborate guitar arrangements" evoke the European heritage of Spain, the *sanjuanito*'s "pentatonic melodies, colloquial lyrics about everyday life," and "preference for high-pitched timbres" in vocal and instrumental arrangements carry indigenous associations. In Wong's words, "The inclusion or exclusion of musical genres and styles associated with indigenous, *mestizo*, and/or Afro-Ecuadorian populations in the notion of *música nacional* reveals how different social groups envision the ethnic and racial configuration of the nation." Such changing perceptions not only "mirror the social, economic, and political transformations that Ecuador has undergone" during the 1900s and early 2000s, but have involved a major reconceptualization:

> from a white-*mestizo* (a term signifying racial and cultural mixing) nation that required ethnic groups to assimilate to the dominant culture as a prerequisite to Ecuadorian nationality ... to a multiethnic nation whose indigenous and Afro-

Ecuadorian populations strive for cultural recognition, respect, and participation in the decisions that affect the country.

Chapter 3 takes the reader to the Puerto Rican communities of Hawai'i, where author Ted Solís documents how modifications to the stylistic attributes of the local Jíbaro repertory track concomitant social changes and elucidate an evolving self-awareness in which Jíbaro, Puerto Rican, and Latino subjectivities are at play. Hawai'i's Puerto Ricans are descended from laborers imported to cultivate the state's sugar plantations in the early 1900s. There they developed a unique, creolized music and dance culture whose stylistic vocabulary—including instrumentation, performance techniques, formal musical structures, lyrics, and choreography—originated largely among the Jíbaro, Iberian peasant farmers living in the Puerto Rican highlands during the early 1900s. Notably, as Solís explains, for Hawaiian Puerto Ricans "Jíbaro" is an in-group term embracing the aesthetic and emotional locus of their Iberian heritage, while "Puerto Rican" conveys "a more abstract sense of political identity and geographic origin, in the sense of the modern nation-state." Despite Jíbaro music's valorized origins, however, with time the repertory's parameters have broadened to include new instruments, influences, and pieces derived primarily from Latin and jazz sources. Curious about how such accretions are rationalized, Solís finds that musicians self-consciously assess their appropriateness while invoking a flexible Jíbaro subjectivity as reference point. Historical circumstances pertinent to the modifications are documented in musicians' commentary and relate to radical shifts in community lifeways; among these are the population's migration from plantations to urban areas in the 1930s and 1940s, the impact of mass media and consequently, resumed communication with Puerto Rico proper in the 1950s and 1960s, and their encounter with and subsequent accommodation (and mitigation) of Afro-Cuban influences in contemporary Puerto Rican culture and music-making. The nature of these changes has caused Hawaiian Puerto Ricans to rethink their self-image according to a broader Puerto Rican rubric in which Latin, African, Jíbaro, Iberian, Puerto Rican, Hawaiian, and American sensibilities and historicities resonate.

While the emphasis in Part I is on repertory and socio-musical change, or how the history of musical repertories maps changing social relations, that of Part II, "Performing Practice: Style and the Politics of Subjectivity," is the fluid, emergent quality of performance itself. The articles in this section, which examine the creative dynamic of jazz improvisation in Austin, Texas and gender discourse in Chilean *canto a lo poeta* (sung popular poetry), consider musical practice as an expression of personal subjectivity in situated contexts. As such, they mark an important shift in analytical focus from how the mechanics of performance practice exemplify large-scale identity politics, to the poetics of performativity and the ontology of the individual, acknowledging the dialectical, temporally bound nature of performance-in-process and its articulation of a feeling, responsive, ephemeral Self.

Drawing upon phenomenology, hermeneutics, cybernetics, systems theory, general semantics, the Confucian/Daoist/Buddhist philosophical traditions of China, and ethnographic research in Texas, in Chapter 4 Tim Brace launches an inquiry into the experiential character of improvisation, positing new ways that this process might be theorized, understood, and described. At issue is the "thick improvisational moment" in which the process is played out—a locus of "situated practice" or "web of action" where indeterminacy vies with choice, divergence and convergence define the ebb and flow of the performative dynamic or groove, and "patterns of relationship" emerge from a sea of interactive and referential contextual, historical, physical, and social variables to create an ever changing event structure. Using commentary from his consultants in Austin's jazz club scene to illustrate and extend his argument, Brace contends that jazz improvisation is not just an aesthetic act, but "an act of transformation in communion." It is a dialectically integrative, communal, and transpersonal experience in which musicians "mutually help each other transcend previous understandings and therein transform the selves involved." Such a musically "affecting presence" (after Armstrong 1971), Brace asserts, which musicians both create and are created by, "is the ultimate human experience, involving both the personal and the transpersonal, simultaneously, as two dimensions of the same reality." The saliency of Brace's remarks reach far beyond Austin or any single improvisatory practice, interrogating the very ontology of communal music-making as interactive social practice.

The sung popular poetry or *canto a lo poeta* of central Chile occupies a central position in a post-dictatorship folk revival in which women's participation, while welcome, is prompting new reinforcement of and challenges to the formerly masculine orientation of the genre's gender boundaries. Rooting her analysis in extensive field research in Santiago and rural Chile, and her own expertise as a vocalist and performer of the *guitarrón*, a 25-string guitar-like lute that provides *canto a lo poeta*'s accompaniment, in the anthology's fifth chapter Emily Pinkerton explores the gender discourses framing the genre's performance in sacred (*canto a lo divino*) and secular (*canto a lo humano*) contexts. These include all-night vigils of devotional song and public gatherings of *payadores*, or improvising poets, in venues ranging from small-scale community events to international showcases in major theaters and festivals. Pinkerton focuses especially on the *paya*, a competition in which *payadores* improvise poetic responses to a particular theme and each other's verses, for the resulting poetic banter is often cast in ways that illuminate how male and female performers are negotiating and remolding gender dynamics through their performances. Here, too, the "thick improvisational moment" is key. Pinkerton details the unique challenges encountered by women who enter the *paya*'s masculine musical space, which includes public (re)framing of their physical appearance, sexuality, and professional identities. She attends closely to "sonic differences" in the performances of established male and female singers, noting the divergent ways in which each employs "aggressive language and sexual allusion as poetic tools." Ultimately, she claims, the power asymmetries evident in *canto a lo poeta* performance are symptomatic of "larger discursive imbalances" characterizing Chilean society after Pinochet.

The analytical subject of Part III, "Situated Events and Performance Politics: Fiesta, Festival, Stage, and Street," is the performance occasion. In this section, anthropologists Michelle Wibbelsman and Thomas Solomon take the reader to sacred and secular festivals in highland Ecuador and Bolivia, respectively, where they investigate the strategies, motivations, agendas, and aspirations driving participant performance and event structuration. In their analyses, both authors distinguish between public, staged presentations of rites or customs as spectacle and their more peripheral, local, community-based practice, but the emphasis, in each case, is on understanding "how performance aesthetics come to sustain competing moral-religious, ethnic, and ultimately political discourses that both reflect and influence divergent systems of interpretation and experience" (Wibbelsman). The fact that the more public events are folkloristically situated— framed and choreographed in accordance with ideological, commercial, or touristic objectives—makes them no less real or meaningful to their actors who, the authors remind us, must be understood not as helpless objects, but as thinking, strategizing individual agents in the folklorization process that typically informs such community festivities.[32]

In Chapter 6, Michelle Wibbelsman compares two renditions of the *Via Dolorosa*, or Way of Sorrows, that occurred during Holy Week in Cotacachi, Ecuador during 2001. The *Via Dolorosa* is a Christian, Catholic tradition in which participants reenact the Stations of the Cross and the tortuous agony and persecution experienced by Christ prior to and during his crucifixion. As Wibbelsman explains, at a contentious meeting in advance of Holy Week, municipal leaders advocated producing the Stations of the Cross as a major urban tourist event, while indigenous catechists mandated the opportunity to enact the Catholic rite as an act of faith rather than tourist pageant, while utilizing an "unprecedented script in Quichua," the local indigenous language of the highlands. The impasse resulted

---

[32] In her 2011 book, Ruth Hellier-Tinoco proposes the term "performism" to similarly describe how particular discourses about a nation or social group, such as indigeneity or notions of ethnic or national identity, are socially deployed and become reified through a manifold network or roster of often mutually redundant or informative, and therefore mutually reinforcing, "presentational and representational processes and practices involving signification, meaning, and experience, for political, ideological, economic, social, and experiential functions and objectives." For her, performism is a multiplicitous discursive phenomenon encompassing whole complexes of pertinent but diverse presentational and representational objects, actions, or behaviors, including "written and spoken linguistic text, corporeal practices, geographical locations, visual and sonic images, and material acts" (2011:36–40), to which, to provide an impromptu example, culture brokers (such as tourist agencies and festival producers), tourist advertising brochures, national museum displays, history textbooks, souvenir manufacturers, and music ensembles may all contribute to differing extents, in different ways, for their own reasons, in varying contexts or circumstances. See also Silverman 2012 for a complementary study.

in two different renderings of the custom, "one performed by *mestizo* actors in the city as a dramatic spectacle, the other relegated to the periphery of the canton and undertaken as a religious pilgrimage by indigenous devotees." Wibbelsman argues that the expedient abbreviation and editing of the Stations of the Cross for tourist packaging, together with its dramatic qualities, presented this otherwise solemn devotional practice as a form of professional entertainment, thereby thwarting "an experience of social transformation or religious reflection among actors and public alike." However, she continues, "the semiotic multivocality, superfluous detail, generalized participation, and sensual experience of the indigenous procession affirmed the Christian ritual not as simple representation but as lived experience." The "pronounced repetition, rhythmic movement, and collective prayer, along with extended temporal duration and spatial range" of the indigenous observance, Wibbelsman contends, joined catechists in "an empathetic community centered on an evolving moral claim as brothers with Christ in suffering," thereby effecting ritual practice as "transcendental affective encounter."

Thomas Solomon, in the volume's concluding chapter, asks how subaltern performers in staged, juried, folkloric festivals sponsored by governmental and non-governmental organizations understand their participation and strategically employ performative agency to successfully navigate the power-laden expectations, perceptions, and agendas of diverse publics. His ethnographic focus, the Quechua- and Aymara-speaking indigenous peasants of Bustillo province in the highlands of Norte Potosí, Bolivia, provides an instructive case. Bustillo's nine *ayllu* communities identify two major coexisting performance occasions: *ayllu*-specific fiestas that are annual celebrations of the local agricultural-religious calendar at which participants perform for themselves and in which competition is implicit and emergent; and folkloric festivals like those described above, at which participants perform on stage in explicit competition before a mixed audience of (often urban) *mestizos*, sponsors, local *ayllu* residents, indigenous groups from nearby communities, and a panel of evaluators. Drawing upon his lengthy experience as a participant-observer of indigenous music-making and a one-time judge of a *festival* in the early 1990s, Solomon shows how *ayllu* performers adjust and re-tool various elements of indigenous performance practice for the stage, including the modification of song lyrics, ensemble instrumentation, and dress styles, strategically deploying them in a re-presentation of their own indigeneity "that meets the expectations they perceive [*mestizo*] festival audiences have of what 'indigenous culture' is about."

Solomon terms this sort of self-presentation "strategic auto-essentialism," a "self-conscious acting out of the folkloric stereotypes *mestizos* have of indigenous culture, in order to succeed in this moment of articulation with the *mestizo* world."[33] In its creative, poietic replication (re-ply-ing) of a certain "active subjectivity"—an

---

[33] The "auto" element of the equation is crucial here, for as Solomon noted in correspondence with me, it makes the performers' agency and self-reflexivity that much more apparent.

active self-awareness of themselves as indigenous, peasants, and *ayllu* members—it is also, he observes, an example of Ricoeurean mimesis. The performative qualities of such re-presentations render them particularly affecting and effective. In Solomon's view, they tender "what might be called a multimedia 'subjectivity package,' embodying identities not just in words, but in sights, sounds, and other feelingful sensations, creating a synesthetic experience that is powerful precisely because of the aesthetic appeal and pleasurable embodied experience they offer." "Music is an important part of this package, he writes, "organizing this multisensory experience as a process in and through time." Therein lie the power, poetics, and ontology of performance, what Steven Friedson describes as "a musical way of being-in-the-world," a "musical mode of being," a musical way of experiencing life-time (see Friedson 2009:8–9, 139–40, 188–9).

In keeping with the book's overall engagement with performativity, each chapter might be understood as a soundscape narrated by its author—a portrayal of performance and performance context in a particular moment and place. Such an orientation approaches performance as processual action rather than static object, situating musical sound within the larger sonic kaleidoscope of the everyday while also paying homage to the analytical rooting of performance studies in oral literature: tale-telling, epic poetry, the ethnography of speaking, and the ethnography of communication. In the most fundamental terms, then, the book's contents illustrate analytical moves from genre and repertory to practice and praxis, from stylistically bound understandings of performance practice to an ontology of subjectivity expressed via an active, emergent poetic performativity, and from event-circumscribed treatments of performance context to an anthropological inquiry into the experience and embodiment of sound in place.

PART I
Genres, Histories, and Discourses of Power Performed

Chapter 1

The *Teatro Bufo*: Cuban Blackface Theater of the Nineteenth Century

Robin Moore

Introduction

Given Gerard Béhague's strong support of research involving performance ethnography, it may strike some as odd to begin a volume dedicated to his influence with a historically oriented essay. Yet such a conclusion would be misguided. Béhague's interests always included history, initially with studies of eighteenth-century *modinhas* [a lyrical salon music form], Baroque classical repertoire from Minas Gerais, biographies of particular Brazilian composers, and of course his influential history of Latin American music published in 1979.[1] Even after 1980, as Béhague's work became increasingly informed by ethnographic method and an interest in contemporary popular music, he retained a strong interest in Latin American historiography.[2]

The last three decades have witnessed an increasing interpenetration of the fields of anthropology and history, as Béhague was well aware. The importance of intersecting axes of historical and contemporary study has been recognized by anthropologists since at least the 1950s;[3] more recently, prominent figures such as Marshal Sahlins have built their reputations primarily on historical analysis,[4] and topics such as individual and collective memory have become fashionable within anthropological inquiry. Conversely, the rise of interpretive anthropology inspired an entire movement of "new cultural history" in the 1980s and continues to impact the discipline. What William Sewell (2005:179) has called the "revelation of anthropology," the notion that there exist radically different forms of behavior, ideology, and social organization that must be analyzed on their own terms to be fully understood, has led to entirely new sorts of historical work. Researchers increasingly understand the past not only in terms of synchronic processes but also as discrete synchronic moments; they recognize that individual or group behavior

---

[1] The title of the latter volume is *Music in Latin America: An Introduction* (Béhague 1979). Among his other historical music studies are Béhague 1968, 1990, and 1997.

[2] This is seen in essays such as Béhague 1982, 1986, and 1991.

[3] For instance, as made evident in Edmund Leach's classic *Political Systems of Highland Burma* (1954).

[4] E.g., Sahlins 1981 and 1987.

26 *Soundscapes from the Americas*

at such times can be understood in much the same way as that of a community under direct observation. Cultural performance in the past may thus be subjected to the same sorts of analyses involving power, class, gender, and other factors with which the ethnography of performance has been concerned.

In the spirit of such interdisciplinary work, this essay provides an overview of the most popular genre of nineteenth-century Cuban stage entertainment. The blackface comic theater or *teatro bufo* is virtually unique in all of Latin America; no other Spanish- or Portuguese-speaking country developed anything similar, with the possible exception of the *sainete rioplatense* and its references to figures from the urban underworld in Buenos Aires and Montevideo.[5] The Cuban genre can be easily compared to U.S. minstrelsy, however, and in fact North American traditions influenced its development for a time, at least in the 1860s. Substantial differences exist between the North American and Cuban traditions, but in at least two respects their histories parallel one another: both flourished during roughly the same period, and both changed substantially over time, depicting African descendants in different ways as the result of changing socio-political contexts.

In North America, the greatest changes to depictions of black characters came before and after the Civil War. As discussed by Saxton (1975), U.S. minstrel troupes prior to the mid-1860s portrayed southern blacks as happy, servile, and docile. Many sketches suggested that blacks enjoyed work on plantations. Characters such as Jim Crow expressed gratitude to their masters for the latter's generosity and kindness, even as they manifested their inferiority to whites through buffoonery, incorrect speech, and dull wits. Portrayals such as these fed directly into an ideology perpetrated by those anxious to justify slavery. Following abolition, depictions of black characters tended increasingly to foreground their promiscuous, unscrupulous, and potentially dangerous nature, especially as manifest in so-called "coon songs" of the 1880s and 1890s. This latter period seems to have supported a particular ideology as well, one embraced by those who promoted segregation.

Changes associated with blackface character types in Cuba, by contrast, fall into three stages. The initial stage, 1812–67, foregrounded recently arrived African slaves who spoke only a broken form of Spanish. The term used to describe such an individual was *bozal* (pl. *bozales*), the same term also applied to their pidgin language. During these decades, depictions of blacks tended to be ridiculous and clown-like yet happy, similar to early minstrel characters in the United States. During the second period in the late 1860s, the genre skyrocketed in popularity as insurrection against Spain began in earnest. Stage actors adopted a *negro catedrático* or "black professor" persona as a central figure, apparently in

---

[5] Stereotyped characters in the *sainete rioplatense* included working-class figures such as the *gaucho* [cowboy] and *cololiche* [Italian immigrant], as well as others who spoke *lunfardo* dialect. None of the roles as presented by seminal authors such as Carlos Mauricio Pacheco (1881–1924) involved donning blackface, however. For more information about this genre, consult websites such as: www.biblioteca.clarin.com/pbda/ teatro/disfrazados/b-613807.htm and www.liceodigital.com/literatura/desalojo.htm (both accessed 3 June 2014).

imitation of the North American Zip Coon. The phenomenal appeal of blackface at this time seems to have resulted from the fact that they incorporated local customs, singing, and dancing that defined the genre as Cuban rather than Spanish. Blackface characters continued to be buffoons, but many audience members also read them as symbolic representations of the Cuban people.

The final period of the genre's popularity, 1880–95, corresponds to a diversification of racialized characters to include white and mixed-race figures as well as a wider range of blackface types. The *teatro bufo* continued to depict black and mixed-race individuals in a decidedly negative manner, but also commonly parodied white characters. Representations of blacks (*negritos*) began to include drunks, hustlers, and razor-wielding thieves, corresponding in a sense to post-abolition representations of blacks in the United States.

The following essay briefly explores these stylistic changes in the *teatro bufo* and relates them to local racial and political discourse. Three representative stage works serve as the basis for much of the analysis; all three have been reprinted in recent years within Cuba in anthologies such as *Teatro bufo siglo XIX* (1975) and *Antología de teatro cubano, tomo 3* (1989), edited by Rine Leal. Specifically, the essay examines early *bozal* blackface as manifest in the writings of Bartolomé Crespo y Borbón's *Un ajiaco o la boda de Pancha Jutía y Canuto Raspadura* (1847), the *catedrático* period as represented by Francisco Fernández Villarós' *Los negros catedráticos* (1868), and *fin-de-siècle* sketches as exemplified by Ignacio Sarrachaga's *En la cocina* (1880).

Race and Society in Nineteenth-Century Cuba

Nineteenth-century Cuban society has been described as extremely stratified and hierarchical (Deschamps Chapeaux 1970:16), controlled by a small number of white elites including Spanish military authorities, colonial functionaries, and plantation owners. A slightly larger group of urban middle-class professionals such as doctors, lawyers, and bureaucrats supported the elites, also white. The bulk of the population consisted of individuals employed in the blue-collar and service professions, including tobacco and sugar workers, shoe makers, tailors, construction workers, dockworkers, musicians, etc. Black and mixed-race Cubans predominated in this group. Some Afro-Cubans employed in blue-collar and entertainment sectors achieved a surprising level of affluence, though their numbers dwindled significantly after 1844. Slaves constituted the bottom of the social hierarchy; their numbers peaked during the height of the slave trade in approximately 1830.

Black and mixed-race Cubans constituted a substantial majority of the population during much of the nineteenth century: nearly 60 percent between 1820 and 1845, and roughly 50 percent into the 1860s. This strong demographic presence, proportionally larger than in the United States or Brazil at the time, generated concern among colonial elites. Many early abolitionists in Cuba such as José Antonio Saco (1797–1879) advocated an end to the slave trade, not because they objected to the practice on moral grounds, but because they recognized a need to increase the white population and felt too many blacks lived in Cuba already (Helg 1990:39). The Cuban leadership lived in fear of a mass slave revolt such as had recently taken place on the island of Hispaniola (Kutzinski 1993:5). And in fact a series of bloody slave uprisings did take place within Cuba, though none ultimately proved successful for long. The first such documented event took place in 1812, led by a free black and former colonial soldier, José Antonio Aponte. Other uprisings date from 1825, 1830, 1835, 1837–38, and 1841–45 (Deschamps Chapeaux 1970:20). The most widespread of these, the so-called Escalera or Ladder conspiracy of 1844, resulted in widespread repression of the Afro-Cuban community, the killing of approximately 1800 suspected conspirators, and the torture, imprisonment, and exile of thousands more (Paquette 1988:229).

Historians have effectively documented the brutal history of the Atlantic slave trade throughout Latin America, the inhuman practice of treating Africans as property in the New World, buying and selling them, breeding them, working them to death and replacing them with others. Somewhat less attention has been devoted to documenting the ways in which white colonial society justified such practices, and it is in relation to this issue that cultural forms such as the *teatro bufo* provide potential insights. By means of blackface theater, *costumbrista* literature and painting, and pseudo-scientific studies, colonial elites seem to have convinced themselves that Africans were inherently inferior. Throughout the nineteenth century, even the most progressive of Europeans and Latin Americans ascribed to notions of European superiority and evolutionism. Most characterized Africans as morally weak, lazy, overly emotional by nature, inclined to criminality, and unfit for citizenship. Helg quotes a prominent author who described blacks at the turn of the twentieth century as "a race vegetating in childhood," adding that they had only brought to the Caribbean "their musical sense, their exhibitionism and lasciviousness, and their lack of foresight" (Helg 1990:48). Clearly, notions about African-influenced music and culture contributed to an ideology of racial subjugation. Lane (2005:44) suggests that the *teatro bufo* in particular served as a form of socio-political containment in this sense: by assuming the role of a *negrito*, the comic actor both defined and circumscribed black behavior, crafting a representation charged with implications beyond the theater stage.

Eighteenth- and nineteenth-century elite Latin American society rejected all references to African or indigenous heritage as part of their nationalist projects (Turino 2003). Zea (1986:1345) describes Latin American elites as wearing a mask, adopting the latest fashions of Europe or the United States while turning a blind eye to their own local cultural realities. Fornet (1967:49–50), writing specifically on Cuba, confirms that the nineteenth-century bourgeoisie actively deprecated or ignored Afro-Cuban culture.

> ... the first ideologues of the nineteenth century, "founders of the nation" and representatives of high creole culture, were complicit in the slave trade and the colonial regime that guaranteed those interests. ... every time those patriarchs

spoke of nationality and liberty, they imagined a white nation in which the white oligarchy would be free to rule. ... Afro-Cuban folklore was rejected as "a black thing," a foreign element in the nation that hearkened back to a barbarous pre-history.

Given this context, it is noteworthy that "reinvented" Afro-Cuban culture in the form of blackface shows came to hold such a prominent place in Cuba's cultural life even after abolition in 1886. The reasons for its broad appeal for over a century derive in part from persistent racial tensions and white bias against the black population. The genre continued to perform ideological work, helping to justify white privilege. However, the *teatro bufo* also survived in part by altering its representations of blacks at particular moments in conformity with changes in racial discourse.

Early *Teatro Bufo*, 1810–1867

Most theater historians (e.g., Robreño 1961:20) suggest that the basic format of the *teatro bufo* derives from Spanish *tonadillas escénicas*, *sainetes*, and *entremeses*—short comic works of a satirical nature that often depicted working-class characters, music, and dance—and perhaps also from the French *buffes parisiennes*. The most important author in the early years of the Cuban genre's development was Francisco Covarrubias (1775–ca. 1850). Considered the "father" of the *teatro bufo*, for many years he enjoyed great celebrity. Joining the comic theatrical troupe of Andrés Prieto in 1811, Covarrubius brought to his roles a knowledge of Spanish theater; he realized quickly that the many local character types used in Spain—Gypsies, Moors, etc.—could be substituted by Cuban figures (Carpentier 1946:229). As of 1812 he began to do so, filling the stage with *guajiros* (farmers), *monteros* (backwoodsmen), *carreteros* (cart drivers), and other personalities. He was the first to debut a character in blackface as part of an 1812 stage play called *El desengaño feliz o el negrito* (Lane 2005:29). Interestingly, this took place sixteen years before Thomas Rice popularized his Jim Crow character in the United States, and almost thirty years before Dan Emmet created the first formal U.S. minstrel show. By 1814, Covarrubius had incorporated local Cuban music into his theater pieces as well, including the *guaracha*, the *décima campesina*, and the *canción cubana*.

As mentioned, the first recurrent black character type to gain broad popularity on the Cuban stage was the *negro bozal*, or recently arrived African. Carbonell (1961:114) notes that blackface *bozal* characters became popular at a time when most African slaves lived in the countryside on sugar plantations and often learned little Spanish over the course of their short lives.[6] The *bozal* emerged as

---

[6] For an extended discussion of the transformation of Castilian Spanish in *bozal* parodies, see Cruz 1974:10.

Figure 1.1   The painting depicts a black domestic servant who seems to be obsessively attracted to white women, and thus furtively kisses an alabaster statue in the absence of his masters. Víctor Patricio Landaluze, *The Kiss*, oil on canvas, ca. 1880. Photo used by permission of the Museo Nacional de Bellas Artes, Havana, Cuba

part of a broader *costumbrismo* movement in the 1830s and 40s, derived from Europe and involving humorous middle-class representations of working-class culture in various forms, including visual art. The most well-known *costumbrista* painter in nineteenth-century Cuba was Víctor Patricio Landaluze, a Spanish national who spent many years creating rather superficial and dehumanizing oil paintings of Cuban blacks between the 1850s and the 1880s. His most important collection is *Tipos y costumbres de la isla de Cuba* from 1881. The oil painting reproduced in Figure 1.1 comes from that publication. It currently hangs in the Museo Nacional de Bellas Artes in Havana.

The author who did most to promote the *bozal* in mid-nineteenth-century theatrical works was a poor Galician immigrant to Cuba named Bartolomé

Crespo y Borbón; he typically wrote under the pseudonym "Creto Gangá" (Díaz Ayala 1981:62). Crespo y Borbón established himself as an author through a column published in *La Prensa* newspaper in which he commented on political and social events of the day in Cuba while impersonating and writing in the style of a slave. His first incorporation of a *bozal* into a stage work came in 1839 with the publication of *El látigo del anfibio* [The amphibian's whip], and his first major commercial success in the same vein came in 1847 with *Un ajiaco o La boda de Pancha Jutía* and *Canuto Raspadura* [A stew or The marriage of Pancha the Jutía (a rodent) and Canuto Sugar Scrapings]. Music played a prominent role in his works for the stage; ironically, he often wrote musical texts in *décimas*, a Spanish-derived ten-line poetic form, but also incorporated the *guaracha*, with broader working-class and mixed-race associations.

For those who do not speak Spanish, *bozal* lyrics can be difficult to evaluate. Here is a *décima* written by Crespo y Borbón in the 1840s that illustrates the sorts of song lyrics incorporated into stage works at that time. The original *bozal* text appears first, then a version of them in standard Spanish for comparison, and finally a translation into English. This excerpt comes from Crespo y Borbón's *Trifuca de Canavá* [Carnival ruckus], reprinted in Cruz 1974:52–3:

Original lyrics	Standard Spanish
Allá va cun Dio! Allá va,	*Allá va con Dios! Allá va,*
Letó, lo que tanto ipera	*Lector, lo que tanto espera*
Allá va pate tesera	*Allá la parte trasera*
Trifuca de Canavá	*Trifulca de Carnaval*
Cun música te lo da	*Con música te lo da*
Pa que ma te lo divieta	*Para que más te lo diviertas*
Ma tú también uno peseta	*Mas tú también unas pesetas*
Lo frojará, cumparito	*Las aflojarás, compadrito*
Poque en jamá tú lo ha vito	*Porque jamás tú has visto*
La trifuca ma cumpreta	*La trifulca más completa*

English translation

There it goes, by God, there it goes,
Reader, what you were so waiting for
There goes the end of it
Carnival ruckus
With music it comes to you
So you'll enjoy it more
But you also will lose
A few coins, friend
Because you've never seen
A ruckus as complete as this one

The lyrics provide many examples of the ways black Spanish was parodied through stage representations, for example the substitution of *letó* for *lector* [reader], or *ipera* for *espera* [to hope, wait for]. A final quote of *bozal* speech as manifest in Crespo y Borbón's writing comes from *Un ajiaco o La boda de Pancha Jutía* (*Teatro bufo siglo XIX*, vol. 1:91). The libretto indicates that this segment is to be sung and danced, but no further information about the musical accompaniment is provided other than that it should "imitate the music of the *negros de nación*," meaning blacks born in Africa rather than in Cuba. Discourse in this second example corresponds more directly to the happy-go-lucky plantation blacks in many early U.S. minstrel shows.

Original text	Standard Spanish
La tiera branco son groria	*La tierra de blancos es una gloria*
Cuando se jalla amo güeno	*Cuando se halla un amo bueno*
Jah! La mio son critiano	*Ja! Los míos son cristianos*
Y como súcara memo	*Y como azúcar misma*
Ya yo son libre	*Ya yo estoy libre*
Yo ta casá	*Yo estoy casado*
Mi su amo memo	*A mí mi amo mismo*
Me libetá	*Me libertó*

English translation

The land of white folks is glorious
If you find yourself a good master
Hey! Mine are Christian
As sweet as sugar
Now I'm free
I'm married
My own master
Has given me liberty

Little information has survived about the specific kinds of musical accompaniment incorporated into nineteenth-century *bufo* presentations. Notes in the libretti frequently indicate that actors should sing: in many, no information about particular instruments are provided; in others, references are made to string instruments such as the guitar and *bandurria* or to street instruments such as the crank organ, cornet, or small bass drum (*bombo*). References to working-class Afro-Cuban dances such as the *cambujá* also appear, along with indications that performers should interpret or mimic them, but it is unclear whether the representations made any attempt to adhere to folkloric practice.

On the basis of available recordings from early twentieth-century blackface sketches, it appears that the music accompanying song and dance of the *teatro*

The Teatro Bufo*: Cuban Blackface Theater of the Nineteenth Century* 33

bufo often consisted only of a few instruments and that in stylistic terms it contained little that marked it as overtly "Afro-Cuban." The comic sketch "La mulata en el precinto" [*Mulata* in the police station] (Victor 78 #6781-1, music by Jorge Anckermann, 1916), for instance, ends with a *guaracha*-style song accompanied by guitar only. Arquímedes Pous's "El melonero" [The melon vendor] (Monteagudo 1924) begins with a stylized *pregón*, or street vendor song, without accompaniment; Ramón Espígul's "El Ford" [The Ford] (Espígul 1916) ends with a vocal duet accompanied by solo piano. The accompaniment style of both the *guaracha* and the piano music cited incorporates some overt syncopation, for instance rhythmic punches on beat 4 of the $\frac{4}{4}$ measure, or *tresillo* rhythms that emphasize the and-of-two of the $\frac{4}{4}$ measure. Only in this sense can they be linked aurally to local hybridized popular music.

The Early Revolutionary Period, 1868–1880

Though detailed research on the topic remains to be undertaken, blackface theater presentations in the 1850s and early 1860s seem to have gradually changed in meaning for local audiences. Increasingly, as the independence movement gained momentum, *negrito* actors and entire comic sketches seem to have been used as a vehicle for political commentary. By means of local slang and oblique metaphor, pro-independence sentiment could be expressed in a manner that Spanish colonial authorities did not recognize. Writing music in Spanish *décima* form, but "corrupting" it with the use of *bozal* speech, apparently constituted part of this overall trend (Lane 2005:46). Oblique political commentary grew in importance owing to censorship of all literature and public entertainment by colonial authorities in their attempts to suppress anti-colonial sentiment. Indeed, the Spanish government forced several well-known authors of stage works such as Miguel Salas into exile during periods of revolutionary struggle (Robreño 1961:27). Blackface characters took on new associations in this context: their words and personae continued to belittle Africans and free blacks, but they were also perceived as an iconic link to Cuba itself, a symbol of something distinct from Spain (Leal 1989a:75). The practice of using the comic theater as a veiled form of political commentary continued well into the twentieth century, especially in the Teatro Alhambra (Robreño 1979), an influential venue for blackface comic theater through 1935.

Most writings on the *teatro bufo* emphasize the meteoric expansion of blackface over a period of only eight months, from May 1868 to January 1869. During this period, seven new *bufo* troupes formed and staged works to immediate popular acclaim. This profusion of such entertainment coincided almost exactly with the onset of the Ten Years War (1868–78), the beginning of widespread armed conflict against Spain. Carlos Manuel de Céspedes spearheaded this effort, famously freeing his plantation's slaves in eastern Cuba and then asking them to voluntarily join him in the rebellion. Popular authors who wrote for the comic theater at the time included Pancho Fernández, Luis Cruz, José Castellanos, Jacinto Valdés, and Miguel Salas. Spanish authorities expressed immediate suspicion as to the potentially seditious nature of *bufo* stage plays after 1868, and in fact banned them entirely in 1869. Not until the Pact of Zanjón (1878) created an uneasy truce between revolutionaries and the Spanish crown did such presentations appear once again. The audiences attending blackface plays consisted primarily of white Cuban men, but some black and mixed-race men came as well. Leal (1989b:165) notes that through 1885 theater audiences remained segregated in Havana, with the non-white public confined to balcony seats.

References to local, working-class culture seem to have become more prevalent in the 1860s. Dances such as the Afro-Cuban rumba and Euro-Cuban *zapateo* appeared frequently, as well as folk melodies from the period such as "El anaquillé." To Jill Lane, local elements with populist resonance played a crucial role in the new prominence of the genre:

> Against the pretenses of European opera at the imposing Teatro Tacón in the city center, against the random, sensational entertainments—acrobats, contortionists, dancing pigs, bullfights— ... the newly popular *teatro bufo* offered an array of especially 'Cuban' performances: original, lively *guarachas* and a flood of new plays that claimed to represent "typical" "Cuban" mores, humor, and figures of everyday life. (2005:13)

Blackface characters in this pivotal period began to change, becoming more varied and three-dimensional. They adopted the role of free urban workers with some disposable income, and thus had profiles much more similar to those in the audience. This framing of blackness, distinct from the earlier *bozal* character, seems to have been performing the "delicate preparatory work" (Lane 2005:14) required to construct a new national culture.

While Lane's commentary serves as an important point of departure for thinking about the changing meanings of the *teatro bufo*, it should be noted that working-class culture still often appeared on stage in a decidedly negative light. While the themes of many plays centered around working-class characters, their actions displayed a lack of morals. In fact, transgressions of morality might be considered a leitmotif of sorts in mid-century *teatro bufo*. Virtually all working-class characters, black or white, are seen to be motivated largely by greed, lust, a desire for revenge, and so forth, with little thought to the constraints of decency or social convention. The genre may document the gradual democratization of society and challenges to bourgeois morality in a certain sense, even if some of the authors themselves came from the middle classes. Leal (1989b:159) stresses that middle-class Cuba remained decidedly conservative in the mid century, even in comparison to other Latin American nations: it was strongly Catholic, it had not accepted abolition or the writings of Darwin, had not given women the right to vote or to divorce, and could not even embrace creolized dance music such as the *contradanza* and *danzón* without controversy. *Bufo* stage plays, with

The Teatro Bufo*: Cuban Blackface Theater of the Nineteenth Century* 35

their humorous depictions of libertine love and youthful rebellion, may have served as a vehicle of sorts for coping with social change.

Along with emerging Afro-Cuban ballroom dance genres, the *guarachas* mentioned above became a central form of national musical culture in the 1860s and may in fact be the very first form of working-class music to have been accepted by broad segments of society through their dissemination in the theater. The *guaracha* of this period was a simple strophic song form with a frequently repeated chorus that could be listened to or danced, as appropriate. To Leal, *guarachas* grew in popularity because their irreverent, bawdy, and parodical "street-savvy" texts fit in well with a stage genre that had come to represent opposition both to bourgeois moral codes and to Spain. "If the *teatro bufo* parodied 'sacred' texts of the stage, the *guaracha* created opposition to the *zarzuela* [light opera] and commented on our reality ... the *guaracha* functioned as a mechanism of escape and frustration related to our habit of making light of serious situations and our resistance to authority" (Leal 1989b:163–4).[7] Certainly many blackface comedies did take inspiration from classic literature or light opera, as was the case with North American minstrelsy (see Levine 1988). One example in the case of Cuba is the sketch *La duquesa de Haití* (The Duchess of Haiti), a parody of Offenbach's *The Grand Duchess of Gerolstein* from 1867.

Leal's insightful analysis notwithstanding, published collections of nineteenth-century song lyrics suggest that the most common topic of discussion in *guarachas* was amorous love, especially of attraction to sensual mixed-race women (*mulatas*), and by extension topics such as marital infidelity, machismo, interracial relationships, and the like. Other references link the genre to the Afro-Cuban community through mention of *caleseros* or coach drivers, the rumba, and *ñáñigo* masked dancers (e.g., Hallorans 1882:23, 31, 38). Below is an example of a *guaracha* text that appears in Sarrachaga's *Un baile por fuera* (1880), sung by a group of blackface actors posing as carousing street musicians. Note that numerous *guarachas* in stage plays from the 1860s exist as well, for instance a piece sung by blackface actors to a *mulata* named Tomasa in Pedro Pequeño and Francisco Fernández Vilarós's *El negro cheché o Veinte años después* (Leal 1989a:250).

La mujer es dulcesita	Women are sweet
Ya yo lo he dicho aquí	I've said it here now
Y si es como Rosa	And if they're like Rosa
Tan linda cosa	Such a lovely thing
¡Válgame Dios!	So help me God!
Yo la quisiera tener	I would like to have her

---

[7] *"Si el bufo parodió los textos 'sagrados', la guaracha se antepuso a la zarzuela, comentó nuestra actualidad ... la guaracha queda como un mecanismo de escape y frustración que tiene mucho que ver con nuestro tradicional choteo y falta de jerarquía y autoridad."*

Siempre contenta a mi lado	Always happy at my side
Para evitarme el enfado	To avoid the trouble
De adorar a otra mujer	Of adoring another woman
Porque yo soy también hijo de Dios	Because I am also a child of God
Que no me contento nunca sino con dos	I'm never satisfied with one, only two
Rosita, linda cubana	Rosita, lovely Cuban woman
Responde a mi tierno amor	Return my tender affections
Asómate a la ventana	Come to the window
Y escucha tu trovador	And listen to your troubador

As mentioned, the most common new blackface character type of the 1860s was the so-called *negro catedrático* or "black professor," similar to the U.S. Zip Coon. It does appear as if the inspiration for the *negro catedrático* figure came from the United States, though its specific depictions and meanings differed somewhat. Carpentier (1946:145) defines the *catedrático* as a "refined" black man who resorts to wild affectations of dress as well as uncommon and extended turns of phrase in order to express the simplest of ideas. "Deprived of adequate education, [the urban black] has sought out in the conversations of learned whites those words that, because of their obscurity, seem to be profound and distinguished" (Carpentier 1946:145). In effect, the *catedrático* represented an aspiring social climber who nevertheless fell short of integration into white society. The impression he created with his affected speech and dress, of course, was laughable rather than erudite. Ironically, the white power structure in Cuba did not allow even free blacks much access to education though it ridiculed them on stage for their lack of refinement. Cuban law prohibited masters from teaching their slaves to read, and through 1878 did not permit free blacks from attaining education beyond the level of primary school (Lane 2005:145). Many occupations were prohibited to free blacks outright, including the clergy and prominent musical roles in the church (Carpentier 1946:145).

Francisco Fernández Vilarós represents one of the most well-known authors of blackface theater in the late 1860s. His play *Los negros catedráticos* (1868) proved an overwhelming commercial success and helped establish the *catedrático* as a standard character type. Little is known about Fernández today; no birth and death dates are available for him in theater history books or in dictionaries of Cuban literature (e.g., García 1980), but he clearly took inspiration from the minstrel troupes of Campbell, Christy, and Webb that toured Cuba during the Civil War in the U.S. south (Díaz Ayala 1981:63). A reprint of *Los negros catedráticos* is made available by Leal (1975:131–63). Its plot revolves around interactions between *bozales* and *catedráticos*; in this case, a *catedrático* family "stoops" to accepting an offer of marriage from a *bozal* because he is rich. The two stylized *negrito* types thus appear side by side, each ridiculous in its own way. Protagonists of this particular stage work include Aniceto, a *catedrático*, Dorotea, his daughter, and José, the *bozal*.

Below is a sample of *catedrático* speech from Fernández Vilarós's play (Leal 1989a:240). It is spoken by Aniceto as he accuses José of being the cause of all

The Teatro Bufo*: Cuban Blackface Theater of the Nineteenth Century*   37

his family's problems (despite the fact that Aniceto has stolen most of his money). A caveat: as in the case of most joking, colloquial language, *catedrático* speech is difficult to capture in translation.

> *Porque es usted la causa de estos trastornamientos de familia; porque es usted un ignorante tópico: porque si sus bémbicos labios no hubieran conquistado el virgíneo corazón del fruto de mis amores conyugales, no sufriría yo estos bochornos en medio de las frecuentadas calles de esta populosa capital. Usted tiene la culpa de estos escándalos escandalosos. Usted es la llave que ha dado cuerda a esa máquina horrísona e infernal. Usted no tiene más que sebo y manteca, dentro de su voluminoso cuerpo. Usted es un indígeno ingrato y desagradecido, que no ha sabido apreciar en lo que vale el honorífico honor que se le concediera, ligando sus acuáticos sentimientos con los glóbulos homeopáticos de las bóvedas incógnitas y sensibles de mi degraciada hija. Usted es un pusilánime. A usted le falta lo que me sobre a mí.*

Because you, sir, are the cause of these family disturbances; because you are a topical ignoramus: because if your fat African lips hadn't conquered the virginal heart of the fruit of my conjugal loves, I would not suffer these embarrassments in the middle of the frequented streets of this populous capital. You are to blame for these scandalous scandals. You are the key that has wound up this terrifying and infernal machination. You have nothing but tallow and lard in that voluminous body. You are an indigenous, disgraceful ingrate who has not come to appreciate what the honorific honor is that I have conceded to you, linking your aquatic sentiments with the homeopathic globules of the hidden and sensitive caverns of my disgraced daughter. You, sir, are pusillanimous. What you lack is what I have in plenty.

A famous theater shooting took place on January 22, 1869 that resulted in the complete colonial ban on blackface entertainment and underscores the manner in which overtly revolutionary sentiment manifest itself through the theater, at least at times. The shooting event took place in the Teatro de Villanueva during a presentation of *Perro huevero aunque le quemen el hocico* [An egg-eating dog, even when they burn its snout] by Juan Francisco Valerio (Carpentier 1946:252).[8] Pro-Spanish militia members in the audience do not seem to have taken issue with the content of the comic sketch itself. Rather, they directed their anger toward a comedian performing that day named Jacinto Valdés. Contacted earlier by insurrectionist groups, Valdés was persuaded to yell out "*viva* Céspedes" [long live (Carlos Manuel de) Céspedes] at the end of a song. It was this act and the repetition of the cry by the audience that led Spanish militia members to fire indiscriminately into the crowd, resulting in multiple deaths (Leal 1989b:168).

---

[8]   The libretto of this work is available in the *Teatro bufo siglo XIX* collection (Leal 1975), vol. 1:231–62.

38   *Soundscapes from the Americas*

Many *bufo* troupes disbanded after the incident, and those that survived (such as the troupe of Miguel Salas) left the country for Mexico.

The Late Nineteenth Century, 1880–1900

With the formal end of slavery in 1886 and the movement of rural Afro-Cubans to urban areas in search of better work and an education, racial tensions surfaced in Cuban society that had their corollary in the comic theater. Black Cubans living in slums and tenement houses tended increasingly to be viewed as a threat, and prominent discourse emerged about the (primarily black or mixed-race) Cuban underworld and its pathologies. Examples of such discourse are found in Urritia y Blanco's *Los criminales de Cuba* (1882) and in Fernando Ortiz's *Hampa afro-cubana: Los negros brujos* [Afro-Cuban underworld: The black witches] (1906). On stage, black characters no longer assumed the principal role of protagonist, but rather adopted secondary roles.

> ... black characters were displaced as heroes and transformed into buffoons ... If legally Spain accepted by 1880 the equality of the races, in the theater it indicated the contrary. It is in this context that the *mulata*, the black witch, the *ñáñigo* or fearful masked black dancer, bullies or thugs, and a marginal, delinquent milieu began to contextualize a great deal of the repertoire ... on stage one found "bad living," sinister characters with razors, quarrels, and drunkenness that left the *bozal* of Creto Gangá and the *catedrático* of Fernández far behind.[9] (Leal 1989b:172)

Teatro bufo stage plots and scenarios became more varied in the late nineteenth century and somewhat more reflective of Cuban society as a whole. They incorporated white and/or Spanish characters, and middle-class professionals appeared with some frequency alongside those from the working classes. Female protagonists also assumed a prominent place for the first time along with more overt sexual innuendo. Nevertheless, the short structure of one-act *sainete* shows did not permit a great deal of character development. For that reason, authors often continued to write for pre-established character types based largely on race and class (López 1979:692). The three most common, found in variation, were the *negrito*,

---

[9] *"El bufo se hace marginal tras el Zanjón y el negro fue desplazado como héroe al tranformarse en bufón, en una maniobra discriminative que alcanzó la república neocolonial ... Si legalmente España acepta en 1880 la igualdad de razas, en el teatro había que demostrar lo contrario. Y es en ese contexto donde aparecen la mulata, el negro brujo, el ñañiguismo, la chulería, y ese ambiente marginal y delincuencial que nutre gran parte del repertorio ... en la escena se le ubicó en la 'mala vida', el matonismo y la delincuencia, convertido en un siniestro personaje de navajas, pendencias y borracheras, que debaja bien atrás al bozal de Creto y al catedrático de Fernández."*

The Teatro Bufo: *Cuban Blackface Theater of the Nineteenth Century* 39

mulata, and *gallego*. Others included the Chinese immigrant, the white *guajiro* farmer, and so forth. Authors poked fun at local political events in theater sketches of the 1880s, a tendency hearkening back to the 1860s, though they avoided discussion of revolution. At this time the use of a rumba or similar dance piece at the end of a *sainete* in order to bring all actors out on stage together became standard practice, another element adopted from the *tonadilla* (Carpentier 1946:252).

Negrito characters proliferated and diversified, though in a manner that continued to portray blacks negatively. In addition to the figures mentioned above such as the witch doctor or *brujo* and the *ñáñigo*, other stock *negritos* included the *negro pendenciero* or troublemaking black, the *chévere cantúa* or marginal black, the *negro curro* or flashy-dressing street hustler, and so forth. As mentioned, *negritos* during this period generally represented a threat to society, a disruptive or dangerous element. Very few demonstrated any degree of education and continued to occupy overwhelmingly subservient or marginal roles. Their lowly social status was generally presented as the result of personal limitations rather than broader social forces. In Ignacio Sarrachaga's *En la cocina*, for instance, drunkenness among black characters emerges as a prominent theme, as well as various sorts of threatening behavior, interspersed with song. Álvaro López's essay on character types of the comic theater (in López 1979) is one of the most insightful for analyzing the implicit ideologies behind various *bufo* characters.

A majority of the (white) women that appeared on stage late in the nineteenth century tended to portray *mulatas*, sensuous mixed-race women. As mentioned, *mulatas* had long been discussed in Cuban popular song; they began appearing in prominent literary works also as early as the 1830s. *Mulatas* of the comic theater often appeared as domestic servants or as predatory *mulatas de rumbo*, frequenters of mixed-race dances who sought out white, affluent men for romantic relationships. Such women often served as the focus of amorous attention on the part of various male actors at once, black and white, married and unmarried, and thus inspired endless comic interactions. In general they, like the *negrito*, came from humble origins and had little education or money. At times they were portrayed as quite innocent or naïve, as in the case of Juliana in *En la cocina*, or as self-centered and manipulative. In stage works, *mulatas* represented a danger to colonial society as imminent as that of the *negrito*, though of a moral rather than physical nature. And yet Lane (2005:124) believes they simultaneously referenced *cubanía* in important ways; she describes the character type in this way:

> New to the stage in this period [after 1880] was the mulata, a highly eroticized figure whose proliferation in the theater—as in lithography, painting, narrative, and scientific discourse of the same period—made her the literal and figurative embodiment of Cuban *mestizaje*, replete with the complex anti-colonial investment, racist panic, and nationalist desire that this implied. She was ... at once a pathologized figure of dangerous racial encroachment ("Africanization"), a miscegenating temptress, and a symbol of the innocent, tropical Cuba to be rescued from the lascivious Spanish imperialist.

White characters appeared in many forms in the late nineteenth-century theater. One common stock figure was the *gallego* or Galician Spaniard, a working-class immigrant often owning a corner store or other small business. *Gallegos* often spoke with a heavy and comical Spanish peninsular accent. They had a bit more education and a more stable economic position than *negritos* or *mulatas*, but lived in the same working-class environment. In general they tended not to dance or sing terribly well, in contrast to black or mixed-race individuals. In *En la cocina*, white characters include a well-to-do professional named Mauricio who takes *danzón* dance lessons (associated with the black community) on the sly when his wife isn't around; Don Antonio, a shopkeeper more in keeping with the typical *gallego*; and Bejuco, a "*blanco sucio*," or working-class "dirty white" (light-skinned, usually with some racial mix), depicted as a conniving and treacherous figure who lusts after Juliana and will say or do virtually anything to get what he wants.

Tensions between social classes became an increasingly prominent theme in the comic theater as the twentieth century progressed. Many *catedrático* shows of the 1860s had involved interactions between *bozales* and *catedráticos*, as mentioned, focusing on divisions within the black community itself. In later works, blackface actors tended to interact with individuals from the middle class while maintaining clear social distance from them. Action could take place in a shoe repair shop, in the kitchen of an affluent home, in a restaurant, or any other venue in which individuals from various classes and races might logically meet. One notes a populist aspect to the sketches in that most of the individuals portrayed came from the working poor. And yet those same individuals became the brunt of numerous jokes and appeared in a less-than-flattering light, to say the least. Discussion of *adelanto*, racial and/or social betterment, appeared frequently from the 1860s onward. Issues of morality, especially the "loose morals" of the streets and their potentially detrimental effects on "decent people" (i.e., white, educated people) represented a recurrent theme.

Conclusion

The character types depicted by the *teatro bufo* in the late nineteenth century created an elaborate "mythology of the slums" (Carpentier 1946:233–4), one that has continued to inform Cuban popular culture to the present day. Many of the characters that first appeared on the theater stage in the 1880s reappeared to great fanfare in music, poetry, and other artistic forms associated with the *afrocubanismo* movement of the 1920s and 1930s (Moore 1997). These include "La negra María Belén," described as an elegant dancer and depicted in the 1930s by poet Emilio Ballagas and later in song by composer Rodrigo Prats; the party-loving, singer/dancer *rumbera* figures of various sorts as immortalized in countless films of the 1940s and 50s from Cuba and Mexico; the black hustler Candela with his razor; and the *mulata* María la O, protagonist of a famous *zarzuela* by Ernesto Lecuona.

This brief overview of nineteenth-century comic theater has suggested both that its meanings changed significantly over time and that, especially in later years, blackface stage works functioned as complex signs that signified in multiple ways. On the one hand, the *teatro bufo* must be characterized as a "consummate theater of humiliation" (Trexler in Lane 2005:9), codifying a white, middle-class ideology that justified racial subjugation and slavery. This was especially true of the early period typified by *bozales*. Playwrights depicted *negritos* as ignorant, laughable, childlike, something less than human. Even in the 1880s and beyond, authors ascribed lust, greed, and other base motivations to most of their black and mixed-race characters. The stage served as a Geertzian model for and of behavior (Geertz 1973:93), simultaneously codifying racist views held by the dominant classes and serving as a form of indoctrination by which they were disseminated to others.

However, some blackface stage plays simultaneously contained other messages of a more populist sort. The *teatro bufo*'s use of local character types, local forms of speech, and uniquely Cuban music and dance resonated with the public in the 1860s and beyond as they began struggling for an end to Spanish colonial rule. Scholars suggest that blackface characters came to represent Cuba itself on an abstract level, serving as a potent oppositional sign. This is difficult to prove definitively on the basis of existing information, but seems to be borne out by the fact that the genre peaked in popularity precisely during the first period of armed conflict.

Later in the 1880s, blackface stage plays came to depict a wider array of actors. White middle-class and working-class characters appeared alongside the *negrito* and became the butt of various jokes themselves. The racism of theater works earlier in the century did not disappear, but developed more nuance and was complicated by other themes, including references to contemporary politics and frequent sexual innuendo. Interactions between classes and races on stage continued to reflect tensions, but most resolved themselves harmoniously by the end of the play, often in collective music-making and dance. In this sense, the *bufo* theater proposed a certain model of social harmony, a vision of colonial life that downplayed the significance of difference even as it reified racial categories (Leal 1989b:176).

Much research remains to be undertaken on Cuban blackface entertainment of the nineteenth and twentieth centuries, and especially on the music and dance that accompanied stage shows. Initial studies by Cuban and North American researchers suggest that fascinating connections exist between the social realities of the colonial era, its racial politics, and the depictions of characters on stage. Additional work on this topic may provide new insights into the significance of blackface entertainment within Cuba and also on the development of similar traditions of representation within the United States and elsewhere.

Chapter 2

La Música Nacional: A Metaphor for Contrasting Views of Ecuadorian National Identity

Ketty Wong

Studies on musical nationalism have examined the constructed nature of national identities, which are (re)articulated, performed, contested, imposed, imagined, and labeled in different and often contradictory ways. Following Anderson's view (1991) of the nation as an "imagined community," Mallon (1995) reminds us that nations can be imagined in multiple ways depending on who does the imagining. Although hegemonic national identities reflect the ideologies and aesthetic values of the dominant classes, Chambers (1991) suggests that in times of political and economic instability there is "room for maneuver" for non-dominant groups to contend with or alter the official images, sounds, and rhetorical discourses of power, which he regards as a "disturbance" in the system that creates the conditions for changing the way things are. While popular expressions of national identity do not threaten to topple existing power structures, they have "a particular potential to change states of affairs, by changing people's 'mentalities' (their ideas, attitudes, values, and feelings) ..." (1991:1).

Changes in "mentality" and attitudes toward national identity are particularly observed in Ecuadorians' changing perceptions of what constitutes their música nacional. These mirror the social, economic, and political transformations that Ecuador has undergone throughout the twentieth century and into the twenty-first—from a white-mestizo [racial and cultural mixing] nation that required ethnic groups to assimilate to the dominant culture as a prerequisite to Ecuadorian nationality (Stutzman 1981), to a multiethnic nation whose indigenous and Afro-Ecuadorian populations strive for cultural recognition, respect, and participation in the decisions that affect the country. The way in which indigenous movements have shaped national debate and policy making since the indigenous uprising in 1990 have shattered the elites' idea of Ecuador as a homogeneous, Roman Catholic, Spanish-speaking, white-mestizo nation. The fact that Ecuador's national soccer team qualified for the 2000 and 2004 World Cup competitions also challenged this perception, as most of the players were Afro-Ecuadorians from the Chota Valley, people who are now considered role models and whose hard work and discipline Ecuador needs to achieve its national goals.

This chapter examines *música nacional* as a metaphor for varied perceptions of Ecuadorian national identity.[1] Throughout this chapter, the phrase *música nacional* cannot be generically translated from Spanish as "national music"; rather, it is a term widely used in Ecuador as a surrogate appellation for a specific anthology of songs composed between the 1920s and the 1950s that eventually came to be recognized by the elites as Ecuador's emblematic music. This anthology comprises urbanized renditions of *mestizo* musical genres, most prominently the *pasillo*, considered Ecuador's musical symbol *par excellence*, but also the *pasacalle*, the *albazo* and, to a lesser degree, indigenous musical genres such as the *sanjuanito*, the *danzante*, and the *yaraví*. Since the 1990s, however, the popular classes have been using the phrase *música nacional* to refer to a broader repertoire of songs that the elites pejoratively call *chichera* and *rocolera* music, which emerged in the 1970s–2000s among primarily indigenous and working-class people. In this context, the repertoire comprises working-class renditions of older *música nacional* and entirely new pieces in *sanjuanito* rhythm.[2]

What do the elite and working-class constructions of *música nacional* tell us about Ecuadorians' perceptions of their national identity? Has an old music label merely been appropriated for a new style of music? What images do both types of *música nacional* convey to their audiences and how are these images encoded in the associated music? Following Béhague's approach to the study of performance practice as an event and a process, I examine "the actual musical and extra-musical behavior of participants (performers and audience), the consequent social interaction, the meaning of that interaction for the participants, and the rules or codes of performance defined by the community for a specific context or occasion" (Béhague 1984a:7). I will show that the differences between the elite and working-class styles of *música nacional* are perceived more in extra-musical terms (for example, the performer's ethnicity, dress, and performance contexts) than in specific musical features.

I argue that Ecuadorians' naming practices and attitudes toward the music they feel represents them as a nation are symptomatic of their outlook on their nation and on co-nationals. The inclusion or exclusion of musical genres and styles associated with indigenous, *mestizo*, and/or Afro-Ecuadorian populations in the notion of *música nacional* reveals how different social groups envision the ethnic and racial configuration of the nation. Rather than pointing to a singular and hegemonic national identity that seeks to mold homogeneity from diversity, I focus instead on

---

[1]   Research for this article was supported by a Graduate School Continuing Fellowship and a College of Fine Arts Dean's Fellowship from the University of Texas at Austin, which I gratefully acknowledge. Further discussion of the material presented in this article may be found in Wong 2007. I would like to thank Donna Buchanan, Thomas Turino, and Michelle Wibbelsman for their comments on an earlier draft of this article.

[2]   It is worth noting that Afro-Ecuadorian *marimba* music and indigenous music from the Amazon region are considered ethnic and regional, rather than national musical expressions.

the coexistence of multiple expressions of national identity that represent different interests, aesthetics, and social groups vying for national representation. I consider both the hegemonic and popular notions of *música nacional* as two sides of the national identity coin which are not mutually exclusive because nations are made up of heterogeneous social groups capable of articulating their own images of the nation from their respective positions of power (Wade 2000).

In this chapter, I explore how the elite notion of *música nacional* marginalizes the indigenous, Afro-Ecuadorian, and lower-class *mestizo* population from the imagined nation, and how the working-class *música nacional* constitutes a more accurate portrayal of Ecuador's heterogeneous population. To these ends, I present brief histories of the *pasillo* and the *sanjuanito*, the musical genres that are widely recognized as most representative of the European and indigenous heritages, respectively, of the Ecuadorian *mestizo* nation. I trace their histories from archival sources, recordings, songbooks, oral histories, and examination of live performances and public discourses in the media. I focus on the 1960s, the golden period of the elite *música nacional* and the *pasillo* in particular, and the late 1990s, the period in which the working-class notion of *música nacional* emerged, with the *sanjuanito* as its dominant genre. Research for this study was conducted in Guayaquil and Quito between 1997 and 2004.

A *Mestizo* Nation

Ecuador's republican history is divided into three periods defined by distinctive nationalist ideologies: the Creole nation (1830–90s), led by *criollos* [Ecuadorians of Spanish descent] who marginalized the "dark skin of society"; the *mestizo* nation (1895–1960s), which legitimized Indians, *mestizos*, *cholos*, and Afro-Ecuadorians as members of the nation; and the multiethnic nation (since the 1960s), which recognizes ethnic diversity as one of Ecuador's assets (Ayala Mora 2008:79). The Liberal Revolution of 1895, which most Ecuadorians consider the beginning of modern-day Ecuador, established the foundation for the emergence of a white-*mestizo* national consciousness that included new social actors who had supported the revolution—peasants, artisans, and workers—in the vision of the nation. The Revolution transferred political power from a conservative, land-owning, religiously devout highland elite to a liberal coastal bourgeoisie, which sought the modernization of the country through the expansion of a market economy and secularization of society.

The new dominant classes articulated their sense of nationhood around the ideology of *mestizaje*, a problematic nation-building discourse that claims racial and cultural mixing as the essence of the nation, because ethnicity in the Andes is defined by social status and cultural practice, rather than by ancestry or biological factors (Romero 2001:30). The determination of who qualifies as a *blanco* [white], *mestizo*, or indigenous person is highly situational and will vary enormously depending on the criteria of classification and the social positions of both the identifying and the identified person. Thus, indigenous people may turn into *mestizos* by changing their lifestyle, language, and style of dress; *mestizos* can become *blancos* by acquiring pertinent education, economic status, and cultural practices. *Blancos*, in turn, may distance themselves from *mestizos* by adopting cosmopolitan lifestyles not accessible to *mestizos*.

Stutzman (1981) rightly notes that the ideology of *mestizaje* styles itself as inclusive but is exclusionist in practice because it overlooks the indigenous and Afro-Ecuadorian populations within the nation due to their "unmixed" condition. Whitten (1981) points out the inequality inherent within this ideology because it requires indigenous people to exchange their ethnic identity in order to gain access to the privileges denied to indigenous people, a process known as *blanqueamiento* [whitening]. According to Espinosa Apolo (2000), this assimilation does not necessarily imply acculturation because, while indigenous people adopt the lifestyles of *blancos* when in public, in the private sphere they maintain their cultural traditions and cosmovision, which he calls a "genuine cultural consciousness." As a result, Espinosa Apolo regards Ecuadorian *mestizos* as indigenous people with a high level of "Hispanization," who live a life of continuous simulacra and, as a result, have developed a low esteem for their indigenous heritage.

A colonial history of oppression of the indigenous population survives through stigmatized images of "Indianness" and also explains to a great extent Ecuadorian *mestizos*' disdain for their indigenous heritage. Colonial documents depict indigenous people as primitive, submissive, degenerate, and a vanquished race defeated by a triple conquest—that of the Incas, the Spaniards, and the "crazy Andean geography" (referring to the hostile living conditions in the high plateaus) they were unable to control—presumed to have transformed them into introverted, apathetic, and melancholy people (Silva 2004). These images, which were reinforced and perpetuated through the school system throughout the twentieth century, help account for why *mestizos* do not value their indigenous roots (Espinosa Apolo 2000).

This lack of esteem is culturally manifested in Ecuadorians' attitudes toward *música nacional*. The *pasillo* and the *sanjuanito*, in their traditional forms, represent contrasting views of the Ecuadorian *mestizo* nation. Both genres have undergone stylistic changes and have generated new meanings and new images of the nation for the upper-middle and popular classes. While the elite *pasillo* points to a European heritage through its refined poetry, waltz-derived rhythm, and elaborate guitar arrangements, the *sanjuanito* points to indigeneity with its pentatonic melodies, colloquial lyrics about everyday life, and its preference for high-pitched timbres in the vocal and instrumental arrangements.

La Música Nacional

It is common for a musical phenomenon, such as a particular genre, musical instrument, or song repertoire, to be considered as capturing the essence of a

Figure 2.1   Disc rack of *música nacional* in Almacenes Feraud Guzmán, Guayaquil. Photo by Ketty Wong

country's national character. However, in its adoption of the term *música nacional*, Ecuador is unusually frank in its acknowledgment of the link between a musical symbol and ideas about nationhood. Elsewhere in Latin America, people identify their national music by the country's name, regardless of the geographic or ethnic origin of the music. For example, Mexicans apply the term *música mexicana*, not *música nacional*, to their *corridos*, *mariachi*, and *norteño* music; Peruvians use *música peruana*, not *música nacional*, to designate their Creole music (*vals criollo*) and Andean music (*huayno*). Ecuadorians, however, seldom label their national music as *música ecuatoriana*. Here I wish to make a distinction between "national music" as a generic, descriptive concept that denotes any type of music that may be seen as embodying the national sentiment of a people, and the prescriptive concept of Ecuadorian *música nacional*, which designates selected renditions and repertoires of Ecuadorian music that the elites have raised to the status of "official" national music. It is worth noting that middle- and upper-class Ecuadorians frequently use the term *pasillo* as synonymous with *música nacional* and Ecuadorian music.

The hegemonic meaning of the term *música nacional*—i.e., that associated with elite values—is common parlance in Ecuador. Musicians and listeners often refer to the deep sentiments that *música nacional* arouses in them; intellectuals talk of the need to keep the *música nacional* tradition alive among the younger generations; music stores have a rack for Ecuadorian popular music labeled *música nacional* (Figure 2.1). In addition, one can frequently hear statements such as "*La música nacional hace llorar*" [*Música nacional* makes you want to cry] or "*La música nacional está en crisis*" [*Música nacional* is in crisis], which show that the concept is associated with profound sensibilities and that it is of contemporary relevance and subject to public debate.

A striking feature of elite *música nacional* is that, once urbanized renditions of indigenous and *mestizo* songs have been raised to the status of *música nacional*, they resist regional or ethnic classification and become emblematic of both the *Costa* and the *Sierra* (Espinosa Apolo 2000:84). It is safe to say that no Ecuadorian would venture to identify the *pasacalle*, an Ecuadorian duple-meter dance song derived from the Spanish *pasodoble* and the *polka*, as a coastal or highland music because it is perceived as *música nacional* and thus is not identified with any particular region. This point is underscored by the fact that a well-known medley of *pasacalles* and *albazos* praising cities and provinces across Ecuador is frequently performed in concerts and civic parades to represent the unity of the Ecuadorian people.[3] Even the few urbanized renditions of *sanjuanitos*, *danzantes*, and *yaravíes* that have entered the *música nacional* corpus—once stylized and cleansed of overtly indigenous musical features—are perceived as *nacional*, rather than as ethnic or folk music.[4] For the elites, however, the music that the popular classes have called *música nacional* since the 1990s is not representative of the nation; instead, they consider it *chichera* or *rocolera*, two pejorative music labels that the elites employ to refer to indigenous and working-class popular music.

What images or stereotypes do naming practices reproduce? Who has the power to name a style of music, and for what purposes? In his examination of the events known in history as the "discovery" of America, Trouillot argues that "names set up a field of power" that shape our way of looking at things (1995:115), and challenges us to examine what kind of power is at work in our naming practices.

---

[3] The medley usually starts with the *albazo* "Esta mi tierra linda" [This is my beautiful land], followed by a set of *pasacalles* devoted to the cities of Quito ("El chulla quiteño") [The *mestizo* man from Quito], Cuenca ("Chola cuencana") [Beautiful indigenous woman from Cuenca], Guayaquil ("Guayaquileño, madera de guerrero") [Guayaquilean, warrior's heart], Ambato ("Ambato, tierra de flores") [Ambato, land of flowers], and the province of Carchi ("Soy del Carchi").

[4] The *danzante* "Vasija de barro" [Clay pot] is an example of a stylized rendition of an indigenous musical genre, which is sung and listened to by the elites rather than by indigenous people. The Dúo Benítez-Valencia set to music a poem that was written by a group of renowned poets and artists—Jorge Carrera Andrade, Jorge Enrique Adoum, Hugo Alemán, and Jaime Valencia—during a social gathering at the house of painter Oswaldo Guayasamín.

The origin of the term *música nacional* as synonymous with elite Ecuadorian music is uncertain. This term may have become popular with the first recordings of Ecuadorian music released by international record companies in the early twentieth century, which local people may have called *nacional* to distinguish it from the international musics in vogue. Currently, Ecuadorians use different criteria to define *música nacional*. Many people I spoke to in the streets (white- and blue-collar pedestrians, vendors, students, etc.) believe that only songs based on Ecuadorian rhythms can be considered *nacional*, while others think that any type of music, as long as it is sung by, for, and with the national sentiment of Ecuadorian people, may be regarded as such. However, music producers and singers have a narrower view of *música nacional*, namely that it only includes certain songs performed in upper-middle-class contexts by *mestizo* middle-class musicians.

My research findings point to two critical moments in Ecuador's history in which the elites, confronted with the need to redefine their vision of the nation, shaped and consolidated the musical genres and song repertoire that are considered today their *música nacional* canon. The first historical moment is the Liberal Revolution of 1895. Writer Juan Valdano (2007) describes the aftermath of the Revolution as a period of *"reconocimiento de lo nuestro"* [acknowledgement of that which is ours] in the arts. Progressive writers and artists denounced in their novels and paintings the exploitation of *indios*, *mestizos*, *cholos*, *montubios*, and *negros*, thus revealing a complex picture of the ethnic and racial configuration of the nation. Following this path of *"reconocimiento de lo nuestro,"* academic and popular composers adopted and stylized indigenous and *mestizo* dances in their music works to represent the white-*mestizo* nationalist ideology, thus relegating to oblivion popular nineteenth-century dances that had been emblematic of the *"nación criolla."*[5] Aristocratic and popular music trends coexisted in the 1920s and 1930s, each trying to redefine "Ecuadorianness" from the particular standpoint of the social groups they represented.[6] The *pasillo* from the 1920s–50s constituted an elite expression in urban popular music.

The second critical moment in the consolidation of the elite *música nacional* anthology is Ecuador's loss of half of its territory to Peru in 1942, which resulted in psychological trauma for the Ecuadorian people. Writer Benjamín Carrión proposed his thesis of the *"Gran nación pequeña"* [Great Small Nation], a national healing discourse which held that if Ecuador could not be a great nation through its army and its economy, it would be one through its culture and arts (2002). This thesis underpinned a newfound pledge to uphold Ecuadorian culture, understood here as "highbrow" culture. It was during this period that a selected repertoire of

---

[5] The *rondeña*, the *quiteña*, and the *alza-que-te-han-visto* are nineteenth-century *criollo* musical genres that have since disappeared.

[6] Academic composers wrote *suites* [cyclic compositions] for piano and symphony orchestra based on indigenous and *mestizo* dances. Amateur musicians in *bandas de pueblo* [town brass bands] and semi-professional musicians in military bands performed their own arrangements of these dances.

pasillos, *pasacalles*, and *albazos* came to symbolize the high culture upon which the elite concept of *música nacional* came to be constructed.

The *Pasillo*

Of all the genres represented within *música nacional*, the *pasillo* stands out as the musical symbol of Ecuador because many citizens have come to believe that it truly expresses the deepest sentiments of the national soul (Wong 2007). Although there is much speculation about its origins, it appears that its musical features can be traced to a local form of the European waltz, which was introduced into current Ecuadorian territories from Colombia with the Wars of Independence in the 1820s. The *pasillo* may be performed in various ways,[7] though the standardized form features duet singing in parallel thirds accompanied by a guitar and a *requinto* [a small high-pitched guitar]. The rhythmic accompaniment consists of a triple-meter waltz-derived pattern (Example 2.1)

Example 2.1 Typical triple-meter *pasillo* rhythmic accompaniment derived from the waltz

waltz   pasillo

The *pasillo* has held different functions and meanings over time. In the second half of the nineteenth century, it was primarily an instrumental genre performed by military bands and *estudiantinas* [ensembles of guitar-like instruments] in outdoor venues; it was also salon music, and an embraced popular dance with short jump-like steps (Guerrero 1997). In the early twentieth century, the *pasillo* evolved into a form of love song that was frequently sung in serenades. It came to be associated with "Ecuadorianness" when it was first recorded (1910s) and broadcast on the radio (1930s).

It is widely believed that the *pasillo*, as a metaphor for the nation, has always been a gentle and romantic expression of love that idealizes the female figure in her roles as mother and lover. In its early period in the late 1910s, however, the *pasillo* was in fact a musical expression of the popular classes; the elites later appropriated and transformed it into what Ecuadorians call a "classy song" (Wong 2007). The lyrics of many early twentieth-century *pasillos*, known in this period as *canciones de maldición* [songs of damnation], depict treacherous women in derogative terms such as "shameless whore" and "daughter of vice."[8] In the

---

[7] *Pasillos* have been performed by military bands, *estudiantinas*, symphony orchestras, piano, organ, and ensembles of harps and guitars, guitars and accordion, or any other combination of instruments.

[8] Lyrics from *El Cancionero del Guayas*, Guayaquil, 1920.

1920s–30s, upper-middle-class poets "whitened" these songs by transforming the vulgar texts into poems depicting nostalgic feelings of love, which were set to music by lower-middle-class composers who had assimilated into the elite culture.

Pasillos that express love and pride for Ecuador's geography and people were first composed on the occasion of the Dúo Ecuador's trip to New York in order to record Ecuadorian music for Columbia Records.[9] With its elegant poetry, metaphors, and musical arrangements that were reminiscent of a European-oriented musical aesthetic (polished singing style in parallel thirds, elaborate guitar accompaniment, instrumental interludes between stanzas), this type of *pasillo* portrayed the elites as cultivated and sensitive people. It was this type of *pasillo* that the elites nationalized in the 1920s–30s with the support of the national and international media and an emerging middle class that listened to the music. "Manabí," a song composed in 1933 by Francisco Paredes Herrera—known as the "King of *Pasillo*" for his prolific musical production—to a poem by Elías Cedeño, exemplifies an elite *pasillo* whose lyrics exalt the magnificence of the coastal province of Manabí (Example 2.2).

Example 2.2   "Manabí," composed in 1933 by Francisco Paredes Herrera; lyrics by Elías Cedeño

Tierra hermosa de mis sueños donde ví la luz primera
Donde ardió la inmensa hoguera de mi ardiente frenesí
De tus plácidas comarcas de tus fuentes y boscajes
De tus vívidos paisajes no me olvido Manabí.

Beautiful land of my dreams, where I saw the first light,
Where the immense fire blazed of my ardent frenzy.
Of your placid regions, of your fountains and woods,
Of your vivid landscapes I do not forget you, Manabí.

---

[9]   This was the first time Ecuadorian musicians traveled abroad to record Ecuadorian music. Until then, Ecuadorian music had only been recorded abroad by foreign artists and orchestras, or in Ecuador by local singers.

The elite *música nacional* anthology was written and performed by a pantheon of authors, composers, and performers whose lives, song lyrics and music are well known to the majority of Ecuadorians because these songs are often taught in schools and listened to on the radio. Renowned artists such as the Dúo Benítez-Valencia, the Hermanos Miño-Naranjo, the Trío Los Brillantes, and Julio Jaramillo innovated and imposed their singing styles in the 1950s and 1960s. Trío Los Brillantes, for example, popularized the three-part vocal arrangement and the guitar-and-*requinto* [small guitar] accompaniment introduced by Mexican Trío Los Panchos in the late 1940s, giving the *pasillo* a more international appeal.

The genre reached its golden period in the 1960s and early 1970s, an era of economic prosperity in Ecuador due to the banana export boom (1948–60) and the discovery of petroleum in the Amazon region (1972). The adoption of the economic model of import substitution to foster the industrialization of the country was a major factor in the development of the local music industry. Licensed to produce records of international music in Ecuador, IFESA (1946) and FEDISCOS (1964), the two major record manufacturers, gained total control of the Ecuadorian market for both national and international music through their records, radio networks, music stores, and publication of magazines, songbooks, and music scores of Ecuadorian popular music.

In the 1970s, IFESA released the recording series "Grandes Compositores Ecuatorianos" [Great Ecuadorian Composers], a collection of 33rpm records featuring the most popular songs of the *música nacional* corpus, many of which were *pasillos* from the 1920s and 1930s. FEDISCOS released "Ecuatorianísima" [The Essence of Ecuador], another recording series that honored the most celebrated *música nacional* performers. Music enthusiasts published songbooks that included not only the lyrics of the most popular *pasillos*, *pasacalles*, and *albazos*, but also biographies, pictures, music scores, and stories about the circumstances in which the songs were created. These songbooks and recording series have greatly contributed to the canonization of the elite *música nacional* corpus.

A revision of the printed media and record production in the early 1960s shows that Ecuadorians were proud of their urban popular music and their national artists, who had plenty of performance opportunities in live concerts and radio and television programs. *Música nacional* competed with the Mexican *bolero romántico* and the modern *balada* for top rankings on the national billboard. In the mid-1960s, recordings of Julio Jaramillo and Trío Los Brillantes sold as well in Ecuador as those of international artists such as Raphael and Los Iracundos. In the 1970s, however, the popularity of the elite *pasillo* declined with the advent of new international musics, such as rock, *cumbia*, *nueva canción*, *salsa*, and disco. Middle-class Ecuadorians, who were the main supporters and consumers of *música nacional*, were awash in new musical options that suggested youth, modernity, dance, happiness, and social protest, in contrast to *música nacional*, which by the late 1970s suggested old, non-danceable, and sad music about despair and unrequited love.

In search of larger audiences, radio and television stations, which had previously promoted and organized *música nacional* contests and festivals, began to devote more time to international music. Music piracy, government policies, and the elite's

La Música Nacional

disdain for the indigenous and working-class overtones that had become grafted onto the new *pasillos* from the 1980s further contributed to the genre's decline. Trying to keep their businesses above water, in the 1980s and 1990s IFESA and FEDISCOS released new albums with selections of old *pasillo* recordings in cassette and compact disc formats, as this was cheaper than releasing entirely new recordings. Since no major performers of elite *música nacional* have emerged since the early 1980s, for the past three decades Ecuador's youth have been exposed to the same *pasillos*, *pasacalles*, and *albazos* interpreted by the same *música nacional* singers who were at the peak of their careers in the 1960s and 1970s. In 2007, for example, I attended a performance in Quito of the Hermanos Miño-Naranjo, who started their singing career in the early 1960s and continue to attract large audiences to their concerts.

A working-class *pasillo* emerged in the aftermath of the rural-to-urban migrations of the 1960s and 1970s that reflected the migrants' life experiences in urban centers. This type of *pasillo* retained the general musical features of the elite *pasillo*, but differed in its musical style and approach to lyrics. The upper-middle classes perceived it as a cheapening of the elite *pasillo* because, according to them, it lacks the poetry and sophisticated arrangements characteristic of elite *música nacional*.[10] In addition, they criticized the performers' melodramatic and sobbing singing style, which is characterized by a pinched, nasal vocal production not typical of *música nacional*.

One example is "Te quiero, te quiero" [I love you, I love you], composed by Nicolás Fiallos in the early 1980s and popularized by *rocolera* singer Ana Lucía Proaño. This song is a declaration of love expressed in colloquial language and devoid of the metaphors and poetic devices commonly employed in the elite *pasillo*. Proaño sings with a high-pitched strident voice, and the musical arrangement incorporates a synthesizer with an organ-like timbre, as well as pentatonic-derived melodies harmonized in the minor mode. These musical traits are reminiscent of indigenous musical features and atypical of the elite *pasillo*, which, as indicated earlier, is normally sung with polished voices in parallel thirds and accompanied by an acoustic guitar ensemble.

Cada día que pasa, cada hora, un minuto	Each day that passes, each hour, each minute
Yo siento que te amo, y te amo mucho más.	I feel I love you, and I love you more and more.
No hay distancia ni tiempo, ni santo en ningún templo	There is no distance, no time, nor saint in any temple
Que impidan que te diga te quiero, te quiero.	That prevents me from telling you "I love you, I love you."

---

[10] Commenting on the state of the *pasillo* in the early 1980s, *El Universo*, one of the main newspapers of Guayaquil, presented the view of a popular musician as follows: "the lyrics and the melodies of many recently composed *pasillos* are banal and tasteless; musicians do not look for poets ... now they are only interested in 'making a hit song' to get royalties." *El Universo*, December 9, 1981.

54   *Soundscapes from the Americas*

Such *pasillos* became associated with a working-class style of music known as *rocolera* music. "*Rocolera*" derives from *rocola*, the Ecuadorian word for jukebox, which is currently found in *cantinas* [lower-class bars]. *Rocolera* music comprises a repertoire of Antillean *boleros* and Peruvian *valses del pueblo* whose lyrics deal with treacherous women, love triangles, break-ups, and drinking as a way of coping with heartbreak. Although working-class *pasillos* like "Te quiero, te quiero" do not refer to these topics, they are nevertheless associated with drunkenness and the *cantina* because, through repeated experiential associations, the songs and the singers who perform them have become indexical signs for *rocolera* ambiences. Applying Peircian semiotics, Turino argues that music typically serves as a powerful index (a sign that stands for something and creates an effect in the observer) for people and situations where one has heard the music, even when this occurs outside of the original social context (Turino 2008). He uses the term "semantic snowballing effect" to describe the multiple significations of indices depending on the past experiences of the perceivers.

In the early 1980s, *rocolera* entrepreneurs organized huge concerts sponsored by Ecuadorian liquor companies. These events, which started in the evening and lasted until the early morning hours, sometimes ended in episodes of violence due to excessive alcohol consumption. The elites regarded *rocolera* concerts as big public *cantinas* where working-class people ventilated their misfortunes in love (Ibarra 1998). The fact that working-class *pasillos* were composed and interpreted by the same composers and singers of *boleros rocoleros* have led Ecuadorians of all social classes to identify the working-class *pasillo* as *rocolera* music (Wong 2007). The co-occurrence of this semiotic connection explains why the working-class *pasillo* is seen as *rocolera* music, rather than as *pasillo*.

Needless to say, the performance contexts and audiences of, and images conveyed by the elite and working-class *pasillos* are quite different. In Quito, for example, the elite *pasillo* is performed for upper- and middle-class audiences at reputable venues, such as the National Theater of the Casa de la Cultura Ecuatoriana, while *rocolera* singers perform working-class *pasillos* for *el pueblo* [the people] in sports arenas and stadiums located in lower-class neighborhoods, such as the Coliseo Julio César Hidalgo and the Estadio Aucas. While the elite *pasillo* is perceived as the musical symbol of Ecuador and as music for listening, the working-class *pasillo* is thought of as a people's music and as music for drinking. These perceptions have been reinforced by the fact that in the 1980s and 1990s informal vendors were allowed to sell inexpensive alcoholic drinks during *rocolera* concerts, while drinking was prohibited in middle-class concert halls. Furthermore, performers who sing elite *música nacional* do not sing *rocolera* music, and vice versa.

The *Sanjuanito*

While the *pasillo* is emblematic of elite *música nacional*, the *sanjuanito* is the prominent genre within working-class *música nacional*. The *sanjuanito* is the most popular indigenous dance-song genre in the Ecuadorian highland region. It is performed during the festivities of San Juan (Saint John the Baptist), which coincide with the *Inti Raymi*, a summer-solstice ritual in which Andean indigenous people give thanks to the *Pachamama* [Mother Earth] for the agricultural blessings she has bestowed (Wibbelsman 2009). The *sanjuanito* is also a folkloric dance and an urban popular music whose many fans comprise indigenous and lower-middle-class *mestizo* people. The *sanjuanito mestizo* displays Spanish influence in its more elaborate musical structure (binary form) and arrangements for instruments of European origin such as guitar, accordion, and violin. Its lyrics deal with a variety of topics about everyday life and may be sung in Spanish or Quichua, Ecuador's main indigenous language.

In the first half of the twentieth century, an urban *sanjuanito* was composed that featured lyrics, musical structure, and a tonal approach that conformed to the elites' European-oriented aesthetics and was thus eligible to enter the *música nacional* repertoire. "Pobre corazón" [Poor heart], a song composed in the late 1910s by Guillermo Garzón, a band director and popular musician from the central highlands, is an example of a "cleaned-up" *sanjuanito* perceived today as elite *música nacional*, rather than as a song of indigenous origin (Example 2.3). The lyrics talk about a person who, with a heavy heart, bids farewell to a dear friend or loved one. This song may have started out as a traditional *sanjuanito*, since the notion of *música nacional* did not exist in the 1910s. However, it was later adapted to the elites' musical aesthetics. This is observed in the structure of the poetic form (alternation of decasyllabic and octosyllabic verses), guitar-and-*requinto* accompaniment, melodic lines, and the short interludes intertwined between the verses.

Example 2.3   "Pobre corazón" [Poor heart], composed in the late 1910s by Guillermo Garzón

Pobre corazón entristecido   Poor saddened heart
Ya no puedo más soportar.   I cannot take it anymore.
Y al decirte adiós, yo me despido   In bidding you farewell, I leave
Con el alma, con la vida   With my soul, with my life,
Con el corazón entristecido.   With a saddened heart.

In the 1950s and 1960s, IFESA and FEDISCOS recorded commercial renditions of the *sanjuanito mestizo*, whose lyrics are generally concerned with everyday indigenous life and include sexual double entendres. The *sanjuanito* "No te has peinado" [You have not combed your hair] tells the story of a woman who finds out when she returns to her home that her husband has neither taken a bath nor combed his hair all day. "El conejito" [Little rabbit] tells the story of a little rabbit that jumped into bed during the night and does not want to leave it. Although these *sanjuanitos* were recorded by renowned *música nacional* singers such as Carlos Rubira Infante, the author of numerous elite *pasillos* and *pasacalles*, they did not enter the *música nacional* anthology because of the ethnic images they portrayed. Other regional and folkloric types of *sanjuanito*, such as those performed by Otavalan pan-Andean ensembles, are also not part of the *música nacional* corpus due to their strong ethnic associations.[11]

In the late 1990s and early 2000s, hundreds of thousands of Ecuadorians from all walks of life left the country in search of better opportunities as a result of Ecuador's worst economic crisis of the twentieth century, which resulted in the failure of most banks and, soon afterwards, the dollarization of the economy. In 1999, Peruvian singer Rossy War arrived in Ecuador and introduced the *tecnocumbia*, an eclectic urban popular music derived from the *cumbia andina*, which combines Andean melodies, *cumbia* rhythm, and electronic instrumentation (Turino 1990). Rather than alienating Ecuadorian popular music, the *tecnocumbia* boom actually revitalized it with the organization of massive concerts in sports arenas and bullfight plazas. It also fostered the emergence of an alternative music industry led by popular singers, composers, and music entrepreneurs who developed their own marketing strategies to promote themselves and their music through concerts that were filmed and released on local (UHF) television channels in Quito with minimal financial investment. Music entrepreneurs who organized these events secured enough performers for the concerts by exchanging free publicity on their television programs for free concert performances. These concerts and videos, in turn, created a star system among Ecuadorian popular singers, who then began to independently produce and sell their own CDs at the concerts. For these singers, the concerts and their video clips and CDs functioned as promotional tools that increased their chances for private presentation contracts (weddings and birthday parties), their main source of income.

Less influential *rocolera* and *chichera* singers switched to the *tecnocumbia* repertoire and became "*ídolos del pueblo*" [idols of the people]. At first, they sang covers of Peruvian *tecnocumbias*,[12] especially those of Armonía 10 and Agua

---

[11] The modern *sanjuanitos* performed by Otavalan pan-Andean ensembles, such as Ñanda Mañachi and the Grupo Peguche, are folkloric renditions often played as musical accompaniment to folkloric dances.

[12] *Tecnocumbias* performed by Peruvian singers are unknown in Ecuador, and the few groups that have attempted to make inroads into the local music market, like Agua Bella in 2002, were not particularly successful.

Marina, two tropical dance orchestras from the northern region of Peru. Then, *chichera* composers, such as Ricardo Realpe and Guido Narváez, began writing their own *tecnocumbias* using rhythmic and melodic features of the *sanjuanito*, the *cumbia*, and other Caribbean genres. The lyrics usually refer to experiences of migration, especially those related to long-distance relationships and nostalgia for the homeland. Song titles such as "El cartero" [The postman] and "Por internet" [By internet] are about waiting for news from home; "Me abandonaste" [You abandoned me] and "Olvidarte jamás" [I will never forget you] are concerned with feelings arising from a couple's separation.

Broadly speaking, the great success of *tecnocumbia* in Ecuador was largely due to the fact that it projected a sense of modernity with its energetic dance choreographies, modern costumes (knee-high and high-heeled boots, small and tight outfits), and electronic instrumentation, elements that are foreign to performances of elite *música nacional*. Most importantly, *tecnocumbia* provided a source of entertainment and an escape valve for the popular classes during a time of economic hardship. It is worth noting that the Ecuadorian popular classes are aware of *tecnocumbia*'s Peruvian origin, but embrace it as an Ecuadorian music when Ecuadorian singers perform it with national sentiment.

In the early 2000s, Los Conquistadores, an indigenous/*mestizo* group from the central highlands, had enormous success among the popular classes with a cover of the *sanjuanito* "El conejito," arranged for synthesizers, electric bass, and percussion, and subsequently recorded by numerous *chichera* singers and music bands such as Rock Star and Star Band. When I arrived in Ecuador in 2001, this song was heard everywhere—on the radio, in buses, and on the streets—though it was scorned and ridiculed by the elites for its simplistic lyrics containing double entendres, and the rabbit ears and tails the dancers wore when performing it (Figure 2.2). Soon afterwards, indigenous and *mestizo* solo singers and songwriters, such as Ángel Guaraca and Bayronn Caicedo, appeared on the local scene, attracting a large following of indigenous people and lower-class *mestizos* by singing original songs in *sanjuanito* and other indigenous genres. Their lyrics refer not only to the experience of international migration, but also to the pride and unity of indigenous people (Wong 2007). Guaraca's song "Campesino de mi tierra" [Peasant of my land], for example, claims the *poncho* as an Ecuadorian cultural symbol.

Gradually, the popular classes began applying the term *música nacional* to *chichera*, *rocolera*, and even *tecnocumbia*. At concerts, I frequently asked people whether a *chichera* or *rocolera* song being performed at the time of the interview was "Ecuadorian music," and they usually responded, "Yes, it is *música nacional!*" Then, when I asked the same people if the music was *rocolera*, most answered, "Yes, it is *rocolera* music," and would then add, "It's *música nacional*." I am less interested here in analyzing the truth of this statement than in examining people's perceptions of the music they identify with the Ecuadorian nation through the use of particular labels.

Figure 2.2 Los Conquistadores performing "El conejito" in the Coliseo Julio César Hidalgo, 2002. Photo by Ketty Wong

Conclusion

Stereotyping and labeling styles of music with derogatory terms have constituted effective "technologies of Othering" that raise social boundaries among different social classes and ethnic groups. In the 1980s, the elite *música nacional* repertoire comprised numerous *pasillos*, *pasacalles*, and *albazos* from the 1920s–50s, and a few *sanjuanitos* stripped of indigenous features and recorded by elite *música-nacional* singers, such as "Pobre corazón." Commercial versions of *sanjuanitos mestizos*, such as "El conejito," were considered *chichera* by the upper-middle classes; similarly, they regarded the working-class *pasillos* of the 1970s–80s, such as "Te quiero, te quiero," as *rocolera* music. The elites used *chichera* and *rocolera* as derogatory terms identifying ethnic groups and social contexts associated with drunkenness, "Indianness," and working-class ambiences, while the term *música nacional* suggested the type of Ecuadorian music that educated, sensitive, and "decent" upper-middle-class Ecuadorians listened to.

Since the late 1990s, however, the popular classes have been using the term *música nacional* to refer to the modern *sanjuanito*, the *tecnocumbia*, and the working-class *pasillo*. This is especially true of younger Ecuadorians who are largely unfamiliar with the old *música nacional* repertoire, and for whom *chichera* and *rocolera* songs may be the only Ecuadorian music they know. It is unlikely that in the early 1980s the popular classes would have referred to *rocolera* and *chichera* songs as *música nacional*, as they frequently do now, because the social boundaries these music labels demarcated were rigid and assumed by everyone. Currently, the popular classes use the term *música nacional* to refer to all types of music sung by Ecuadorian singers, as long as they are sung with so-called "national sentiment," thus showing that it is not the musical genre per se, but a shared "Ecuadorian" aesthetic that brings disparate musics, such as the *tecnocumbia*, the *pasillo*, and the *sanjuanito* together.

As seen in this article, *música nacional* embodies different perceptions of Ecuadorian national identity depending on who is doing the perceiving. As in the ideology of *mestizaje*, the elite notion of *música nacional* is exclusionist and marginalizes the indigenous and Afro-Ecuadorian popular musics in the imagining of the nation. The *sanjuanito mestizo* and the early twentieth-century *pasillo* [songs of damnation] were "whitened" and "edited" to conform to the elites' class ideology and aesthetic preferences. The working-class notion of *música nacional*, however, is inclusive and better portrays the heterogeneous Ecuadorian population with various repertoires and styles of music representing both the elites and the popular classes. Furthermore, the popular classes distinguish between *música nacional bailable*, made up of happy and danceable *sanjuanitos* and *tecnocumbias*, and *música nacional antigua*, which comprises the old *pasillos*, *pasacalles*, and *albazos* from the 1920s–50s. I frequently observed this distinction being made during my stay in Quito from 2002 to 2004, especially when I asked street vendors to show me their CDs of Ecuadorian music. They usually responded, "Do you want *música nacional antigua* or *música nacional bailable*?"

Lower-class *mestizos* have appropriated and resignified *música nacional*, a label that has represented the elites' definition of Ecuadorian music and their sociocultural hegemony in the twentieth century. With their all-encompassing vision of *música nacional*, the Ecuadorian popular classes are indeed providing a more democratic reading of the ideology of *mestizaje* and a better portrait of Ecuador as an ethnically diverse and heterogeneous nation.

Chapter 3
Conserve, Adapt, and Reconverge: Rationalizing a Template in Hawai'i Puerto Rican Musical Performance

Ted Solís

Introduction: Dancing for the Past

The electric echo from the cool, cream-colored plaster walls dies away as the couples finish their waltz, men delivering their partners back to the long tables, seating themselves again among the drinks, ash trays, dishes of *pasteles* (pronounced here, in Caribbean Spanish fashion, as "*pa'tele*") and *gandule* rice. The uninhibited gregarious chatter is all in English, but the accents are pure Hawai'i. The musicians stand, exchanging a few words; one lights a cigarette. Sound hangs; the drinker/talkers are attentive to whatever comes; they are dedicated dancers as much as drinkers and talkers, and they know that whatever this group plays will inspire them to dance— no question about that—no danger of disco, hip hop, rock, or even *salsa*, for that matter. They have a comfortable sound world, immune to unwelcome surprises.

The lead *cuatro* player begins the characteristic rising arpeggiated pick-up phrase of a *seis caliente* and we hear from the assemblage a collective welcoming sigh of warm anticipation. Energized, men move quickly to partners (strict gender protocol), leading them out to the floor in front of the small bandstand. They move in tandem, erectly and smoothly, not too closely entwined physically, looking past one another with non-committal expressions, their pleasure in dancing and in each other subtly expressed mainly in their close coordination. They engage in few *salsa* or *merengue*-like wraps, turns, fancy moves, kicks, or taps; their feet move in a deceptively simple forward and back motion overtly reflecting the bass rhythm and less directly, but more fundamentally and deeply seated, the implied syncopation of the guitar strum—no *salsa* cross-rhythms. Their hip movements, while not stiff, are understated and distinctly not Afro-Latin; the movements would appear, to many Latinos, formal, erect, and somehow archaic, the way they might remember their grandparents dancing.

This is the dance hall downstairs in the United Puerto Rican Association of Hawai'i building in Kalihi, a working-class neighborhood west of downtown Honolulu, on the island of Oahu, and the time is the 1980s. Long ago this used to be Silva's Ballroom; before that it was something else, and before that, something else. The ensemble is typical of 1980s and 1990s Hawai'i Puerto Rican dance bands: a *cuatro*, or five-coursed lead Creole guitar played with flat pick; ordinary six-string guitar for strummed accompaniment; electric bass guitar; *güiro* gourd scraper; and *bongós* and/or *congas*. *Cuatro* and *güiro* players are most typically lead vocalists, the others providing *coros* [responses]. All these instruments are familiar either to contemporary pan-Latin music aficionados, with the possible exception of the *cuatro*, which is more specific to modern Puerto Rican folk music. Its distinctive curvaceous, violin-like appearance and "tinkly" timbre stemming from its unison and octave double courses are almost always important Puerto Rican signifiers whenever added to *salsa* or Latin jazz instrumentation. The core ensemble of *cuatro*, güiro, and guitar is for the most part associated in Puerto Rico with the music of Jíbaro highland peasant farmers, but now primarily in a self-consciously folkloric sense. In Puerto Rico Jíbaro symbols are foregrounded positively: icons such as white, dark-brimmed "Panama" hats, *güiros*, and *cuatros* have become pan-Puerto Rican symbols. Jíbaro musics (especially the *seis* and *aguinaldo* genres) and food (*lechón*, *pasteles*) blanket Puerto Rico during the Christmas season, a time of great communal interaction. This music is also heard in folkloric festivals, hotel folkloric shows, and intermittently sponsored *concursos de trovadores* [sung poetry improvisation contests], which emphasize the *décima espinela*.[1] On the other hand, Jíbaro music is much less commonly heard outside these contexts, even in Puerto Rico, and certainly has been considerably declining in everyday life throughout the twentieth century.[2]

But we are not at a folkloric presentation, or a San Juan hotel, or a *concurso de trovadores*; we are in a dance hall in Honolulu (why Hawai'i?), and people are drinking and socializing. But are music and dance the excuse for this conviviality, or is it the other way around? Why these instruments? Why this ensemble? Why this repertoire? Why these performance practices? Or, to put it another way, why not other, far more hegemonic assortments of instruments, ensembles, repertoire, and performance practices?

---

[1]   The *décima* is a traditional Iberian 10-line octosyllabic or hexasyllabic poetic form found throughout Latin America. A number of *décima* schemes exist, but the most common in Puerto Rico is the *espinela*, whose rhyme scheme is ABBAACCDDC. (Lines 1, 4, and 5 rhyme with each other, as do 2 and 3; 6, 7, and 10; and 8 and 9.) The octosyllabic form was set to the secular *seis*, and hexasyllabically, to the Yuletide *aguinaldo*. Using this complex verse form, *trovadores* were expected to improvise upon topics in real time, sometimes with the additional challenge of a *pie forzado* [forced foot], a final line which was presented to them ad hoc, and with which the preceding, to be improvised, poetic scheme must appropriately fit.

[2]   At the same time that Jíbaro culture was declining in the Puerto Rican countryside, Jíbaros were in the process of becoming at the national level what Kirshenblatt-Gimblett (1995:371) calls "museums of themselves." Successive Puerto Rican governments have found Jíbaros (in their folkloric roles) a safe and useful pan-Puerto Rican symbol.

The dynamics of a Hawai'i Puerto Rican music/dance performance are, like any performance, rooted in the past, present, and even the perceived future. The choice of media, repertoire, the order of pieces, the overall frame of an event, the framing of events within the overall frame, the relationship of *dramatis personae* (audience and performers) all are to an extent culture-specific. In the words of McLeod and Herndon: "The ethnography of musical performance requires, at the outset, the determination of a wider social field which includes not only the physical sounds, but also the actions, thoughts, and feelings of those involved in the conception, performance, and reception of music in a particular cultural context" (McLeod and Herndon 1980:6). To this encapsulation I would add Béhague's "rules or codes of performance defined by the community for a specific context or occasion" (Béhague 1984a:7). Actually establishing clear connections, however, is something else again.

Hawai'i Puerto Rican (hereafter "HPR") music and dance performance is eminently public and designed for communication with an appreciative audience. The basic assumptions and overt *raison d'être* of this performance complex have not essentially changed to any significant degree since the antecedents of this tradition were imported to Hawai'i in the early twentieth century; the music is considered recreational and communal, and apart from rehearsals (and arranged performances for ethnomusicological fieldworkers), has very little of a "high art" or "art for its own sake" mystique.

Musical performance practice in the Hawai'i Puerto Rican community results from a tension between conservatism, or the desire to maintain a particular set of symbolic and aesthetic values, and the impulse to expand upon that set. Adherence to the set appears to have been a particularly conscious decision, while accretions to it seem much less overt, occurring without fanfare, and with an ever-present, although understated rationale linking them to the tradition.

I have elsewhere referred to a kind of "filtering mechanism" relating to HPR self-image, in which members of this community evaluate their own cultural performance and cultural artifacts relative to Jíbaro self-image, within an overall Puerto Rican rubric. Puerto Ricans are accepted in Hawai'i as a small "local" ethnic group. In Hawai'i parlance the word "local" refers to traditional ethnic groups of long standing and cultural critical mass: native Polynesian Hawaiians (hereafter "Hawaiians") or descendants of long domiciled non-*haole* [Anglo/Caucasian] populations such as Chinese, Japanese, Portuguese, Filipinos, Koreans, and others brought to the islands as plantation workers. HPRs refer to themselves as Puerto Rican in the general sense, but many find the locus of emotional and aesthetic values in the more specific term "Jíbaro." This term is well known to all HPRs, but is relatively unknown to other locals lacking specialist knowledge or strong connections to the HPR community.

The term "Puerto Rican," as HPRs apply it to themselves, conveys a more abstract sense of political identity and geographic origin, in the sense of modern nation-state, and virtually all official documents use the term. "Jíbaro," on the other hand, is almost exclusively used within the group, and is heavily weighted with emotional and aesthetic valuation. We can find within this concept the rationales for virtually every aspect of contemporary HPR performance practice, whether organological, choreographic, or sonic. In this chapter I will interrogate the narrative and reality of this performance practice, noting its arc-like chronological contour. By this I mean that during the 1930s and 1940s urbanization process, when HPRs began leaving the plantations in large numbers, they diverged considerably from the early 1900s plantation musical culture transplanted from Puerto Rico, facing more squarely mass media and the demands of a broader American society. Their reaction to these influences and challenges involved, on the one hand, adaptation of material culture and a variety of performance practices and, on the other, loss, homogenization, and amalgamation of traditional forms. Later, beginning in the 1950s and 1960s, under the further influence of mass media and a resumption of physical communication between Puerto Rico and Hawai'i HPR musical culture, HPRs more directly re-engaged with the Jíbaro music of the Puerto Rico their forebears had left six decades earlier, re-establishing a negotiated musical orthodoxy. However, the tradition they re-joined had meanwhile perforce adapted some Afro-Cuban instrumentation and performance practices; these were apparently palatable to HPRs because they experienced them via "bona fide" Jíbaro mass mediation. HPRs, however, have largely resisted attempts by their Caribbean or Nuyorican brethren to overtly "correct" their musical and linguistic archaisms. Béhague speaks to these sorts of dynamics in the context of his Brazilian *candomblé* scholarship: "It is clear ... that any effort toward the re-Africanization of the local religions, particularly through language, is bound to fail because its artificiality goes against well-established cultural dynamics, resulting from the whole complex of local cultural and historical contexts" (Béhague 1984b:249). For younger HPRs, poignantly aware of the broken link with Puerto Rico (barely a handful of immigrants from early in the century, brought to Hawai'i as infants, survived into the early 1990s), recordings in a sense had come to serve as surrogate ancestors. They constituted what, in another context, I have neologically called "a 'pathoscape,' an emotional [sound] landscape" (Solís 2004:234).

"Jíbaro" as a State of Mind: Demographics of the Hawai'i Puerto Rican Migration

The "local" HPR population primarily derives from contracted sugar plantation laborers brought to Hawai'i in 1900 and 1921, and in the 1990s numbered some 15,000. These immigrants did not represent a cross-section of Puerto Rico's population at that time; rather, they were drawn almost entirely from among the highland Jíbaro peasants, many of whose small subsistence farms had been recently devastated by Hurricane San Siriaco, leaving them without food and income, and thus amenable to migration in the pursuit of employment. Jíbaro emphasized their "white" Iberian (and, to a lesser extent, Amerindian) heritage (obvious and inevitable cultural and racial contact with Afro-Puerto Ricans notwithstanding) and styles of cultural production, especially poetic, music, and dance forms and performance practices, and linguistic archaisms.

The Jíbaro in Puerto Rico experienced upheaval due to the hurricane, which exacerbated the longtime gradual drift to the cities from their relatively isolated highland yeoman holdings. The Jíbaros who then left Puerto Rico for Hawai'i were doubly isolated as Spanish-speaking Catholic Latins on a Pacific Polynesian island where, in 1900, many still spoke Hawaiian, with a small *haole* Caucasian English-speaking population effectively in charge of the economy (including ownership of the plantations), education, and government at virtually every level. Their first fellow plantation workers were primarily Asians—Japanese and Chinese, followed within a few years by importations of Koreans and Filipinos. Jíbaros were separated from the *haole* owners by a rigid social hierarchy as well as from the Portuguese, early settlers mostly from Madeira and the Azores. Most had already left the plantations, but as privileged Europeans, those who remained worked primarily as supervisors.

Economic class structure and physical isolation during the plantation period laid the groundwork for and coalesced with subsequent social/class marginalization associated with urban migration. Many of the sugar plantations were for long periods relatively segregated by ethnic group. The resulting "Japanese camps," "Filipino camps," "Puerto Rican camps," and so on, were nurturing islands of traditional ethnic culture. Workers lived with their families in company residences and enjoyed "house dances" (in the small living rooms) that for decades tended to preserve the music and dance practices of the immigrant generation.

In the more than ninety years since the principal migrations to Hawai'i, extensive urbanization and homogenization have blurred Puerto Rico's inherent Iberian-African polarity. The great cultural gap between highland Jíbaros and lowland Afro-Puerto Ricans that existed at the time of the first migration has considerably narrowed in Puerto Rico itself, under the impact of large incorporated plantations and industrialization. These processes effectively drew Jíbaros from their individual shareholdings, ultimately urbanizing the island, and threw disparate racial groups together. Much of this Puerto Rico and concurrent New York cultural coalescence bypassed HPRs, who strongly embrace what they perceive as the Iberian-derived aspects of Jíbaro culture, and often substitute the word Jíbaro for Puerto Rican in referring to themselves. These cultural elements point toward what earlier generations of ethnomusicologists might have happily embraced as a study in conservatism, but I prefer to approach this study, in Bruno Nettl's words, somewhat less as "areas of agreement in ... society" than "as the arena of debates" (2002:192).

The "debate" in this instance consists almost entirely of HPR-conflicted and negotiated conceptions of "appropriate" Jíbaro musical identity. The obvious and indisputable Africanisms and Afro-Caribbean creolizations inherent in physiognomy and cuisine have striking parallels in music and dance, and, of course, subvert HPRs' Iberian cultural narrative. In the Caribbean, Creoles, the populations most sensitive to the precariousness of racial position, are often most prone to somewhat equivocal explanations of their racial heritage. Note Creole musical genius Jelly Roll Morton's famous first words in Alan Lomax's classic oral history *Mister Jelly Roll*: "As I can understand, my folks were in the city of New Orleans long before the Louisiana Purchase, and all my folks came directly from the shores of France" (1993:3). HPRs tend to cling to a perceived and idealized Iberian and Taino Caribbean Amerindian heritage. In much of Latin America, actual, living Amerindians are marginalized and exploited, and occupy a social level comparable to that of Afro-Latins. By contrast, the Caribbean islands for the most part provide only distant, highly mediated memories of the all-but-vanished Amerindian population. Importantly, such vanished Amerindians often have more cachet than the live variety—certainly in the Caribbean.[3] HPRs commonly claim part-Taino ancestry to explain away dark skin or "nonwhite" features.[4] Analogously, they have implicitly and sometimes explicitly rejected overtly African or Afro-Latin musical and dance features, while embracing Iberian-derived qualities of their past. Musical selection procedures at every level, whether with regard to genre, improvisation practices, dancing style, or musical instruments, have been influenced by this general preference schema.[5]

HPRs seldom allude to the matter of African heritage, which is clearly (especially for those of the older generations who do not subscribe to the black cultural cachet so pervasive in modern America) a painful and embarrassing subject. In June 1990, for example, I asked a prominent musician born in the early 1930s to compare his style with that of "X," a somewhat older, noted performer of the same instrument. I was in no way intentionally probing the racial issue. Yet he seemed uncomfortable, looked around him to see whether we would be overheard (we were in the UPRAH hall), lowered his voice, and said,

> X plays different from me ... . Puerto Ricans are all kinds of colors: red, white, brown ... . White folks like my grandparents played *seis*, *villarán* [i.e., Iberian-oriented Jíbaro genres] ... . Certain people, I don't like to name names, some play music more on the slave side. *Salsa*[6] ... is from the dark side of the music,

---

[3] Note, in an early 1950s Cuban *guajira-son*, the philo-Amerindian refrain, in praise of the Taino chief and rebel leader Hatuey, burned at the stake by the Spanish in the early sixteenth century: "*Cubano de raza pura soy, la muerte es gloria para mi, recuerdo al indio Siboney que dió su sangre como Hatuey.*" (I am a Cuban of pure race; death is glory for me; I remember the Siboney Indian [chief] who gave his blood [i.e., was martyred by the Spanish].")

[4] Duany (1994:69), Largey (1994:112), and Lewis (1963:501) refer to this same rationalization for the Dominican Republic, among Haitian Creoles, and West Indian immigrants to New York respectively.

[5] See Solís 1995 for an examination of how these attitudes affect musical instrument choices.

[6] I should make clear that, like virtually all HPRs, X did not play *salsa* per se, but rather earlier *típica* [folkloric] and popular Caribbean forms that are either peripheral to or

from the slave side; that's where *plena* [important coastal Afro-Puerto Rican genre] comes from, and *salsa* comes from that [*plena*] ... . X likes the *negrito* style more.

This musician considered mainline (i.e., non-African derived, at least in his opinion) Jíbaro music to be the appropriate standard, although he was willing to accept *plenas, merengues*, and other non-traditional genres as played by "Ramito" (the late *trovador*, i.e., singer/poetry improviser Flor Morales Ramos), Odilio Gonzalez, and "Chuito" in what he considered "Jíbaro style." As we will see below, these Jíbaro idols inadvertently served as Trojan horses for the almost inevitable introduction of genres and performance practices hitherto considered dubious by the community.

Conscious rejection of Afro genres has not, however, by any means precluded the gradual and occasional abrupt adoption of instruments and performance practices from that world; clearly, contemporary HPR music/dance culture is by no means frozen in time, but contrasts dramatically with that of the early 1900s, change having primarily been negotiated through the mediation of the Jíbaro filter mentioned earlier.

I will now examine the basic framework of the traditional HPR ensemble, and organological and stylistic accretions to that framework, beginning with what we must assume was an instrumentarium, repertoire, and performance practice identical (within the obvious limits of material culture[7] and personnel restrictions) to that left behind in Puerto Rico.

Plantation Musical Culture as a Template for Change

The examination of early plantation musical culture of 1900–20 is problematic. I have never seen a cohesive written description of dances; scarcely any written observations of musical life remain from the early Puerto Rican plantation period in Hawai'i, nor are many photographs or *any* recordings available. Only a small handful of people who were young children in the early 1900s survived into the 1990s, and virtually all are now dead. My research in general has been heavily dependent upon oral history; few plantation workers early in the century possessed even the simplest technology for documenting their lives.[8] Few letters

---

partly contribute to the evolution of salsa. HPRs often use the term *salsa* anachronistically, in that it clearly postdates these genres. It can serve as a symbol for Afro-Cuban/Afro-Caribbean music in general, without a strict adherence to the sorts of formal, harmonic, and instrumentation criteria marking the word's more specific context in recent years.

    [7]   See, for example, initial botanical limitations on *güiro* construction, below.

    [8]   "Who [on the plantations of her childhood] had a camera?" rhetorically remarked the daughter (84 at the time) of a near legendary Puerto Rico-born musician, *cuatro* player Juan Rodrigues, who died in his nineties in 1951.

or diaries exist, virtually no photos of musical activities before the 1930s, no home recordings before the 1940s (very few) and 1950s, and no commercial recordings (all for local, in-group distribution) before the 1970s.

Many plantation workers came from a functionally illiterate milieu and did not communicate by mail with their relatives at home. Few had the financial means to visit Puerto Rico, although some returned permanently. The Asian and European immigrant model of making good and returning to the motherland to distribute largesse and/or retire in comfort did not apply to poor Puerto Rican plantation workers with few opportunities for upward mobility. I never met any HPRs with personal connections to Nuyoricans or New York, or, for that matter, with tangible connections to family in Puerto Rico.[9]

My reconstruction is thus by necessity a composite, drawn from the recollections, often hagiographic, of musicians and dancers who were children sixty, seventy, and even eighty years earlier, of conditions from the 1910s–30s, when many Puerto Ricans were still on plantations. My own self-conscious involvement with HPR music began in the mid-1980s, by which time it had already changed considerably from the plantation period. I produced two CDs with very different goals (Solís 1989, 1994), in an order that might seem somewhat counterintuitive in the context of ethnomusicology's historical trajectory: the Smithsonian album was an eclectic, predominantly Latin overview of contemporary (mid-1980s) HPR musical culture, recorded live in living rooms, bars, a wedding, a mass, and a luau with various traditional and non-traditional instrumentation, and with very mixed acoustics. I happily embraced what I saw as a holistic presentation of typical HPR musical life, and required of myself little rationalization, other than that the music be Latin HPR in some way.[10]

The 1994 album, produced for the late John Storm Roberts's now-extinct Original Music company, was very different; an artifact of activist ethnomusicology on my part,[11] it represented my attempt to re-create plantation music, preserving older styles and repertoires. The album notes state that,

---

[9]   This strongly contrasts with the situation of New York Puerto Ricans, whose culture has long been paradigmatically one "of commuting, of a ... back and forth transfer between two intertwining zones [New York and Puerto Rico]" (Flores 1993:104). Flores borrows Luis Rafael Sánchez's (1987) metaphor of the *guagua aérea* [air bus] that transports Puerto Ricans: "a people who float between two ports."

[10]   The Catholic Mass that I recorded for the Smithsonian album, however, represented a considerably reconstructed artifact, one in which certain folklorically inclined individuals in the community thought it would be nice to reconstitute a Spanish-language version. However, as far as I know, HPRs virtually never had access to Spanish-language Catholicism during plantation days, attending churches with multiethnic congregations. They have never had parochial-ethnic churches of, say, the American Polish model, either during or after the plantation period.

[11]   I even harbored quixotic ambitions of staging an early 1900s house dance in a plantation house living room, with *dramatis personae* including dancers, musicians,

> In the interest of obtaining as traditional a sound as possible, we generally limited the instrumentation to that most commonly heard on sugar plantations before the Puerto Ricans dispersed to larger urban areas and began using Cuban-derived percussion and (from the late 1930s) electronic amplification. The basic ensemble featured in this recording is therefore the standard trio of 10-string *cuatro* melodic lead guitar, ... six-string Spanish guitar strumming an accompaniment, and *güiro* gourd scraper. (Solís 1994)

I certainly know much better than to seek any sort of proto-authentic *Ur*-style, preferring "explorations of horizontal relationships among related forms rather than searching vertically for unprovable origins" (Cook 2003:206, citing Schechner 1998:28), but nonetheless, surprisingly, found myself (like countless ethnomusicological and folkloric forebears) in search of a sort of Garden of Eden.

Oral accounts have a tendency to distill and simplify, and oral accounts of reality are often really collages and distillations, as Lise Waxer states, citing Roach 1996, "in which certain objects, images, or personae are substituted for some imagined original located in the past" (Waxer 2002:11). However, since we are in actuality concerned here with the relationship between a cognitive construction and the development of reality, it seems perfectly acceptable to me that we adopt what seems to be a rather consistently arising trope of Jíbaro appropriateness as a template. I thus found myself, as the researcher and producer of this recording, attempting to conform to my interpretation of the preconception.

The Narrative: Basic Ensemble of the Plantations

The basic assumption which I adapted was that of the primary HPR Jíbaro narrative: that the kinds of music and dance heard on early 1900s plantations were those popular in parts of Puerto Rico which the immigrants had recently left. The basic ensemble in this schema, attested to by most, not all, elderly HPRs, consisted of a trio led by a plucked string soloist playing the *cuatro*, a six-string Spanish guitar strumming an accompaniment, and a *güiro* (Figure 3.1).[12] The *sinfonía* button accordion was also a frequent presence on plantations and sometimes (although relatively infrequently) replaced the *cuatro* as the melodic lead. Later, in the 1930s, HPRs introduced *maracas*, which they frequently used along with *güiros* until the 1950s, especially for performing *boleros* and *rumbas*/rhumbas,[13] broadly defined.

---

traditional instrumentation, and traditional genres. This proved impossible—"gone with the wind."

[12] In the course of my research I met only three HPR accordionists in this traditional style, all born between about 1912 and 1921, all now deceased. Accordionists were rare enough in collective memory that only one, Juan Fiol (d. early 1950s), stood out as a well-known specialist from the 1920s through the 1940s.

[13] "Rhumba" is a common mainstream American spelling of the Cuban word *rumba*.

Figure 3.1   Charlie Vegas, plucked lead violin-shape modern *cuatro*; August Rodrigues, strummed Spanish guitar; Ted Solís, *güiro*. Lawai Valley, Kauai, Hawai'i, June 1990. Photo by Virginia Rodrigues

The Cuatro

The *cuatro* of the 1901 immigrant generation was very different from the modern curvaceous, five double-coursed violin-like instrument shown in Figure 3.1, which supplanted it in Puerto Rico from the 1930s on. It was, rather, generally referred to in Puerto Rico as *cuatro antiguo* [old *cuatro*]. For Caribbean Puerto Ricans, the most famous depiction of this instrument is to be found in the celebrated 1893 painting *El velorio* [The wake] by Puerto Rican artist Francisco Oller. Its general shape, viewed from the front, is similar to that of an old-fashioned keyhole, and is therefore in Hawai'i frequently referred to as a "keyhole *cuatro*." In Figure 3.2 we see an ornate old *cuatro* made and held by Miguel Rodrigues (1904–96), a musician since 1910 who continued to play the instrument occasionally until his death. Such *cuatros* were the most common melodic lead instrument at the time of the 1901 migration and remained so in Hawai'i until the early to middle 1930s, when they were supplanted by the American tenor guitar.[14]

---

[14]   I have seen the following Creole Puerto Rican stringed instruments mentioned as accompaniment, along with the *cuatro*, in nineteenth-century Puerto Rico Jíbaro music: *tiple*, *requinto*, *tres*, and *bordonua* (see Alonso [1849] 1986; Batista 1984; Centro de Investigaciones y Ediciones Musicales 1981). Only the oldest Puerto Ricans (octogenarians

Figure 3.2   Miguel Rodrigues, holding an ornate "old cuatro," standing with musician Tanilau Dias (1908–ca. 1994). Hilo, Hawai'i, July 1990. Photo by Ted Solís

HPRs apparently used both single- and double-string courses at different times. Although double-string courses seem to add resonance and loudness, any sort of logical Hawai'i evolution from single to double strings (an innovation conceivably introduced by 1921 immigrants) is purely conjectural: all available photos of old *cuatros* (the earliest I have found, from the late teens) show four double courses rather than single strings. All modern *cuatros* have double courses, and keyhole *cuatros* built in Hawai'i within living memory have to my knowledge all had double courses, as well. What we do not know is the extent to which instrument builders imposed what they knew of modern *cuatros*, retroactively, and anachronistically, upon reconstructions of old *cuatros*.

The Güiro

Güiro scrapers have long ideally been constructed from long gourds: the particular kinesthetic requirements of scraping appear to require a long, relatively straight

---

and nonagenarians) remembered even the first two. These instruments appear to be the only traditional Puerto Rican strings (as opposed to violin, guitar, mandolin, banjo, and other pan-EuroAmerican instruments) to have been frequently used in Hawai'i in a lead capacity. See the "Electric Bass" section for more on the *bordonua*.

72   *Soundscapes from the Americas*

surface or "long axis." Puerto Ricans in the Caribbean may have deliberately cultivated elongated gourds for the scrapers so essential to their music as basic density referents—what Koetting calls a "fastest pulse" (1970:122). Caribbean gourds were longer and harder than those rounded, globular varieties native to the Pacific, which were more suitable for the gourd gongs and rattles of traditional Hawaiian music (Solís 1995:128). Before the HPRs learned to cultivate suitable gourds (perhaps importing seeds), they often used ad hoc replacements: *tapas* [covers], readily available from old fashioned cans of coffee, shortening and other products, and scraped together, and cylindrical metal *güiros* with open ends from metal cans.

The Six-String Guitar

I am not aware of any particular conceptual restrictions placed upon the Spanish six-string guitars which have, to my knowledge, always served as strumming accompanists to all kinds of lead instruments.[15] They have included full-bodied acoustic, acoustic with simple microphone or pickup amplification, or electric instruments.

The typical guitar accompaniment for medium and fast dances reflects *güiro* rhythm and technique; it consists of strummed block chords in alternating sixteenth-note up-and-down strokes, the first in each set of four strokes being damped with the heel of the right hand. In Puerto Rico and among some of the oldest HPRs the pattern is called *habana[d]o* [lit. "Havana-d"], probably in recognition of the Cuban origin of the Puerto Rican *guaracha*.

Narrative: The Repertoire

Older HPRs with any memory of the plantations spoke of the *vals* [waltz], *guaracha*, *seis*, *danza*, *polca* [polka], *mazurca* [mazurka], and *aguinaldo* or Christmas song. All but the very last are dances, some of which are also sung; the *aguinaldo*, generally of religious content, was sung but not danced. The *polca* and *mazurca* are largely extinct; even the oldest HPRs remember little or nothing of the latter other than the name, and even commonly conflate it with the *polca* as "*mapolca*" (*sic*); both were considered specialist dances, for experts, even during the plantation period (Solís 2005:101). I was able to solicit and record a couple of versions of *polcas* (see Solís 1989 and 1994), but other than one conspicuously Mexicano version of the *polca-ranchera* "Ay, Jalisco no te rajes" in a bar, replete with faux-Mexican *gritos*, I have never heard a *polca* played publicly by HPRs. Of this traditional repertoire one may expect to hear several *seises*, *guarachas* (including some that would have originally been acknowledged as *danzas*—see below—and others from a variety of mostly Latin sources), and *valses*. Two

---

[15]   The guitar occasionally substitutes as lead; see Solís 1989, band 10, "Malditos Besos."

Conserve, Adapt, and Reconverge 73

post-plantation-era dances, the *bolero* (added in the 1930s) and *merengue* (in the 1950s), more or less complete the repertoire one may safely expect to hear in a given evening.

The *seis*, in its rich diversity, named variously for descriptive qualities, towns, performers, composers, or hybrids with other forms, is the genre with which Jíbaros most typically identify. Most variants are composite songs/dances distinguished by a characteristically Iberian nasal vocal technique; one vocal soloist at a time, rather than a group; strophic form without chorus; duple meter; and a repeated harmonic progression (most faster genres employ a tonic–subdominant–dominant sequence in major or minor tonality). Each variant has its emblematic instrumental introduction, interlude, and *cuatro*, guitar, and *güiro* accompaniment figures. Distinctions among variants are sometimes nebulous, and Puerto Rican musicians do not always agree on nomenclature.[16] Most *seises* are octosyllabic, and set to the traditional 10-line Spanish *décima* poetic form (see note 1).

At the time of the first Hawai'i migration, rural Puerto Rican folk *danzas* were among the most popular Jíbaro dances. The *danza Puertorriqueña* stems from the great Euro/Caribbean ballroom continuum originating in the upper-class French *contredanse*, which evolved in Cuba through the *contradanza, danza, danzón,* and (tangentially) the *mambo* and *chachachá*. Like its Cuban relative the *danzón*, the *danza* is usually instrumental; its melodies are longer, and harmonic schemes usually considerably less predictable and more complex than those of any other genres in the HPR corpus, including even the *bolero*. *Danzas* were traditionally sectional, tending toward ABACA... rondo form, and marked by shifts in tonal center and changes in modality; a slower *paseo* [promenade] traditionally served as both an introduction and interlude between sections. Both the instrumental emphasis and the sectionalism stylistically seem to contradict apparent, general, unstated preferences for sung pieces and simple two-part forms.[17] While *danzas* remain in the repertoire, they are seldom acknowledged as such; *danza* is effectively an obsolete category among HPRs. Rather, the very vibrant concept of *guaracha* has expanded to encompass most instrumental pieces of unknown provenience or uncertain genre.

The *guaracha* is unique among traditional genres in its Cuban origins, having probably arrived in Puerto Rico (a closely associated Caribbean colonial partner) in the nineteenth century, apparently via Cuban *bufo* [light theater] troupes (Glasser 1995:23; see also Moore, Chapter 1, this volume), and has been firmly entrenched there ever since. Cubans and other Caribbean Hispanics often appended

---

[16]   For the most part, fast *seis* forms in Hawai'i have coalesced into a relatively standardized "*seis caliente*" [hot *seis*] (Solis 2001: *passim*), a term unknown in Puerto Rico, more or less corresponding to what Caribbean Puerto Ricans call "*seis chorreao*" [gushing or spouting *seis*]. *Güiro* and guitar accompaniments are now *guarachada* and *habana'o*, respectively.

[17]   Note, in this regard, typical structures of the other iconic forms: *seis* (strophic + instrumental interlude); *guaracha* (verse-chorus); and *vals* (ABA).

74   *Soundscapes from the Americas*

to the *guaracha*'s traditional strophic AB verse-chorus a *montuno*: an extended improvisation, often including call and response, over an interlocking ostinato. This heightened rhythmic complexity offsets a harmonic scheme simpler than the initial section. HPRs, however, apart from an occasional self-consciously Cuban-oriented or, later, *salsa* group (usually organized and dominated by Latinos from elsewhere), seldom played *montunos*; such overtly Afro-derived performance practice was generally anathema.[18] Even without *montuno*, however, *guaracha* verse-chorus structure provided space for at least some limited improvisation, typically in the form of ornamentation or limited elaboration of the tune—what Lee Konitz, in his improvisation continuum schema, would refer to as "embellishment" (Berliner 1994:69). As far as I can ascertain from old home recordings,[19] a somewhat more abstract type of melodic improvisation commonly occurred (and still occurs) during harmonically stereotyped *seis* interludes. None of the traditional genres besides the *seis* contained interludes between iterations of "the tune."

Rationalizing the Template

Especially in the 1994 recording project, my personal stamp influenced this traditional template. In 1994 I myself chose the principal *dramatis personae*, which for HPR almost always meant the lead instrumentalist (usually the *cuatro* player), who might or might not be the principal vocalist. Thus, I found myself in the dubious position of deciding who was more "traditional." After this point it proved impossible to control the process of personnel selection. My lead contacts inevitably chose their own harmonic and rhythmic accompanists, with whom they either customarily worked, or who happened to be available, or who they thought would fill the bill within their understanding of my requested requirements. Furthermore, providing typical plantation instrumentation was at least a three-fold problem.

Firstly, I based my assessment of what was typical upon a world conceived and reconceived in the highly creative ways I have described above, in the absence of concrete photographic data from the early plantation period or any recordings whatsoever. I had largely and willfully bought into the community's Jíbaro narrative, which was inevitably shaped, anachronistically, by its rediscovery in recent decades of Puerto Rico and the contemporary state of Jíbaro consciousness there.

A number of my first contacts were those whom I considered primary foci. These musicians were more or less obliged to use modern instrumentation, both

---

[18] Note that the *seis* (as I've noted, the most Iberian of all HPR genres) *is* characterized by an insistent harmonic ostinato which, however, serves rather less as the foil for ongoing improvisation than to foreground its rigid rhyme scheme and literal melodic repetition.

[19] None of the few locally produced and distributed commercial recordings appeared before the late 1970s and early 1980s.

because originals were not available physically, and because the gap between the present and those years when the instrument was in common use was too great. The best example was the *cuatro*. All involved (myself included) from the outset seemed to accept an empirically dictated assumption that *cuatro* meant modern *cuatro*, rather than the old keyhole *cuatro* or the tenor guitar played until the 1970s. All those but one whom I contacted as primary foci had long since committed to the modern *cuatro*, although all had begun their careers playing tenors, as HPRs universally refer to tenor guitars.

My criteria for choosing these initial focus individuals were likewise subjective; they were based upon my own fieldwork assessment that certain people were more committed to tradition than others. Tradition, in a number of cases, however, also implied longevity in terms of Latin music activity in this community, and this sometimes compromised my assessment of their repertoire and performance practices. Very fundamental to my general thesis in approaching HPR material over the years was that tradition represented music and dance culture deemed appropriate to the Jíbaro image at any given time. This resonates with Nicholas Hockin's (2004) query: "Is it possible ... that tradition can be a convenient emblem signifying and/or reinforcing cultural homogeneity?"

1930s–1940s Ensemble Expansion

In testing the vigor of the tradition's underpinnings, we can look to developments in the 1930s and 40s. By that time, the movement of HPRs from plantations to urban centers was well under way. Those remaining Puerto Rican-born musicians with substantial memories of the old country would have been in their sixties or older; most active musicians were now of the second immigrant generation, had never seen Puerto Rico, spoke only English in daily discourse, regardless of whether they knew any Spanish, and may have seen, but probably never played an old keyhole *cuatro*.

By the mid-1930s the simple, functional plantation trio had expanded considerably (and continued to do so into the 1950s before ultimately being reduced in size, in the late 1960s, to an ensemble similar to that of the present day: guitar, *cuatro*, *güiro*, *bongos*, and/or *congas* and electric bass guitar). The tenor guitar replaced the old *cuatro*, and groups added *maracas* and then *claves*. Dances limited to plantation-house living rooms were now held in gymnasiums, lodges, and catered dining rooms in nightclubs, requiring louder and therefore larger ensembles. Gymnasiums provided more room on a stage than had been available along one wall of a small living room, and musicians who hitherto might have waited their turns to contribute to the proceedings at a Saturday night house dance now might be accommodated together. Two or three or more guitars might play simultaneously, plus *claves*, *maracas*, and *güiro*. One musician, born in 1928, remembered the pre-amplified days of the last house dances in the early 1930s, and that sound volume was always a problem: "As you'd approach the house, first you could only hear the *güiro*, then maybe *claves* [these perhaps most appropriately later in the 1930s], but you could only hear the guitars when you went into the house … . That's why you needed more than one guitar." He insisted that both guitars (see Figure 3.3) would strum the same chord to reinforce volume, although commonly in different positions and voicings.

Groups adapted *maracas* and *claves* in the 1930s largely after hearing recordings of Cuban *son* and *bolero*, which prominently featured them, and of viewing "Latin" musical episodes in Hollywood films. The two small hand-percussion instruments played important visual and musical roles, symbolizing, in my view, a sort of early acceptance of Jíbaro music's position as a dialect in the pan-Latin musical language. *Maracas* largely doubled or elaborated the *güiro* part in most genres (see "Ensemble Flamboyance," below); in the 1950s and especially 1960s, as groups reduced in size, one musician might play both, switching to *maracas* specifically for *boleros*.

The *claves* most stereotypically played an eponymous two-measure *son clave* pattern consisting of x. x. x rest x x rest. The first three values consist of the syncopated "Caribbean triplet" pattern referred to in Latin America as *tresillo* (but measures are often reversed, with two preceding three, depending on the piece). The earlier mentioned characteristic *habanao* guitar strumming pattern can in a kaleidophonic or variously interpretable way imply the *tresillo*; some genres (notably the Puerto Rican *danza* and its Cuban cousin *danzón*) typically allude to it, and many Latin compositions subtly incorporate it in their phrases. Before the introduction of the *claves*, however, no instrument in the traditional ensemble presented the *tresillo* so overtly and repetitively. This helped set the stage for anticipated bass in the late 1960s and early 1970s (see below), in which the *tresillo* rhythm is crucial.

"Eva the Rhumba Queen": Post-World War II Neo-Cuban Ensemble Flamboyance

An advocate and ongoing practitioner of this expanded style was the late Eva Rodrigues, the "Rhumba Queen" of the 1940s and 1950s, whom I recruited for the second album. She represented a stage of the HPR musical world long faded, namely the large ensembles, perhaps swing bands, which were common from the late 1930s until World War II and then around 1945–50s (Figure 3.3). The presence of such groups for nearly two decades renders them "traditional" by our earlier definition. Within the parameters of what was considered appropriately Jíbaro (i.e., "white" and "Spanish"), HPR musicians were, as usual, able to rationalize a means of embracing musical styles they found attractive. This expanded HPR ensemble style is rich in referential material, including its instrumentation, presentation, and associated dances. This greater number of personnel—two or three six-string guitars, one or two tenor lead guitars, singer, dancers, *maracas*, *güiro*, *claves*, and *bongós* and/or *congas* and frequently the *marímbula* lamellophone (called "box

Figure 3.3   Boy and His Family Troubadours, 1947. Joseph "Boy" Sedeño and his brothers-in-law. L–R: Sebastian Fernandez, *marímbula* lamellophone played as bass; Luciano Perez, guitar (probably "running bass"); Arthur Fernandez, *maracas*; "Boy" Sedeño, Rickenbacker tenor guitar (converted from electric steel guitar); Raymond "Moncho" Fernandez, *güiro*; Jack "Tito" Fernandez, guitar; Carmelo "Melo" Fernandez, *claves*; Anton "Tony" Fernandez, *bongós*. Honolulu, Hawai'i. Photo gift of Joseph and Maria Sedeño

bass")—reflected available manpower in the late 1930s and following World War II (Figure 3.3). Neither *congas* nor *bongós* appear to have significantly affected either repertoire or performance practice, but served rather as vague visual and sonic signifiers of the mainstream Latin music world. The *congas* did not assume a solo, showy role (which would have been too Afro), but rather maintained an ongoing *tumbao* pattern very closely related to the guitar strum. *Bongós* provided a rather free, rhapsodic filigree emulating the performances heard in Hollywood Latin music episodes, as a sort of add-on, without affecting basic ensemble textures.

The exhibition rhumba was frequently associated with these large ensembles. Often performed in shows, at dance intermissions, prize fights, and other public events in and for the HPR community, this dance style was largely derived from the Havana cabaret style (Moore 1995:175) that first appeared in New York about 1930 (Roberts 1979:76). It most likely developed in Hawai'i during the late 1930s and 1940s through exposure to escapist Hollywood musicals.[20] In Hawai'i one man and one woman usually danced, often barefoot, in typical ruffled rhumba costumes such as those in Figure 3.3, accompanied by enlarged ensembles—Hawai'i versions of American cabaret rhumba bands. The exhibition rhumba's flamboyant Afro and individualistic (i.e., open, solo position) qualities were totally opposed to those of the established Jíbaro dance culture. HPRs, while enjoying the wild, jungle image as spectacle, seldom, if ever, engaged in it as a social dance. Its popularity indicates the ongoing—and often resisted—allure of Afro-Cuban music and dancing. It is worth noting that, even during its heyday as a national craze, HPRs never embraced the *mambo*, which in its 1940s New York Palladium Days heyday was often danced in open position (albeit not nearly as freely and wildly as the exhibition rhumba).

Five factors, the first choreographic, the others musical, probably were most responsible for this. (1) All of the traditional Jíbaro dance corpus, compared with the open position *mambo*, used tightly coordinated and relatively conservative couple steps. (2) Unlike all traditional HPR genres but the *polca* or *mazurca*, the *mambo* was largely instrumental, without the either generic-innocuous or Puerto Rican-identified Spanish texts preferred by HPRs. Such vocals as typically existed in 1940s–50s *mambo* (apart from mainstream novelties of the "Papa Loves Mambo" variety) tended to be Afro-Cuban calls and cries of distinctly, vaguely, or presumably African origin (e.g., Tito Puente's "Ran Kan Kan," Machito's "Tanga," and others). They directly referenced Afro-Cubanism, which was of course anathema among hard-core Jíbaro-identified HPRs. (3) The heavily foregrounded Afro-Cuban percussion reinforced the ideas in item (2). (4) The jazz-oriented wind solos typical of most *mambos* were a distinct non-Latin marker; note that virtually all the repertoire adapted by HPRs originated in Latin music, mostly Cuban and Mexican. (5) The *montunos*, extended improvisations over an interlocking harmonic and rhythmic ostinato, had no counterparts in traditional repertoire.

Having said this, I reiterate that the exhibition rhumba avoided these conceptual pitfalls for the most part by foregrounding the dancers themselves as a show of exotic Cubanism, and that the models for this style presented themselves to HPRs from what appeared to be impeccably white Latin sources: Hollywood films of the *That Weekend in Havana*, *That Night in Rio*, or *Down Argentine Way* homogenized-Latin variety.[21]

---

[20]   These films typically featured white Latin cabaret bands, their personnel reflecting the contemporary strict segregation of casinos in Cuba. Many of these musicians were Cuban émigrés who had played in such casino bands in Cuba.

[21]   Musicians simultaneously wearing Valentino-style Argentine gaucho hats, ruffled-sleeve Cuban rhumba shirts, incorporating Mexican-referenced *marimbas*, and singing about Brazil provide a typical filmic neo-Latin potpourri.

Thus, the liminal quality of the show itself creates a sort of protective barrier against dangers of self-identifying with the racial category "which dare not speak its name." The ensemble performance practice, however, included one very significant departure from the relatively self-effacing, lyric-serving musical presentation style (analogous to the quietly harmonious community couple dance eschewing showy virtuosity). This was a flamboyant *maracas* style involving intricate rhythmic patterns, deep smiling, arm and hand intertwining, bodily contortions including splits, and other *shtick*. The highly foregrounded *maracas* seemed to symbolize this concept of presentation, so different from that of the plantation era.

Signifiers of Reconvergence: Modern *Cuatro* and Electric Bass

By the 1960s HPRs were beginning to establish the first, modest, direct physical connections to the Puerto Rico their parents and grandparents had left six decades earlier. A few people flew to Puerto Rico in attempts to re-establish long-lost contacts with relatives. They returned with *cuatros*, *güiros*, LPs, photos, home movies, and other items important for cultural transmission. The Jíbaro music scene they encountered there was of course a very different one from that of their grandparents.

From the early 1960s HPRs had had increased access to Jíbaro LPs from Puerto Rico. The record jackets were replete with straw hats, machetes, cock fights, stereotypical highland subsistence farms, and Jíbaro-style *bohío* shacks. We might call these "inactive ingredients," sending the message that all was as it had been (or as they had imagined it to have been); the "active ingredients," however—the music—belied this message, in that listeners now heard modern *cuatros*, plus Cubanization such as *bongós*, *congas*, *septeto*-style trumpet playing, and anticipated bass.

As Jim Samson says, "[I]nstruments themselves are social agents; they change music history" (2008:24). The *cuatro* is such an agent, facilitating HPRs' reconnection with their ancestors' Caribbean homeland; in fact, the instrument is a sort of synecdoche for the process of re-acquaintance. By contrast, the electric bass signified a new acknowledgement that Jíbaro music was indeed Latin in a broad sense. However, given that both the *cuatro* and bass derived from Jíbaro sources in Puerto Rico, the older concept of vetting musical features for suitability remained intact.

The Protean *Cuatro*

As noted, after about 1930 younger, Hawai'i-born musicians adopted the tenor guitar as the standard lead instrument for the following reasons. An increasing number of guitar makers offered various tenor models, making many readily and relatively cheaply available; Rickenbacker steel guitars (already wired for amplification), tenor and baritone ukeleles, Martin tenors, and others were all adaptable. The tenor's four-string format may also have attracted HPRs used to four-string (and/or four-double course) *cuatros*. In fact, although very few who played the old *cuatro* remain, most agree that the tenor was tuned similarly, in a combination of a fifth and two fourths, or D–A–d–g (from lowest to highest pitches). The typically narrower tenor neck allowed easier fast chording (a presumably more modern style), while the appeal and, to some extent, prestige of a modern, American instrument may also have served as an inducement. The passing of those who knew how to construct keyhole *cuatros* further prompted the tenor's popularity.

By the later 1930s some musicians were adding strings to create double courses, and by the 1950s photos show most tenors with at least some double strings, usually four sets. In fact, lead instruments invariably featured four double courses or strings; even tenors with six strings, for example, had two single and two double strings. By the late 1970s and early 1980s, however, most HPRs were playing the curvaceous violin-like modern *cuatro*, with 10 strings (five double courses tuned in fourths; see Figure 3.1) This instrument had been evolving in Puerto Rico since 1901, and inevitably, in New York, which had a vigorous and ongoing symbiotic relationship with the home island; HPRs, however, rarely encountered it, a testimony to their physical isolation. Once they became aware of its capabilities, they began switching rather readily from the tenor. One former tenor player told me that he began using the *cuatro* again "because it was more Jíbaro," which, as we can see, meant "because it was what we could see now was *really* Jíbaro."

In addition to being "more Jíbaro," some practical rationales for this change given by those musicians born in the middle 1950s or earlier include "better sound," "better chords," and greater efficiency. The "better sound" may be due to the larger number of strings, which adds richness to the overtone structure (in the same way that double strings were said to "sound better" than single). "Better chords" seems to imply both the potential of wider and more complex voicings inherent in five, instead of four string sets, and a greater choice of string combinations. The modern *cuatro*'s low fifth string set compensates for its shorter neck and provides a range comparable to that of the tenor with less effort.

One implication of the change was an emphasis on fast scalar and single-note figurations at the expense of the fast parallel chording typical of HPR tenor playing. One likely reason is exposure to such musical gestures on the virtuoso *cuatro* LPs that became available prior to the late 1960s. In the words of one *cuatro* vocalist (b. 1929): "We tried to match the tenor to Puerto Rican *cuatro* records. No way—we couldn't match up. We wondered what was going on—we couldn't—we didn't know it, but those guys had 10 strings."

Exposure to the modern *cuatro* coincided with increased physical communication with Puerto Rico. Famous Puerto Rico Jíbaro musicians, such as "Ramito" and *cuatro* virtuoso "Yomo" Toro, performed in Hawai'i from the 1960s

Conserve, Adapt, and Reconverge

81

(en route to Japanese tours), bringing modern *cuatros*. At the same time, as one musician summarized, "a lot of people [in the 1960s] had gone to Puerto Rico, and came back with *cuatros* as souvenirs. There were lots of *cuatros* lying around, but no one knew how to tune them ... ." The instruments were readily available on the US West Coast, with which HPRs were traditionally in close contact. Its "mid-Pacific" location also made Hawai'i accessible to even less expensive Korean-made *cuatros*. Eventually HPRs adopted the instrument one way or another, whether from contacts and musicians from California or Puerto Rico, or from LPs such as that of the famous *cuatro* virtuoso Nieves Quintero (1970s), on which one cut provides (in Spanish) tuning instructions.

The Electric Bass: "If It's Good Enough for Them, It's Good Enough for Us"

The adoption of the electric bass exemplifies the symbolic power of the "Jíbaro filter" in vetting genres, performance practices, and instruments for inclusion in HPR music. HPRs were as aware of the electric bass, well-known in rock music since the 1950s, as any other Americans, but did not include it until it had become commonplace on Jíbaro LPs in the early 1970s.

Although older HPRs mentioned such traditional lead folk guitars as *tiples* and *requintos* as existing on the early plantations, none, even the oldest, mentioned a bass instrument. In general, strong bass lines are not an important stylistic characteristic of the *Jíbaro* versions of genres comprising the nuclear repertoire of the 1901 immigrants.[22] The only stringed instrument associated with traditional Jíbaro music in Puerto Rico in the late 1800s and early 1900s that might conceivably be construed as fulfilling a bass role was the *bordonua*, a lower-pitched version of the *cuatro*. Batista (1984:6) mentions several stringing formats: always five sets, with various combinations of single and double strings. The *bordonua* has never been unequivocally categorized as a bass in the sense of primarily supporting strong chord tones at a slower pitch density; rather, it may have fulfilled, as it often does in academic/revivalist Jíbaro ensembles today, a low-register contrapuntal role. Batista's instrument-maker informants in Puerto Rico indicated that the *bordonua* "*nunca ha sido un instrumento acompañante*" [never had been an accompanying instrument] (Batista 1984:18). The term "accompanying" is interpretable in a number of ways (e.g., bass part or second

---

[22] In other words, whereas the orchestral urban *danza* in Puerto Rico made use of double bass, with a pronounced emphasis upon chord root tones on strong beats, the Jíbaro *danza*, played primarily upon guitar and *cuatro*, placed less emphasis upon bass partly because of the relative acoustical weakness of guitar strings, and probably most specifically because of the Jíbaro traditional small-group orientation, very different from that of the urban dance orchestra. The latter was characterized by complex texture, wide ranges, and sharply defined instrument family ranges, including a bass concept closely adapted from that of pan-European art music.

lead); he does not elaborate upon this statement with supporting data, either verbal or musical.

The earliest form of bass playing in HPR music that I have documented is guitar strumming mixed with single-note bass lines played on the lower strings, as in American Hillbilly string band and country music of the 1930s and later. Such recordings were widely available; many HPR musicians participated in these and other folk and popular musics. HPR musicians refer to this practice variously as "bass guitar," "double bass" (clearly their own idiosyncratic use of those terms in this local context), or, most commonly, "running bass" ("running" being construed both as adjective and gerund; see Figure 3.3). It is not clear that any musician or instrument was formally assigned a "running bass" part within the texture of an ensemble. In recent years I heard "running bass" only in Eva Rodrigues's septua/octagenarian retro group, on my *Puerto Rico in Polynesia* album. HPRs likely never considered the technique essential; one musician (who had also played in a cowboy band) mentioned that when he and his older brother were playing in a prominent ensemble in 1938, his brother complained that he was "playing too much bass—it interfered with the music."

During World War II some groups (under the influence of Puerto Rican and Cuban servicemen stationed in Hawai'i) added the *marímbula*, an Afro-Cuban lamellophone popular in the early twentieth-century Cuban *son* (Figure 3.3). It provided a bass rhythm, albeit linked to a very limited tonal range, with a limited acoustic focus upon which one could aurally/mentally superimpose the harmony at a given moment. By the 1960s the *marímbula* (which may have been adopted as much for appearance as musical contribution) no longer appears in contemporary photos, groups having shrunk in size. However, it served as the principal bass, at least among mainstream HPR musicians, until the incorporation in the 1970s of electric bass guitars under the influence of recorded Caribbean groups and the omnipresent rock guitars played by multimusical HPRs. Most HPR groups now use electric bass guitars.

When playing *guarachas*, *seises*, and their highly transformed versions of *danzas* (but not with *meringues* or *boleros*, which have their own characteristic squared-off bass patterns), HPR bassists typically played—and play—in *tresillo* rhythm. Many also choose to carry the *tresillo* technique one step further, to the "anticipated bass" that Manuel (1985:249) has called "perhaps the single most distinctive feature of Afro-Cuban popular music." The rhythmic pattern is related to the *tresillo* pattern (x. x. x), comprising one measure of the pervasive, iconic two-measure Cuban *son clave rhythm* (x. x. x rest x x rest). The technique demands a considerable musical sophistication, involving the ability of the bassist to: (1) play the one-measure *tresillo* rhythmic pattern (two dotted values followed by a single undotted version of that value), (2) mentally reduce this to a two-stroke, rather than three-stroke, pattern in which the first beat of each measure is silent, the tone having been carried over from the preceding measure; and (3) anticipate by one beat the harmonic structure of the next measure. If appropriately linked to the harmony, an anticipated bass creates an ongoing harmonic tension against a melody and accompaniment patterns (especially, in contemporary HPR music, against the strummed guitar accompaniment), whose chord changes thus trail the bass by a beat. It was not until the reconvergence in the late 1960s that this technique took root in HPR music. As I suggested earlier, the popularity of the *claves* themselves from the late 1930s–50s may have paved the way for the anticipated bass by foregrounding the *tresillo*.

Conclusion: *Plus c'est la même chose*

We have seen how HPRs, while consciously basing their received repertoire, instrumentation, performance techniques, and aesthetics upon those of early twentieth-century plantation culture, consistently—almost certainly from the very beginning—reconfigured them throughout the entire span of HPR history. Beginning in 1900 with the main migration, they had rooted their identities in a kind of Jíbaro and Iberian distinctiveness amid Polynesians, Asians, and color-conscious white Americans. Homogenization and black-white mestization of any cultural stripe threatened this identity. Even when adapting Cuban genres, they eschewed the most obviously Afro performance practices such as the *montuno* ostinato/call and response improvisation section.

Of all the aspects of HPR music, we can follow developments in instrumentation most clearly. Throughout the HPR century, the ensemble nucleus of Spanish guitar, *güiro*, and *cuatro* formed the basis for music and dance. HPRs modeled repertoire and performance practices on those of the Puerto Rico they had recently departed. The most important changes in performance practice resulted from the movement from plantations to cities, with the consequent change of performance venue from small plantation houses to dance halls and gymnasiums. This concentration in larger, noisy spaces required a higher level of sound projection, to which they responded with additional instrumentation and/or (when it became available) acoustic (as with internal guitar cones) or electronic amplification. This urbanization inevitably led to the second main reason for change: greater contact with mainstream American and Latin mass media. Records provided greater access to a wider Latin repertory, and Hollywood films provided some new presentational strategies (costumes, flamboyant movement).

Changes in the ensemble occurred in different ways. Some were what I would call "companionate," in which an introduced instrument coexisted with another performing more or less the same role; others were "surrogate," replacing an earlier version of the same instrument; still others added new musical dimensions, significantly affecting performance practice. Of the three nuclear instruments, the role and technique of the Spanish guitar have apparently changed the least, apart from the introduction of amplification. Guitarists naturally adjusted to the accompaniment requirements of newly introduced forms, such as the new rhythms and complex harmonies of the *bolero*.

The *güiro* itself experienced little change, other than frequent ad hoc scraper substitutions. *Maracas,* introduced in the 1930s as a result of exposure to Hollywood Latin episodes, were companionate to the *güiro*. They did not in any significant way change the rhythmic density referent framework long associated with the *güiro*, nor did they for the most part challenge the *güiro*'s supremacy in providing that role. The main contribution of the *maracas* was in the area of timbre and in its often *outré* visual presentation, through the antics of its performers. *Congas* introduced in the 1940s offered a new visual image while for the most part reinforcing accents of the guitar strum, while *bongos*, closely linked rhythmically and timbrally, added ornamentation without affecting basic ensemble textures or relationships.

The many varieties of tenor guitar that replaced the old *cuatro* provide the best example of surrogate change. It is very likely that the tenor's longer, narrower neck offered possibilities that alleviated the constraints of the old *cuatro*. The *cuatro* is the most tangible musical artifact of the arc of HPR history. Its earliest, keyhole variety, identical to those of the Puerto Rico recently forsaken in the early 1900s; the many varieties of tenor guitar which embody diasporic acculturation; and its modern form adopted by HPRs from the late 1960s on all bear witness to the process of clinging to tradition through adaptation and reconvergence.

The electric bass was the most noteworthy innovation since the introduction of *congas* and *bongós* in the 1940s. Although less arresting visually than the drums, it certainly affected rhythmic texture to a greater extent, by foregrounding the important *tresillo* rhythmic pattern. Even more striking, through the anticipated bass technique it added a characteristically Cuban element of harmonic tension previously only implied.

The variety of repertoire, performance practices, and musical instruments during the HPR century all speak to a vibrant and vital musical culture. In the change from (1) a simple nuclear plantation trio; to (2) a sumptuous post-World War II ensemble with copious doubling and apparent luxury instruments such as *maracas*, *bongós*, *congas*, and exhibition rhumba dancers; to (3) the return to something approximating a plantation trio plus electric bass and *congas* and/ or *bongós* we can still see the template of both instruments and genres which endured to the present. Throughout this period an allegiance to perceived Iberian Jíbaro aesthetic values remained an overt constant, at least cognitively keeping the pervasive Afro world at bay. Modern HPR music now, due to the mass media, more closely reflects contemporary Puerto Rican Jíbaro trends than at any time since the migration. The music itself subtly reflects cultural and racial mixing; that it comes to HPR directly from Jíbaros in Puerto Rico, however, renders it acceptable. The two recordings I produced embody the negotiation between HPRs' avowed aesthetic preferences and the reality of the performed product: even the second of these two, in which I (somewhat naïvely, in retrospect) consciously set out to reproduce the early twentieth-century plantation sound milieu, clearly shows wide deviation from that era in genres, instrumentation, and performance practice.

Thus, as we have seen countless times, in the Americas, African-derived musics (no matter how many chronological generations removed from the original source) have proven potent reverse-colonizers. They have, note by note, beat by beat, permeated or replaced European performance practices. The colonized are in this way often not even aware of their colonization. Perhaps, however, they are more aware than they wish to admit, and rationalize their acquiescence in this cultural seduction process. At any rate, although the reconvergence after the 1960s and 1970s may have resulted in a modern HPR culture somewhat less distinctive than during the long isolation period, the process itself is a story as rich as any musical epic.

PART II
Performing Practice: Style and the Politics of Subjectivity

Chapter 4
Transformation in Communion: Toward an Aesthetic of Improvisation

Tim Brace

"When the innermost point in us stands outside"
Rainer Maria Rilke, "To Music"[1]

Jazz improvisation has, in recent years, drawn the attention of researchers both inside and outside music scholarship. Ethnomusicologists have documented and described the musical details of improvising within a jazz framework and addressed certain questions about its place within human individual and social activity (e.g., Berger 1999; Berliner 1994; Monson 1996; Norgaard 2008); researchers outside music scholarship have approached this topic as an example of coordinated social activity (Borgo 2006; Sawyer 2000) and even as a model for optimizing organizational behavior (Napoli, Whiteley, and Johansen 2005). What is it about jazz improvisation that would attract interest in such disparate fields? What, specifically, is the *experience* of improvising in this setting all about? This article will suggest some answers and some avenues for further investigation, in the hope of fleshing out some of the theoretical descriptions heretofore suggested, and of contributing to a better understanding of—as the general semanticists would say—WIGO (What Is Going On) when jazz musicians improvise.

The starting point for this investigation is improvisation as it is practiced by a soloist within the framework of a jazz combo playing "standards"—tunes within the standard repertoire of a small traditional jazz instrumental ensemble (or "combo"), such as one finds playing in clubs and bars all over the world and in academic performance settings (recital halls) as well.[2] The degree to which the ideas presented are valid vis-à-vis other improvisational contexts such as group improvisation or "free improvisation" will not be addressed here. The primary theoretical and philosophical influences for this work include Western philosophical phenomenology, hermeneutics, cybernetics, systems theory, general semantics, the Confucian/Daoist/Buddhist philosophical traditions of China, ethnomusicological research (mostly in China), and my training in

---

[1] In Mitchell 1982:147.

[2] Much of what will be presented concerns the improvisational experience that players strive for; it is in this sense an ideal. The frequency of this kind of experience is of course variable—but it does occur, it is a common goal, and it is one measure of success for an improviser.

90   *Soundscapes from the Americas*

ethnomusicology under Gerard Béhague, Steven Feld, and Stephen Slawek at the University of Texas at Austin. The terms and categories presented here are some among many possibilities; words must be used to discuss concepts, and these will illuminate some things and obscure others. Concepts, categories, and models are not reality and "the map is not the thing mapped" (Korzybski 1994).[3] Models are useful in helping us organize the complexities of life, and we are "the model-making organism par excellence" (Hall 1981:13); but all theoretical models are incomplete—this includes models constructed by actors in reflecting upon and describing their own actions. Reification of one concept/category/term or another, it seems, is very difficult to avoid; at least we can be aware—mindful—of this tendency so that we can observe the way it colors what we see.

So, experientially, what is going on during improvisation? Where is it going on? And how should we understand it and talk about it?

The Thick Improvisational Moment

Time

Improvisation takes place in what has been called the "thick present" (Berger 1999:132). Through this term—expressing a fundamental premise of Western phenomenology—we see the passing present not as a thin thread flanked by the enormity of the past on one hand and the unknown future on the other; rather, we understand the depth of each moment, which has embedded in it an ongoing, emergent relationship to both the lived (and imagined) past and an anticipated (and imagined) future. *This thick present is all we experience, and where we live our lives.*

There are several types (to use a word) of temporal experiences during improvisation. First, attending to the "creative musical now" involves relating to the flow of sound through retention of the immediate past (what just happened within the group and/or within the solo), as apprehension of the emergent "now" (what is in awareness just now), and as protention toward an anticipated future (where the soloist thinks this might go or where s/he intends to take it). Second, one relates to the wellspring of personal experience that the improviser brings to the improvisation—what one musician referred to as a "personal file cabinet" of motifs, riffs, learned scales, stylistic devices, personal and musical history, and what s/he has learned listening to others, all of which the improviser draws upon during the improvisation (consciously or not). Third, there is the dimension of structuring

---

[3]   During my fieldwork in Beijing, China (1987, 1989) I was initially frustrated by the Chinese aversion to questions about objective substance, such as "What is music?" My Western mind wanted definite answers to some types of questions, but my Chinese friends, colleagues, and interlocutors persisted in laying out the different ways one could approach or view such questions. It took me awhile to learn that this dynamic contextualization of the question was, for them, a natural process and was indeed the "real answer" to my questions.

Transformation in Communion   91

and realizing the music—that is, of playing it. Finally, there is "clock time," which often has little direct experiential influence, but does have a real influence in that it is one of the historical and traditional contexts within which jazz improvisation has developed. (For example, soloists are not necessarily constrained by a preset number of repetitions through the form when taking an improvisation, but there is generally an accepted range within which they know they must fit the solo.) In improvisation, all of these time modalities occur simultaneously as *interrelated flows*.

Place

Jazz improvisation is a *situated practice*; as such, it is an action—or *web of action*—by actors not only in a specific time but also in a concrete location in space. The settings that serve as venues for the practice of jazz improvisation are contexts that both are constituted by and themselves constitute details and directions of the practice itself—that is, jazz settings have influenced, and will continue to influence, the sound of jazz, including its improvisational practices. The mode of interaction—in other words, the structure and pattern of relating— among players and between players and audiences constitutes a tradition owing its structure and practice in part to the social and physical settings in which it has taken place. Verbal and visual cueing and reacting, for example, are part of a general style of presentation that is part and parcel of the sound of jazz as well as of its very structure and repertoire. Shared knowledge of standard tunes, easily interchangeable (and extensible) "parts" of the combo, a general low prioritizing of exactness of details of orchestration and a high prioritizing of spontaneity, a premium on the art of listening, reacting, and creating together—these are direct results of a continuing interaction between jazz players and the real contexts of their practice.

Direction

Indeterminacy and choice
An improvisation can be understood, from the point of view of the performer, as a stochastic system. Stochastic systems combine elements of chance, or randomness, with choice. Improvisatory acts by fellow performers within a performing group are not "chance" or "random" from their point of view, but a soloist cannot predict the acts of all the fellow performers and thus, for my purposes, the differences between this and real randomness or chance are not essential. The point is that the direction of the improvisational moment combines the perception of some level of unpredictable sound events with responses to those events. In the case of an improvised solo, the soloist builds his/her line over the ground of sound being produced by the group, and the members of the group, hearing the soloist's melodic and rhythmic decisions, respond in sound, thus potentially shifting the ground somewhat, and the soloist perceives this shift and reacts to it, again shifting

92 *Soundscapes from the Americas*

the context out of which the next moment emerges.[4] It should be added here that this continuously emerging behavior can be leaderless—that is, it can be (and often is) the result of quickly passing individual responses that together form a moving context, rather than the result of one or another of the group necessarily taking the lead (Borgo 2006:5). All of this happens almost simultaneously,[5] resulting in a dynamic and continuously emerging pattern woven by indeterminacy and choice; but there is more to it than that.

Divergence
Improvisations involve a continuous "moving away" from whatever just took place; that is, a developmental direction is taken and followed, or a reversal, or a new and unrelated idea, or a "mistake" is made.[6] This divergence is part of the indeterminacy and unpredictability of improvisation. I'm reminded here of Keil's participatory discrepancies (Keil 1994) and how they give a "groove" its "grooviness," and of a comment to me from one jazz improviser that he is always looking for a way to "go slightly out of tune" with whatever the main "sound" is at the moment (Klemperer 2009). Jazz players talk of "rubbing up against" the main harmony and "side-slipping"—i.e., moving the improvisation just out of the consonant range of sounds within a given harmony—as common acts to create interest and tension (Brace 2009). These are acts of divergence; but divergence isn't the only tendency of improvisers.

Self-Healing (Convergence)
Along with acts of divergence, improvisers are also continuously bringing the sound back together; that is, an improvisation can be seen to exhibit both divergence and "self-healing": a tendency toward consistency and coherence (Bateson 1979).[7] The human tendency toward synchronic behavior has been remarked upon by others as related to a natural need to create spontaneous order (Borgo 2006; Strogatz 2008). Terms such as "entrainment" and "interactional synchrony" have been used to describe this phenomenon (Sawyer 2000), which is evidently panhuman, though the particular behavioral rhythms used to synchronize are culture-specific (Hall 1981).

---

[4] For an interesting and detailed elucidation on mature improvisers talking about the decisions they make while improvising, see Norgaard 2008.

[5] This "almost simultaneous" aspect of interaction is where the common improvisation-as-conversation metaphor breaks down (Snow 2004).

[6] The subject of "mistakes" in improvisation is fascinating and has been touched upon by Berliner and others (see Berliner 1994:210). Certainly, sometimes a player plays something other than s/he intended, but that event, in the hands of experienced players, becomes "part of the fabric of the solo" (Klemperer 2009); i.e., it becomes a part of the dynamic context, and thus fair game for the ongoing referral/repeating/transforming exploration.

[7] "Real music, when people play together, is like this: you come together, you go away, you come together" (Keith Jarrett as quoted in Yamashita 1999:413).

It is this synchronization that creates the "groove" of jazz —that "intuitive sense of style as process" (Feld 1994:109)—as well as being the ground for participatory discrepancies, the existence of which reminds us both that synchronization exists, and that it is not perfect or complete. In improvisation, synchronization-as-self-healing holds high value (Hall 1981:79, 92) and provides the ground for the next divergence. The convergence/divergence/convergence (etc.) pattern then itself becomes the ground for the next pattern. Creativity, through the contributions and interactions within the group, self-organizes (Nachmanovitch 1990) and brings the experience of the community toward unity (Dewey 1958).

The Body

One of the key relationships while improvising is with the physical environment—not as raw material or passive context, but as "mode of expression" (Dewey 1958). This physical environment includes the physical space, the physical body of the improviser, the instrument as an extension of that body (and through which all musical "expression" takes place), the method of playing that instrument, the resistance applied back toward the player from the instrument, the sounds as they are played and attended to, and the ongoing physical relationships among the players in the group (cueing, smiling, frowning, cajoling, moving with the beat, etc.).

Too often the physical space, body, instrument, and so forth are taken as limitations (and this is how many players refer to them) rather than as a ground that makes the creation of music possible. Playing any kind of music is the enactment of a mind/body unity that is neither solely mental nor solely physical (Varela, Thompson, and Rosch 1991); with improvisation, the face-to-face presence of others is part of the ground of this unity (Fischlin and Heble 2004) and is thus constitutive of the resulting sound itself. In addition, the patterns of sound emanating and emerging during improvisation are not just the result of rational choices. They are felt in the body itself: as physical reaction to and enactment of the ongoing "groove," and as constituting and reacting to the sound of one's own improvised contribution to the whole.[8] It is this mentally/physically unified ground from which, to a large extent, the very joy of making music (and of improvising specifically) emanates—a joy without which one wonders whether music itself would continue to be made. The significance for humans of the material, sensual aspect of making music is "inexhaustible" (Barthes 1985).

Structure

Structure is emergent through time and in space. It is not the result of reflection upon a piece of music or improvisation after the fact, though it is certainly common to take it as just that. Our concern here is the role of structure in the improvisatory

---

[8]   This is where, in some traditions, including jazz, the quality and variance of timbre make a significant expressive contribution.

moment itself. The perception and creation of structure is a core element of this moment. Structure arises from continuous creation and perception, in dynamic context, of patterns (Bateson 1979). But patterns of what? These emergent patterns are *patterns of relationship*. It is the perception and creation of these patterns that give rise to meaning, and to art—and, I would suggest, to the very *self* of the creating performer.

Humans are pattern makers and pattern perceivers; perception itself takes place in a field of relationships we can call a context, or a web of patterns (Merleau-Ponty 1989). Our abstracting, transforming, and assimilating our perceptions is an act of "contexting." This contexting in each moment is a *creative act* through which we dynamically understand our world and constitute ourselves (Bois 1978; Dewey 1958; Goguen 2004; Hall 1981; Merleau-Ponty 1989). In an improvisatory moment, improvisers contextualize that moment through a web of relationships including but not limited to:

- the improvisers' personal history: the ideas they have to mine in each moment; their present state, physically and emotionally; the history of their playing of this piece and understanding of the piece; the cultural, subcultural, and/or regional practices of which the improvisers may consider themselves a part (including training);
- the other musicians and their personal history with the improviser;
- what was just played by the improviser, by previous improvisers, and by the rest of the group (structures of time);
- the unfolding physical and musical relationships among the performers (and with the audience) and the improviser's reflexive consciousness of this process (Berger and Del Negro 2002);
- the improviser's physical and historical relationship with the instrument;
- the physical context, including the performing space, external noises, and the audience;
- the improviser's anticipation of the next moment; and
- the improviser's sense of the emerging pattern(s) of the piece, including the improvisation as it unfolds.

Through the perception (and ongoing creation and transformation) of these elements (and others), the improviser, in the thickness of continuously emerging moments, produces, creates, and explores patterns of these relationships. Through this action, the improviser dynamically creates and transforms him- or herself, and also transforms this moment's context into the context for the next moment. Great improvisers are those who can perceive higher-level patterns (i.e., patterns of patterns) in this emerging and continuously changing "now" and can manipulate—play with—the ongoing flow of relationships through improvisatory contributions. These patterns are not just abstractly conceived; they are physically felt (Nachmanovitch 1990).

It is important to note that our improviser creates these emergent, continuously transforming structures through perception. Any "objective reality" of the structure is irrelevant except to analysts (or performers) reflecting after the fact and trying to explain why things happened the way they did. What is important for our purposes is that the improviser, attending to the context, creates the impression of form and acts upon that impression in contributing to the emerging piece of music. In so doing, improvisation becomes the act, to paraphrase Rilke, of taking what is innermost and bringing it out into the world.[9]

I am sympathetic to Ingrid Monson's (1996) preference for our thinking of this emerging and transforming context as growth rather than as form. Words like form and structure feel too solid, too stable—and yet, the higher the level of abstraction in our pattern recognition, the more stable and unified the patterns do seem. We must not forget that improvisatory context is dynamically emergent and is the result of the *activity* of improvisation (Goguen 2004) in "multiple contextual dimensions" (Béhague 1984a). Form, in this conception, as it emerges and grows, provides material and inspiration for the next moment—the next context (Brown 2006).

Imagine, for a moment, that you have a piece of paper, and you make a mark on it with a pencil. You improvise that single mark, not thinking ahead of time what you are going to do. That marking starts an action, created in an existing context (the paper, the pencil, the surface the paper is on, your physical hand, your emotional state). Next, without thinking about it for too long, you make another mark, and then another; now the first mark is part of the context for the second—you have transformed the original context—and, knowing there will be a third, the context of the second—its "moment"—is "thicker," as it includes an anticipation that there will be a third. As you continue your marks, you become aware of patterns: among the marks, between them and the paper's texture and/or its edges or marks already on it, and maybe you become aware of patterns of those patterns (you perceive a relationship between the pattern of your marks and, say, the way two opposite edges of the paper form another pattern). Finally—and this is crucial, to draw this example closer to our subject—imagine that the paper itself is in flux in its texture and patterns, and that you don't control that, but it is happening in relationship—in response, to some extent—to your marks, and you begin to change the patterns of your own marks in relationship with the changing paper.

Our dynamic contexting—that is, the creation of context through time—is a creative act through which we know and constitute ourselves and, if we are fortunate, create art as well. Creativity is an exercise in creating and relating patterns—not in a traditional Western philosophical sense of the imitation of nature or the reconstitution of a previously existing order that can be recreated,

---

[9] I submit that it is in this sense, and perhaps in this sense only, that music can be said to be "self-expression"—and what is expressed is not the "feelings" of the artist, but his or her artistry.

or of creating and relating abstract entities, but rather—borrowing from traditional Chinese thought—as a way (one of many) of harmoniously correlating what is in fact "at hand" in the moment of improvising (Hall and Ames 1993). Meaning emerges from this ongoing contexting, in which we perceive, create, and transform—and relate ourselves to—patterns through time (Bateson 1979). Through these intentional acts, in which we embody our (enculturated) interiorities in interaction with others, we create "affecting presences": we bring into being forms that have their own meaning, their own energy, and that are not (necessarily) symbolic of anything external to themselves (Armstrong 1971). As our musically relational explorations are transformed into perceived multi-layered structures, we create art (Gadamer 1989).

The Playful Search for Art

It is no surprise, I think, that some cultures use the term "play" to describe the act of making music. The act of making music with others (especially improvisation), to be successful, needs to involve non-threatening relationships, even playful ones. There appear to be good evolutionary reasons for the human activity of play, including adaptability to changing circumstances and the development of trust in community (Brown 2009). Play involves playing *with something* and (often) *with someone*. Play is not what is done, but how it is done (Nachmanovitch 1990). In jazz improvisation, the context for this play is created in the performance situation, routinely and historically a club or bar or (more recently) concert stage. It is within these contexts that jazz improvisation has grown as a kind of group exploration.

One player said to me that the process of improvising within a group setting is an experience of joy, learning, expression, and that "hopefully sometimes art happens" (Brace 2009). The creation of art is among the most human of activities. It involves the intentional creation of recognizable, meaningful layers of patterns of recognizable, meaningful elements, and exploring—playing with—the relationships among them (Bateson 1979). These are not metaphysical acts; they are decidedly physical. Creative play takes place outside the perceived boundaries of the self, but involves that self. This means that art-as-created is in the world and not in the self (or selves) creating—i.e., the art is in the event, and in this way it is *public*. While improvising, the individual player contributes to but does not control the creative movement. In fact, the moment helps to create the player; thus all playing is also, simultaneously, being played (Gadamer 1989). This group creativity is enjoyable partly because it effects a potential in humanity (Bois 1978) and because the result transcends the limitations of the self. I have had many performers tell me, reflecting upon an improvised solo, "I didn't know I could do that." The group creative exploration—play—draws out of the individuals involved something that is not *in* any one of them. This exploration is the search for art, and is not a means to joy, but is joy itself, and the resulting work of art is the performance itself (Maitland 1980). For jazz

Transformation in Communion 97

improvisers, the immediacy of the creative moment, and the search for art in the thick moment of "now," is the ground of this joy: a way to take the self and reach with it beyond it, with others, toward—and in the service of—something greater.[10]

An Aesthetic of the Improvising Act

Mastery of the Moving Moment: Agency/Efficacy in Improvisation

One difference between mature (or masterful) and immature improvisation is in the act of organizing musical elements across time. The mature improviser "feels the form" across multiple recurrences, while a less mature player (incorrectly) sees each time through the form of a piece as a repetition. Another way of saying this is that the mature improviser is more fully present to the "thickness" of each moment, while a less experienced player lives each moment more "thinly," not seeing the flow of how each moment arises out of (and is contained within) the previous one, and contains within it potentials for the next.

This section draws heavily on traditional Chinese thought on individual agency within a flow of events. From this point of view, the moment itself is ever moving, and our very naming it "moment"—thick or not—gives an illusory impression of substance. Mastery involves the ability to see the movement in each moment, those patterns (and meta-patterns) that connect into a continual flow. Mastery does not involve controlling the flow. Western notions of agency have often relied heavily on individual will (Jullien 2004); efficacy in jazz improvisation within a group setting is badly analyzed, I think, if one approaches such efficacy as a function of the willpower of the improviser: one doesn't force oneself into the lead in this kind of group setting, and others don't follow because of the soloist's willpower. The real power, according to Confucius, is in the event, not in the person (Fingarette 1972:12), and the potential for the next moment is in the situation, not in the player. Efficacy is being able to see, through attention, the fullness of the event as it unfolds, and being able to contribute in the right way at the right time in creating a unique, meaningful constellation of relationships that has never happened before (Hall and Ames 1993).

I am drawing a distinction here (which I first read in Krishnamurti 1999:26) between *attention* and *concentration*. Attention widens, concentration narrows. In *Metal, Rock, and Jazz*, Berger (1999) clearly describes the narrowing that occurs in order to bring a jazz group back together when it gets out of sync, and how this kind of narrowing interferes with the players' stated goals of being "in the flow" and letting the music take them away effortlessly. This effortlessness I would call

---

[10] Jazz guitarist Larry Coryell (1998:94): "You never stop learning. Keep this seeking spirit with you. This music we play is rich in choices and nuances; you never (at least in my opinion) will arrive at the ultimate plateau and say, 'I don't need to learn more.'"

attention; it has an open character to it, and is frequently a goal of jazz players.[11] It is an awareness that "thickens" the moment of time by "feeling" both the ground out of which the present arose, and the possibilities of the next moment. It is a creative act, organizing—focusing—what *is* as a unique field, as patterns, as figures and horizons: as a presence (Merleau-Ponty 1989: esp. 26–51).The mature improviser, with this awareness, is able to experience the fullness of each moment and react to it, but is also organizing as s/he goes, and that organization (and all the players' reactions to it and to their own organizations) determines the potentialities of the next moment.

Power/effectiveness/influence is thus co-created, emergent, dynamic. Even the mastery of the mature solo improviser exists within the context of the event. Confucian thought says that this mastery is public: we see a performer's sensitivity and mastery in the performance, not in the person (Fingarette 1972:53). The improviser thus attains a kind of "freedom of mastery" (Maitland 1980) described to me by an experienced player as "like surfing, in that you're on top of waves, and there's lots going on under you, lots of different currents, and you're aware of them, and you just choose which one to enter into" (Klemperer 2009). This speaks directly to the traditional Chinese notion of efficacy, in which true agency is understanding the situation at hand, seeing its potential (i.e., the direction or directions unfolding within it), and being able to act upon that unfolding in just the right way to help determine the next moment's direction(s). The music is constantly moving from something toward something else, and the master player sees this happening and is able to contribute effectively, transforming the next moment. Or, in simpler words, the artist "has a grasp of what was just done and what is to be done next" (Dewey 1958).

Unity, Integration, Communion, Affect, and Transformation

> I have always felt that what the group does together is what makes music happen.
>
> Miles Davis (1999)

I chose the term "aesthetic" in the title of this chapter because it connotes perception—or creation—of order, of meaningful presence, and of *unity*. Gregory Bateson, in *Mind and Nature*, says that the Western knowledge traditions' "loss of sense of aesthetic unity [of the world] was, quite simply, an epistemological mistake" (Bateson 1979:19). The German philosopher Hans Georg Gadamer says in *Truth and Method* that "experience ... is a unity" and further, that "Aesthetic experience is not just one kind of experience among others, but represents the essence of experience per se" (Gadamer 1989:66, 70). If an aesthetic experience—

---

[11] I am reminded here of the concept of "soft eyes" used in disciplines such as Aikido, in which you are aware of what is in front of you but also what is all around you. From photographer Henry Wessel: "It is a physical sensation. You are not looking for something. You are open, receptive. At some point you are in front of something that you cannot ignore" (Gefter 2006:1).

Transformation in Communion   99

and I would suggest that jazz improvising is such an experience—is the essence of experience, and is a unity, then we need to ask: a unity of what? Where does this unity come from?

Aesthetic experience as an act of improvising in the jazz setting here described is a *dynamic integration into the unity of relationships creating an affecting presence*. The relationships are of the elements—constantly changing—in this moment's "field" as apprehended and acted upon by the musicians. Improvisational acts involve dynamically perceiving, exploring, transforming, and focusing these relationships. This starts with being able to perceive the relationships: the form of the piece as it unfolds and grows, interactions (physical and musical) and their relationships with the form, the contexted situation(s) out of which the piece is to be created, and finally, the patterns of all of these as they and their multiple potential directions emerge into the next moment.

The aesthetic act of jazz improvisation is an integration of the improviser with these emergent and continuously changing relationships in the continuously flowing and emerging moment. It is *a creative act of integration of the self with others in time and through aesthetic ordering (form)*. However, it is more than that: the self, others, time, and the aesthetic ordering are not static. The unity of the aesthetic act takes place through an intentional continuous transformation—of the self, of others, of history, of the moment, of the piece of music, of the situation, of silence into sound, of pattern into patterns, of patterns into patterns of patterns—that is continuously anticipating but also relating back and being re-integrated.

This integration of the self with others in time can be described as an act of *communion*. It involves both acting and being acted upon; it transforms and is transformed. Improvisation involves both willing and letting go; moving and being moved; being hard and being soft; the creation and resolution of creative tension;[12] leading and following. Anyone who has been in this sort of setting—when it "happens"—understands how poorly we are able to talk about such things; I recently heard musicians talk of "sharing souls," and Berger's work, following phenomenological precedents, posits and applies the concept of "shared experiences" within various musical performance settings, including jazz improvisation (Berger 1999).[13] Confucian thought holds that it is during these moments of deepest sharing that we are at our most human—that spirituality itself is public (Fingarette 1972:46).[14] We humans often, in our descriptions of

---

[12]   "The danger for genuine [musical] dialogue … is not the *presence* of tension but its loss or imbalance" (Benson 2003:171).

[13]   These references to deep, personal sharing point to how jazz improvisation differs from the other improvisations that make up daily life (e.g., walking down the street): in jazz improvisation, the intention is to create a shared, meaningful, affecting presence—what we call art.

[14]   Lest the reader think the author is being too romantic here, it should be remembered that the medium of this communion is the music. One doesn't have to like the people one is with; one only has to be able to *musically* commune with them.

100 *Soundscapes from the Americas*

such things, venture into poetic language because, as an art, it is a language of meaningful, dynamic unity. Communion and integration of the self with the social, of the deepest personal self with others in a larger world through the creation of meaningful, affective sound structures, lead musicians to say that sometimes it "feels like someone else is playing my horn," or that the instrument "plays itself," or that one is, in these highly valued moments, "in the flow." These comments bring to mind the Chinese notion, useful here, that the unity of a moment is understood—perceived—aesthetically, and is not something achieved (since it is naturally already there) but rather *entered into* (Hall and Ames 1993). In these situated moments of creative communion, it is easy to wonder where the "self" begins and ends—especially when it is extended communally with others in coordinated social action. I suggest that the self is co-created in these events, in an ongoing flow of transformation that is itself communal.

Thus, the aesthetic act of jazz improvisation is an act of *transformation in communion*. It is an integrative act in which the improviser takes part in the creation and transformation of the ground into which s/he is integrating and being integrated. It is the integration of the self into something that is transpersonal. It is a communal process in which the participants mutually help each other transcend previous understandings and therein transform the selves involved. It is an act of opening the self into a situated, communal action frame in which others do the same; and together there is synchronization, integration, freedom, healing, meaning, creation, and transformation. Creating the presence—the piece of music—and being created by it are the ultimate human experience, involving both the personal and the transpersonal, simultaneously, as two dimensions of the same reality. In communally creating and perceiving meaningful patterns of sound, and creating and perceiving the communal layering of patterns and experiencing these relationships, one knows the joy of this kind of exploration, this kind of play. This act—and this should not be underestimated—is an act of human optimism in a context of perceived risk, an act of belief in the efficacy of the self—and of the community—through an intensification of the experience, through creating music, of the flow of life and one's physical, mental, and spiritual involvement in that experience.[15]

Art, created in this way, is a spiritual and expressive *communicative act*, not just a class of objects to be admired. For jazz improvisers, the performance *is* the work—and the *work*—of art. This act, and this work, is fundamentally an aesthetic process, grounded in the physicality of the body, of other bodies, bodily extensions (instruments), and sounds, and the rubbing of all of this against time, space, and tradition in the thick present moment. Within all of this the improviser perceives, understands, correlates, integrates, and transforms the self and, for the duration of the event for those participating in it, the world.

---

[15] This is where improvisation can teach us about how to handle the continuous flow of life in other domains, such as business behavior and, indeed, our own daily life.

Chapter 5

Feminine Flowers among the Thistles: Gendered Boundaries of Performance in Chilean *Canto a lo poeta*

Emily Pinkerton

Nuestra lira que empezó	Our *lira* that began
Con flores de puros cardos	With flowers of only thistles
Y una que otra flor de nardo	And one or another *nardo* flower
Que más mérito le dió;	That lent it more merit;
Ora bien se matizó	Now it is well tinted
Con las flores femeninas	With feminine flowers
Que son perfumada y fina	That are fragrant and fine
Y forman jardín de amor	And make a garden of love
Ternura en su corazón	Tenderness in their heart
Sus versos luz que iluminan.	Their verses light that illuminates.

(Unión de Poetas 1954:64)

With these flowery verses, Miguel Luis Castañeda, "*un modesto campesino de nuestra patria, pero un poeta popular de la más fina estirpe ...*" [a modest peasant of our country, but a popular poet of the finest lineage], paid tribute to Águeda Zamorano, one of the leaders in an historic 1953 gathering of Chile's popular poets. From rural and urban laborers to members of elite academic circles, at this unprecedented event individuals were brought together from distinct socio-economic groups in an effort to foster both the revival of Chilean popular poetry and a climate of cross-class collaboration in tune with mid-century populist movements. While certainly complimentary, Castañeda's lines nonetheless single out women's participation in popular poetry as something unique and unusual, a late addition to a tradition that began as "flowers of only thistles" (*flores de puros cardos*). A strong and eloquent female poet who has assumed leadership of the first national organization of poets and singers in Chile, Zamorano is simultaneously a flower that lends a special sweetness to the tough, poetic world of men.

With this account, I wish to introduce the framing of gender that characterizes Chilean popular poetry's past and present, specifically in the musical arenas of *canto a lo poeta* and *paya*.[1] Although women have played central roles in

---

[1] "Popular poetry," although sometimes used as a general term for any poetic form produced and consumed by "low" socio-economic classes, is generally associated with

102   *Soundscapes from the Americas*

the tradition's revitalization and have been accepted as welcome participants, they continue to be framed as newcomers with a delicate style that stands in clear contrast to *canto a lo poeta*'s "thistle"-like masculinity.[2] Based on 15 months of field research in Santiago, Chile and outlying rural areas, this chapter explores the performative boundaries of gender in Chilean *canto a lo poeta*, contributing to recent ethnomusicological literature that examines women's participation in masculine musical communities (Aparicio 1998; Babiracki 1997; Cornell 2001; Dawe 1996; Moisala and Diamond 2000; Qureshi 1997; Rice 2003; Tsitsishvili 2006). Given *canto a lo poeta*'s prominent spot in a new wave of post-dictatorship folk revival, it is important to consider the ways that this practice reinforces or challenges traditional boundaries of gender and relates to larger discursive imbalances within Chilean society. After a brief introduction to *canto a lo poeta*, including *paya* [improvised poetic competition], *canto a lo divino* [sacred song vigils], and the *guitarrón* [a twenty-five-string, guitar-like instrument], I will describe the unique musical challenges facing women in this tradition. I will also consider the sonic differences between prominent male and female performers, placing particular attention on the experiences of Myriam Arancibia, one of the most active *payadoras* and *guitarroneras* today. In the second half, I will describe how women who enter this masculine musical space navigate boundaries of performance defined by gender as well as the public framing of their physical appearance, gender, and professional identity. More specifically, I will highlight how aggressive language and sexual allusion are poetic tools which women do not employ in the same fashion as many male performers. Finally, I will consider two recent festivals in Pirque, examining how the participation of women has begun to reshape the discursive framework and gendered landscape of performance.

Gendered Difference in the Music of *Canto a lo poeta*

Canto a lo poeta is a form of sung popular poetry in central Chile that encompasses the sacred and secular repertoires of *canto a lo divino* and *canto a lo humano*. Singers deliver their *cuartetas* [quatrains] and the *décimas* [ten lines of octosyllabic verse] with recitative-like melodies called *entonaciones*. Guitar or *guitarrón* accompanies the *entonación* with a corresponding accompaniment (*toquío*) that can include short countermelodies, harmonic-rhythmic vamps, or strumming. While some *entonaciones*, such as *la común* [the common one], are

---

canto a lo poeta [the musical rendering of popular poetry] and *lira popular* [large-sheet printed publications that flourished from the mid- to late nineteenth century]. *Verso* is another term used interchangeably with *canto a lo poeta*. For more information on the history of popular poetry, see Grebe 1967; Lenz 1919; and Lizana 1912.

[2]   For a full discussion of the history of women's performance in *canto a lo poeta*, see Pinkerton 2007.

Feminine Flowers among the Thistles

part of a repertoire shared across Chile's central valley, other melodies, such as *la principalina* [the one from Principal] are closely tied to specific localities. For many singers and instrumentalists, individual style is a deliberate expression of cultural and personal identity. Through musical detail (embellishment, tempo, vocal timbre, volume, strumming technique), they demonstrate before colleagues and audiences their connections to a region or a certain performer, as well as their individual creativity within the harmonic and melodic structure of the *entonación* and *toquío*. The importance of defining an individual style is notable in the most common types of *canto a lo divino* and *canto a lo humano* performance: all-night vigils of devotional song (*cantos*) and gatherings of improvising poets (*encuentros de payadores*). In both sacred and secular contexts, the performance space can become a competitive arena where musicians attempt in subtle or overt ways to outshine, or at least distinguish themselves from, their colleagues.

Across Chile's central valley there are dozens of sacred vigils throughout the year to commemorate saints' days and important events in the Catholic calendar, such as Easter and Christmas. Singers arrange themselves in a semi-circle before a small table where a religious icon stands amid candles, flowers, and other decorations. From sundown to sunrise, they exchange rounds of *versos*, poems comprising five to six *décimas* that address a specific religious theme or story. Each singer performs only one 10-line verse of a poem before his or her turn is over and the next person begins to sing. Prior to the 1970s, *cantos*, also called *vigilias*, were small community gatherings in private homes involving five to ten singers. Whereas today the majority of singers provide their own guitar or *guitarrón* accompaniment, *cantos* in the past often featured only one instrumentalist. This performer occupied a powerful position as the first singer of the evening; he could sing the *entonación* or the *fundamento* [religious topic] of his choosing, and—according to the unwritten rules of performance—the rest of the performers who sang *de apunte* [without an instrument] had to adhere to the same melodies and themes throughout the evening or drop out of the circle. *Guitarrón* player Osvaldo Ulloa describes how players of his father's generation could use their instruments to their advantage in performance:

> It was in the *entonaciones* ... because not all poets know all the *entonaciones*. They can't sing them ... to skip someone, for example, you know more than me, more *versos*. So, I would come and I'd change the *entonación* so that you couldn't sing ... and I'd just leave you out. (personal communication, March 10, 2005)

Drawing from field research in the 1950s and 1960s, folklorists Juan (1962) Echevarría and Violeta Parra (1979) described similar processes of "natural competition" in rural *cantos*. When all singers performed the same *entonación*, in the same key, and on the same religious subject, this facilitated comparison of performative prowess. Traditional *cantos*, although solemn and devotional in tone, often spurred an undercurrent of competition where singers sought to project themselves, their musical skill, and their poetic knowledge in the best light.

Beginning in the 1970s and 1980s, the Catholic church took an increased interest in this devotional rural expression, and it is common today for *cantos* to be held in chapels and large cathedrals where anywhere from 20 to 100 singers might participate. At these larger events, singers often travel from distant communities, and one will hear pronounced regional differences in repertoire, vocal style, or in the rendering of *entonaciones*. Unlike *cantos* of old, it is much less important to follow the *fundamento* or the *entonación* of the first singer. In addition to uniting singers from multiple localities, church leaders have also sought to quell competitive tendencies amongst traditional singers and to discourage the singing of verses with humorous sexual double entendre embedded in a sacred story. Although these larger church *cantos* have undergone significant changes in size and spirit, they share a similar format with their smaller predecessors.

Like *cantos*, *encuentros de payadores* vary in scope, ranging from small-scale community events to national and international showcases in major theatres. These confrontations of singing poets existed in Chile as early as the 1700s, peaked in the second half of the nineteenth century, but began to wane, particularly in urban areas, by the early twentieth century. Between the 1950s and the present there have been various movements to revitalize the tradition, building alliances between rural practitioners and urban newcomers to *paya* and *canto a lo poeta*. In the decade prior to the military coup of 1973, these folk expressions captured the imagination of artists and intellectuals from both extremes of the political spectrum and—unlike genres and instruments of the northern Andes— were not explicitly censored during the early years of the dictatorship. Several *payadores* associated with the left, however, did find their projects curtailed by the restrictions placed on television, radio, and public performance. The most recent revitalization movement began in the 1980s and has attracted young urban musicians to a burgeoning community of poetic improvisers that continues to grow in the twenty-first century. Today's *encuentros de payadores* involve multiple improvisers (between four and twenty) and include a variety of poetic games: questions and answers, role-playing, *el banquillo* [where one *payador* is assaulted with a barrage of questions from all of his colleagues], and duels in *décimas*. In most facets of performance, the audience is invited to participate by suggesting topics and characters for the performers to represent. Like *canto a lo divino*, the public figures of *paya*'s history and revival are mostly men. The most talented of these improvisers represent the country at international gatherings of poet/singers throughout Latin America and Spain.

Within Chilean *paya*, the twenty-five-string *guitarrón*[3] is the instrument of choice, lending a significant aura of respect to a musician's performance. Like

---

[3] Although we lack definitive historical sources about the *guitarrón*'s origins, its European predecessor most likely arrived to the southern cone in the hands of soldiers,

Figure 5.1   *Guitarrón* of Fidel Améstica made in the mid-twentieth century. Photo by Emily Pinkerton

the song it accompanies, the *guitarrón* is also primarily a man's instrument. Narrower but deeper than the guitar, its numerous strings are distributed in irregular courses of five, six, four, three, and three (Figure 5.1). The remaining four strings are grouped in pairs that extend from the bridge to pegs on each side of the neck where the fingerboard meets the body of the instrument. *Guitarrones*

---

bards, settlers, or missionaries during conquest and colonization (1540–1810). Barros and Dannemann (1961) draw links between structural elements of the *guitarrón* and forms of the European archlute. They trace characteristics such as the body size (smaller and deeper than the guitar), five courses of multiple strings, and unfretted strings to the side of the neck to European instruments of the early sixteenth century (1961:3). In contrast, Pérez de Arce proposes, through comparative studies of timbre and sonority, a close link with indigenous musical traditions of Chile's central valley in order to foster a *mestizo* (mixed indigenous and European) identity for the instrument (2002). For most players, the *guitarrón* is first and foremost Chilean and *criollo* [local, rural]. Because the *guitarrón*'s revival stems from its "rediscovery" in the rural area of Pirque and Puente Alto of the 1950s, the *guitarrón*'s origins are generally perceived as rural. Dannemann (2004), however, suggests that cultivation of the instrument radiated from urban centers to the countryside through the travels of prominent players in the nineteenth century and later.

are most commonly tuned and played in the keys of G and A—a range that accommodates male voices in the standard repertoire (Example 5.1)

Example 5.1 Standard *guitarrón* tuning in A

For a woman studying *guitarrón*, however, this tuning poses a significant problem. In order to sing in a comfortable range, she has two options. Either she must create unique *toquíos* recasting the subdominant or dominant chord as the tonic, or she must restring the entire instrument using a combination of nylon guitar and *charango* strings to play in a higher key. Both of these factors give a female performer's instrument a sonority that is different than that of her male colleagues.

Below are two brief instrumental accompaniments for *la común*, the most frequently performed *entonación/toquío*, and one that is rendered distinctly in masculine and feminine performance. In the first example (Example 5.2), Alfonso Rubio performs a standard variation of *la común*, with core harmonic movement between I, V, V/V, and IV. Many of his movements between tonic and dominant are accentuated by the high *diablitos* tuned to each chord. Alfonso plays on a *guitarrón* tuned to A to best accommodate the upper end of his vocal range, giving volume and presence to his performance.

Example 5.2 *Entonación la común* in A, played by Alfonso Rubio

In the next example (Example 5.3), Myriam Arancibia also plays on a *guitarrón* tuned for a man, this one in G (notated and analyzed in A to facilitate comparison with the last example). To reach a suitable vocal range, she tonicizes a D, the subdominant in the usual "tonic" of the instrument. She tunes her upper *diablitos* down three scale degrees to the third and fifth of her tonic chord, but uses them very sparingly to mark her arrival on I. Close in pitch to the main courses of strings, these lowered *diablitos* sound less chime-like, and the return to the tonic does not carry the same sonic impact of a man's *entonación* in A. Her primary vamping pattern on the tonic also lacks the third degree (compare the four initial eighth note pulses of line 1 in each example), lending an open and resonant sound to this place of harmonic arrival. Her unique arrangement is further distinguished by a special resting pattern on the subdominant (line 4). On a *guitarrón* in standard A tuning, Myriam's *entonación* moves from G to A (IV–V in the key of D) using the same sequence of notes that is employed as a final cadence (♭VII–I in the key of A) in modal *entonaciones* of central Chile. The association of this particular G to A pattern with a modal ♭VII–I cadence is so strong, that although G is the subdominant in Myriam's *entonación*, it can be perceived as a momentary departure from *la común*. Audiences attuned to the typical movements and timbres of *la común* on a *guitarrón* in standard tuning find Myriam's *entonación* striking and different. In comparison with standard renditions of *la común* by male musicians, Myriam's recreation of the *entonación* serves as a marker of gendered musical difference in performance.

Example 5.3 *Entonación la común* in D, played by Myriam Arancibia (original key: C)

108 *Soundscapes from the Americas*

Myriam, born in the late 1970s, grew up in a neighborhood to the north of the capital Santiago and began playing *guitarrón* as part of her studies in music education at the Universidad Metropolitana. Along with studying Western classical instruments, students at this institution have the option to specialize in traditional folk performance as part of the core curriculum. When she initiated her *guitarrón* classes and practiced *paya* with her classmates, she was not aware that she was stepping into masculine musical terrain:

> I would get together to practice with Hernán Ramírez and with Américo ... we were always the same group of three friends, and with them we always improvised as equals. I was never the "woman" of the group. We challenged each other and answered back. [In poetic improvisations] they would hit me, and I'd hit them. (Interview with author, 2008)[4]

When she later started to attend rural and urban performances of *canto*, she realized the full extent of the tradition's masculine character, facing unique challenges in both her apprenticeship and professional life.

When Myriam began performing publicly in both *paya* and *canto a lo divino*, she sang *de apunte* [with accompanist] for an extended period of time. For older generations of singers, this practice is part of an important unwritten code of conduct for new singers. Although she was already an accomplished *guitarrón* player at the time, she wanted to enter the community with great deference to her elders, showing respect for their beliefs about traditional practice. To heed the rules of tradition proved challenging at times, requiring both flexibility and innovation. She often sang with instrumentalists who only played *entonaciones* in keys suited for male singers, either straining her voice to reach the notes, or inventing higher melodic patterns to fit her vocal range. Most importantly, Myriam describes the discomfort of coordinating her verses to the instrumental rhythms of other players:

> I feel better playing my own accompaniment because you have a handle on your timing, how long you take to start singing the *décima*, to think it up, so you're in charge of your own rhythm ... . Sometimes it wasn't easy to sing *de apunte* ... one time ... Santos Rubio accompanied me on guitar. He's an excellent guitarist, but I wasn't used to him. I felt strange; he used so many patterns, so many things over here and over there, that I felt uncomfortable. (Interview with author, 2008)[5]

---

[4] *"Me juntaba a practicar con Hernán Ramírez y con Américo ... éramos ese grupo de amigos los tres siempre, y con ellos payábamos de igual a igual. Tampoco yo pasaba a ser la mujer del grupo. Nos hacíamos preguntas, nos respondíamos. Los chiquillos me pegaban, yo les pegaba a ellos."*

[5] *"Yo me siento mejor tocando mi propio acompañamiento ... porque uno sabe los tiempos que maneja, cuanto demora en empezar a cantar una décima, en pensarla,*

While Myriam performs to her own *guitarrón toquíos* today, other contemporary *payadoras* tend to sing with an accompanist. She speculates that this circumstance affects a singer's comfort and confidence, perhaps contributing to the perception of women as more timid and delicate in their musical style. Playing to her own accompaniment gives Myriam a sense of control, confidence, and ease in performance.

In my observation of several *payadoras*, I noticed that these women tended to sing with a more relaxed tone and less volume than *payadores*. While aesthetic preference and individual vocal technique certainly influence this tendency, I believe that a woman's timbre and projection may be closely related to where the tessitura of an *entonación* sits in her vocal range. If we look at the melodic range for *la común* in the keys typically used by male and female performers, we see that the pitches correspond to the upper end of male registers, whether one is a tenor or bass (Example 5.4). For soprano or alto voices, the melodic span of *la común* sits relatively low in their range. This results in less vocal tension and less volume, hence a more relaxed and "sweet" sound. This musical distinction may also contribute to perceptions of men as more aggressive performers and perceptions of women as deferential "flowers."

Example 5.4 Standard male and female vocal ranges (left) compared with the melodic range of *la común* in D, C, A, and G (right)

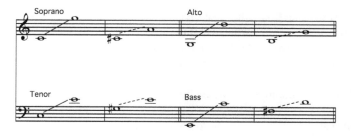

Gender Roles and Poetic Style in *Paya*

Female performers are marked not only by a distinct musical sound in *canto a lo poeta*, but by discursive practices that separate them from many masculine norms of competitive poetic exchange, particularly in the performance of *paya*. A female performer's presence at an *encuentro* often receives extended commentary: a narrative framing by both emcees and fellow musicians who call attention to her gendered "difference." She is a "rarity," a "flower," a "beauty,"

---

entonces uno maneja su propio ritmo … . A veces no era muy favorable cantar de apunte … una vez … me acompañó Santos Rubio con la guitarra, que es un excelente guitarrista, pero yo no estaba acostumbrada con él, me sentí extraña, que hacía tanta postura, tanta cosa por acá y por allá, quedé incómoda."

or a professional colleague depending on the authoritative male voices who interact with her. Both on stage and off, social interactions and poetic choices demonstrate how 1) a woman's physical appearance and sexual identity are terrains where men speak more freely than women, and 2) women tend to embrace a less aggressive poetic style largely in accordance with the audience's, and their own, expectations.

"Room In My Heart for Everyone": A Young Woman's Poetic Approach

In performance today, the metaphors and descriptors that frame female performance are not so different from the flowery introduction included at the beginning of this article. As Ingrid Ortega approached the microphone at the twelfth annual *Encuentro Internacional de Payadores* [International Gathering of Payadores] in Casablanca, the emcee highlighted the significance of her participation in this event, commenting further: "see how pretty she is, and young, too" (*mira que es linda, y joven también*). Accompanied by Dángelo Guerra on *guitarrón*, she intoned her *cuartetas* in a round of *preguntas y respuestas* [questions and answers] in which four singers took turns challenging their opponents. With a high, clear, and relaxed voice, she posed the following existential question to her older male competitor:

Que me responda su alma	May your soul respond to me
Con mucha sinceridad	With great sincerity
Le hago ahora esta pregunta	I ask you this question now:
¿Diga qué es la libertad?	Tell, what is liberty?

To this, he replied that freedom is the joy he finds in being close to her:

... Estar tocando el cielo	... To be touching heaven
Y siempre juntito a ti.	And always right next to you.
	(Audience laughs.)

Later, it was Ingrid's turn to answer her opponents' questions, and the following series of verses were exchanged:

Payador 3	*Payador* 3
... Dime cómo hoy día te sientes	... Tell me how you feel today
De ser una payadora.	To be a *payadora*.

Feminine Flowers among the Thistles

Ingrid

Contenta desde San Carlos
Hoy recibo su calor
Con el corazón hinchado:
Felicidad y amor.

Payador 2

Aunque yo ya soy casado
Y ya que habló del amor.
Di si en tu corazoncito
Hay lugar para un payador.

Ingrid

... en mi corazoncito
Hay un lugar para todos.

Ingrid

Happy from San Carlos
I receive your warmth
With my heart swelling:
Happiness and love.

Payador 2

I am already married
But since you spoke of love,
Say if in your little heart
There is room for a payador.
(Audience laughs.)

Ingrid

… in my little heart
There is room for everyone.

To her competing *payadores*, 20 to 40 years her senior, Ingrid posed thought-provoking questions and riddles. She responded to their humorous and suggestive quips with a consistent gravity of manner and a pronounced positive tone. Without exaggerating the salacious character of the male *payadores'* comments, I do want to emphasize the difference in the discursive terrains that the young *payadora* and her male counterparts occupy. Ingrid's poetry, her gender, and her physical appearance were all open arenas for commentary by the *payadores* in the form of endearing jokes to which the audience responded with pleasant chuckles. They described the personal pleasure they felt at the side, or as the object of affection, of this talented young lady with whom they performed. The young *payadora*, however, did not respond in a similar tone to her competitors. Rather, she circumvented acknowledgment of gendered relationships by keeping her comments to generalized descriptions of love, beauty, and happiness. In this poetic interchange, women's gender and sexuality were a topic about which the men voiced their opinions, but with which the female participant avoided direct engagement.

"What Did You Like About the Gringa?": Professional versus Sexual Identity

During my dissertation research in Chile, I studied both *guitarrón* and *paya*, on several occasions improvising publicly. My first performance on *guitarrón* inspired a series of improvisations laden with sexual double meaning, and metaphors related to feminine identity. In *Music and Gender* (Moisala and Diamond 2000), scholars from a variety of disciplinary and feminist perspectives are united in their efforts to sustain a dialogue about their own individual subject positions in the

112 *Soundscapes from the Americas*

field: how their understandings of gender shape their research as well as their interpretations (Koskoff 2000:xi). I include the following anecdote because of its value as a defining moment in the field (Kisliuk 1997:39), calling my attention to gendered divisions in discursive terrains of *canto a lo poeta*.

At the *Encuentro de Payadores* in the Plazuela Independencia in Puente Alto on February 10, 2005, my contribution was to perform three original *décimas* with *guitarrón*, showcasing what I had been studying with my teacher Alfonso Rubio, organizer of the event. He introduced me as a young woman who had come from the United States to study Chilean musical culture. After I exited the stage, the public suggested I be the topic of the next "*banquillo*" [bench]—in other words, the subject of the next competitive exchange of verses—during which the youngest *guitarronero* was grilled with questions by the other poets:

Payador 1	*Payador 1*
Con tu verso que repunta *Que ante todos se distinga* *El público te pregunta* *¿Qué te gustó de la gringa?*	With your verse that sums up May it distinguish itself before us all The audience asks you: What did you like about the *gringa*?
Payador 2	*Payador 2*
Me ha gustado de la gringa *De que escribe versos miles* *Y de un interés profundo* *Por conocer nuestro Chile.*	About the *gringa*, I have liked That she writes verses in the thousands And for her deep interest In getting to know our Chile. <div align="right">(Audience applauds.)</div>
Payador 1	*Payador 1*
	(Spoken, interrupting next *payador*'s music):
Tu respuesta fue bonito *Tu repuesta fue muy bella* *Pero mas yo no lo creo* *Yo creo que te gustó ella.*	Your answer was pretty Your answer was very beautiful But I don't believe it however, I think you like her. <div align="right">(Audience laughs.)</div>
Payador 3	*Payador 3*
A usted se le felicita *Por sus respuestas tan buenas* *Di qué hace esa gringuita* *Que no hacen las chilenas?*	You are congratulated For your very good answers. Say what does that little *gringa* do That Chilean women don't? <div align="right">(Audience: "ooooo …")</div>

Feminine Flowers among the Thistles

Payador 2	*Payador 2*
	(Big pause while playing *guitarrón* and
	thinking of an answer; audience laughs.)
La diferencia no importa	The difference is not important
Permítame que me centre	Allow me to focus
Una mujer es la flor	A woman is the flower,
No importa donde se encuentre.	No matter where she is.
	(Audience applauds.)

Prior to the above exchange, I was introduced as a foreigner who had come to engage in serious study of the *guitarrón*, rapidly learning to play and improvise. My verses were received with respectful applause, particularly as I sang of my dedication to Chilean music. Immediately following my performance, however, my identity as a serious student and respected guest was juxtaposed with my sexual identity as a young, and presumed single, woman, united through floral metaphor with women worldwide.

Sexual double entendre is such a prevalent mode of humor in Chile and in *canto a lo poeta* that I felt it might be difficult to challenge it without alienating my teachers and my fellow students. I did approach Alfonso, however, gently indicating that I had not expected such a suggestive verse from him. He responded that he was trying to give the *payador* on the *banquillo* an opportunity for a really humorous response. In detailing what the *gringa* does that Chilean women do not, he should have said "she plays *guitarrón*." Such an interchange would succeed because Alfonso's verse—at first glance rife with sexual innuendo—would be reduced in the end to an innocent observation. In other words, with such a response, Alfonso's verse would not have exceeded any limits for the respectful treatment of his female student. Addressing the young man on the *banquillo*, the other *payadores* could show their dominion of sexual double entendre. Addressing his comments to the audience (of which I was part), the young *payador*, however, was under pressure to produce respectful comments that would neither offend nor be ungallant. This interchange juxtaposed several social images of a woman: 1) an "eloquent woman"[6] and serious student of Chilean tradition, 2) a sexual object, and 3) a "flower" that should be treated with chivalry in verse.

A Feminine Example of "Making Tradition"

Along with the *paya* of Ingrid Ortega, I attended multiple performances of Cecilia Astorga and Myriam Arancibia, women who are *payadoras, cantoras a lo divino,*

---

[6] I am borrowing a term used in *Discurso, género y poder* (Grau, et al. 1997). The authors describe how the "eloquent woman" emerges as a metaphor of femininity in the transition to democracy, citing the examples of influential women in political arenas.

114   *Soundscapes from the Americas*

and *guitarroneras*. They are also sisters-in-law; Cecilia is the sister and Myriam the wife of Francisco Astorga, who is a prominent figure in contemporary *canto a lo poeta*. While this status may have influenced the absence of any suggestive sexual humor in regard to their performance, their presence at a *paya* would always inspire commentary from emcees or from fellow musicians; they were "the first" or "the only" women in Chile to shine in the masculine arena of *canto a lo poeta*. Beyond these introductions noting their gendered "rarity," they frequently assumed a distinct performance posture on stage, maintaining a less direct and aggressive poetic style than their male colleagues.

Let us take as an example a common element of an *encuentro de poesía*: the *contrapunto en décimas* [counterpoint/duel in *décimas*]. In many gatherings, an older poet, generally regarded as an authority in *canto a lo poeta*, will be paired with a young poet to improvise. The *contrapuntos* of this kind that I have observed follow a similar progression. After respectful introductions, the *payadores* acknowledge the talent of the other for several *décimas*. Approximately half way through the improvisation, one person will suggest that they return to a *contrapunto*: a confrontation of poetic skill. They will exchange a series of challenges, witticisms, or subtle slights for several more *décimas*, after which they will conclude by reaffirming the tradition that unites them as brothers. Although more often than not these confrontations do not turn bitter, there is use of confrontational language and direct contestation. At the 2005 annual *Encuentro de Paya y Poesía* in Codegua, Francisco Astorga was paired against a former student, Hugo González. In their exchange, Hugo attempted to draw Francisco into a debate with provoking comments such as: "You spoke of horses / And I'm a very good horseman / My poetry attacks / And I am strong when I improvise ... ." In one *décima* he thanks Francisco for his valuable instruction on *guitarrón*, but ends by saying "you teach *guitarrón*, but I'll teach you to improvise." Francisco responds to both affronts in a light-hearted manner by teasing Hugo about the hat he's wearing, and by reaffirming their common dedication to tradition. Depending on the participants, this kind of *contrapunto* can turn more or less polemical, but most often ends peaceably. In this case the two poets concluded their farewell verses by offering that in the end, "our poetry" wins the *contrapunto*. We see from the character of the exchange an eagerness on the part of the younger *payador* to initiate animated debate with self-aggrandizing and aggressive verse. Although the older *payador* responds with less forceful language, he does not shy away from overt slights about the other *payador*'s physical appearance and boldness. While their style of confrontation differs, both poets were prepared to refute the other's stance with direct language.

At the same performance, *payadora* and *guitarronera* Myriam Arancibia was paired with don Arnoldo Madariaga, considered an authority by fellow poets. Here there was no rise in tension, nor any allusion to the need to make their improvisations more confrontational. Rather, it was a series of verses expressing mutual admiration, respect, and optimistic visions of motherhood, youth, women, and tradition.

AM

... Antes que llegue la hora
Rápido como una cometa
Hoy ya Myriam es poeta
Excelente payadora.

MA

... Porque viajo en esta barca
Y pronto seré madre
Hoy saludo a este padre
El padre entre los patriarcas.

AM

Orgullo de mi nación
Es cumplir con mis deberes
Porque hoy día las mujeres
van haciendo tradición ...

MA

En esta precisa hora
Mi palabra no se enreda
También fue Rosa Araneda
Gran poeta y payadora ...

AM

... before the hour arrives
Quick as a comet
Today Myriam is now a poet,
Excellent *payadora.*

MA

... because I am traveling on this ship
And will soon be a mother,
Today I salute this father,
The father among the patriarchs.

AM

Pride in my nation
Is fulfilling my duties
Because today women
Are making tradition ...

MA

In this precise hour
My words do not tangle
Rosa Araneda was also
A great poet and *payadora ...*

Compared to the previous example, this *contrapunto* lacks the same degree of blatant, confrontational language. It comprises a progression of reaffirming stanzas in which the elder singer confirms the poetic talent of the young *guitarronera* and expresses great pleasure to be singing alongside one of the women who is "making tradition" today. Unlike her young male counterpart, Myriam never uses directly challenging or arrogant language, and always addresses the elder singer with respectful and complimentary verses. There is no explicit debate; the *contrapunto* is, rather, an exchange of uplifting commentary on tradition, youth, motherhood, and family. The tone of their poetic exchange was further reinforced by spoken commentary following the *contrapunto*, where Madariaga again declared that Myriam, like Cecilia, is a future *payadora* of great talent, requesting an additional round of applause. Myriam returned the gesture in an emotional expression of her gratitude for the teaching and support she has received from this "father" of *canto a lo divino* and *a lo humano.*

116   *Soundscapes from the Americas*

Offstage, in a 2007 interview with journalist David Ponce, Myriam's observations confirmed the same respect she showed onstage to her poetic elder: "That's the best thing to be able to sing *a lo poeta*. To have respect for the elder singer, who is the one who best knows the tradition."[7] She also emphasized the importance of family and tradition in *canto a lo poeta*:

> David Ponce: Is it a coincidence that you are both *payadoras* [Myriam and Cecilia] and you are both connected to the same family?
>
> Myriam Arancibia: … more than coincidence, the family tradition is present there. Cecilia learned from her family, I learned from my husband and that is what unites us, family tradition through poetry.[8]

At the *encuentro* in Codegua, Myriam's participation as a woman in *canto a lo poeta* was framed by her male colleagues as something "rare," and her performance in great part remained within a safe discursive zone of issues relating to motherhood, family, and tradition. Within her poetic improvisation however, I would also like to indicate how in a non-polemical way she was able to project an alternative image of women in the history of popular poetry. In this poetic discussion, "the father of the patriarchs" affirmed this young woman's poetic merit and participation in a masculine tradition. Although the exchange was non-confrontational in character, I would like to call attention to one specific pair of *décimas*. Madariaga observed that "today women are making tradition." Implicit perhaps in this statement is the idea that yesterday women were not making tradition. In response, Myriam named Rosa Araneda, a prolific popular poet of the late nineteenth century,[9] indicating that through this woman's participation in *canto a lo poeta*, she has also inherited the tradition. Within a masculine discourse of performance, Myriam discreetly contested the discourse of "rarity" that frames her participation. In a 2005 conversation with me she reaffirmed that she wants the public to know that she, Cecilia, and Inés are not a novelty of popular poetry today: there is a history of female participation:

---

    [7] *"Eso es lo mejor para poder cantar a lo poeta. Tener respeto por el cantor más antiguo, que es el que más conoce la tradición."*

    [8] David Ponce: *"¿Es una coincidencia que sean dos payadoras [Myriam y Cecilia] y tengan que ver con la misma familia?"*

    Myriam Arancibia: *"… más que coincidencia ahí está presente la tradición familiar. Cecilia aprendió de su familia, yo aprendí de mi esposo y eso es lo que nos une, la tradición familiar a través de la poesía."*

    [9] See Navarrete 1998 and Dannemann 2004 for two distinct perspectives on the life and poetry of Rosa Araneda. The former is a compilation and discussion of her verses, and the second includes biographies of golden age poets, and asserts that "Rosa Araneda" was a *nom de plume* for poet Daniel Meneses. For analysis of this debate, see Pinkerton 2007.

Feminine Flowers among the Thistles   117

… that's a bit what I wanted to say with that *décima*, because I see that there are a lot of people who think that Cecilia, that I, that we're the only *payadoras* that have ever existed, that we are, I don't know … that we are … a rarity. That's also why through the song [*canto a lo poeta*] I like to talk about the *payadoras* that have been, because historically there have been women—few, but they've been there.[10]

Although her performance was heavily framed by the historical and cultural weight of male dominance in popular poetry, Myriam employed a unique non-confrontational mode of critique with an improvised verse intended to reshape public perception of women's roles in the history of *canto a lo poeta*. She voices this alternative image of popular poetry's history, however, within the normative expectations for peaceable, non-aggressive, female performance.

Both Myriam and Cecilia told me that in general, they have sensed a warm reception as *poetas* and *guitarroneras* within the community of male *cantores*. Cecilia indicated to David Ponce (2007) that the process of becoming a *payador* is not easy for women; she has had to earn her title:

It's [*la paya*] got more challenges for a woman … . A woman doesn't allow herself to do lots of things, despite having so many capabilities, so much to say, so much talent. I know girls who write super well and say "no, no I can't" [improvise]. It's like there's a fear. Because on stage in improvisation, it's like you leave yourself bare. Woman is much more fearful than man in this. She is too cautious.[11]

Cecilia highlights the challenging internal process of building the confidence to get on stage and improvise. Myriam, on the other hand, commented to me about her treatment by colleagues after entering the performance arena. More specifically, she feels less welcomed by younger *payadores*, as opposed to older singers. In 2005, she recounted to me how after leaving the stage one day, a fellow *payador* congratulated her on her performance, but said that he would never improvise with her in public. She attributes this behavior to the idea that men are expected to be genteel with women in all contexts:

---

[10]   "… *un poco eso fue lo que quise decir con esa décima, porque yo veo que hay mucha gente que piensa que la Cecilia, que yo, somos las únicas payadoras que han existido, que somos, no sé po, … que somos … una rareza. Por eso también a través del canto a mi me gusta hablar de las payadoras que han habido porque historicamente han habido mujeres, pocas, pero han habido.*"

[11]   "*Es que tiene* [*la paya*] *más dificultades para una mujer … . La mujer no se permite muchas cosas, teniendo tantas capacidades, tanto que decir, tanto talento. Conozco chicas que escriben súper bien y dicen 'no, no puedo.' Hay como un miedo. Porque uno en el escenario en la improvisación como que se desnuda. La mujer es mucho más temerosa que el hombre en eso. Tiene demasiado cuidado.*"

118   *Soundscapes from the Americas*

I imagine that it's because in order to improvise with a woman, he can't fall back on certain recourses. I don't know, like saying things with double meaning, or to be very aggressive with her, because he'd not look like much of a man before everyone else … Pancho [her husband, Francisco Astorga] told me, "it's that he has to raise the bar" … .[12]

Societal gender expectations restrict the performative strategies that a young *payador* would use against a female adversary. He must avoid conflict or vulgar humor. These comments illustrate that *payadores* are aware of how gender expectations will impinge upon their performance style. When improvising with a woman of the same age range, a young man does not have the option of an older singer to engage in polite exchanges of compliments and gratitude. In a true *contrapunto* exchange of critical ideas, a young performer may look bad whether he wins or loses. While *payadoras* today express critical ideas about women's roles in Chilean society and within *canto a lo poeta*, it remains a cultural space where gendered boundaries delimit significant aspects of performance structure and style; men and women do not always participate on the same terms.

"Criticizing with Kindness": Recasting Gender Roles at the *Encuentro Nacional de Guitarroneros*

Through the discussion above, my intent has been to outline the tendencies related to performance practice and gender that I observed in the context of *paya* performance between 2004 and 2005. I would like to emphasize that this is not a monolithic pronouncement about gender dynamics within *canto a lo poeta*. In our 2008 conversation, Myriam, in particular, pointed to important exceptions to the circumstances described above. She has a deep respect for younger *payadores* who agree to improvise against her, avoiding excessive gentility on stage:

One time, I did a *contrapunto* with Manuel Sánchez here, and I made a mistake. I repeated a rhyme, and he told me right away … . "She studied with me and she messed up her rhyme … . I didn't teach her that," he says. Right away, just like that … not [with] too much delicacy … because he said it in front of everybody and bluntly.[13]

---

[12] "*A mí se me imagina que es porque para payar una mujer, no puede recurrir a ciertos recursos, no sé po, como decirle cosas en doble sentido, o ser muy estrellero con ella, porque quedaría como poco hombre delante de los demás. … Pancho me dijo, 'es que tiene que subir el nivel' … .*"

[13] "*Yo también una vez acá hice un contrapunto con Manuel Sánchez y yo me equivoqué. Repetí una rima y Manuel al tiro me dijo … . 'Aprendió conmigo y pisó la rima … eso no se lo enseñé' me dice. Al tiro, así … no [con] tanta delicadeza … porque me lo dijo delante toda la gente y fuerte.*"

Feminine Flowers among the Thistles

In addition to exceptions such as these, an argument can also be made that women have begun to play a principal role in reshaping the character of *paya* and *canto a lo poeta* in recent years.

In 2008, I returned to Chile for two months to participate in the *Encuentro Nacional de Guitarroneros* [National Gathering of *Guitarrón* Players]. During this time, I met with *payadoras* Myriam Arancibia and Pepita Muñoz, whose recent performances at the festival had caused great excitement. I solicited their opinions on the conclusions I drew during previous research. While they acknowledged a *payadora*'s tendency toward less aggressive language in performance, they also described how their personal styles are progressing toward modes of performative engagement that redefine the parameters of poetic confrontation and permit a feminine framing of masculine *and* feminine style and identity. For both Myriam and Pepita, the national gathering in Pirque was the stage for these revelations.

With several years of *canto* under her belt, Myriam has become an imposing figure on the stage: a rapid, deft poet and an accomplished instrumentalist. Although she continues to be framed as a rarity, she encounters floral metaphors of femininity with less frequency, which she feels may be due to the way she "plants" herself on stage:

> That hasn't happened to me ... excessive flattery, no. And I think it depends on you. If you carry yourself like one who's going to receive praise and flattery, of course you'll receive it ... but, if you place yourself on stage with a guitar, or even better, with a *guitarrón*, and you sing *contrapuntos* in *décimas* like you're singing to your equal, that is striking and leaves an impression. (Interview with author, 2008)[14]

In 2005 Myriam was invited to be the first female *guitarronera* to participate in the national *guitarrón* festival. The evening before the main stage performance, Santos Rubio, an elder among performers, suggested that Myriam compete in a *contrapunto* in *décimas* against a younger *payador*, well known for flaunting his inflammatory, aggressive style. At this particular performance in Pirque, Myriam's poise and dominance of the *guitarrón* set the young male performer in question off balance, and he found himself nearly mute in a duel against her:

> ... that time in Pirque, I think that the Pircanos intentionally put me against him to teach him a lesson: that how he improvised with other *payadores*, saying certain things, that that's not how it's done ... and afterwards they teased him .... I realized that a lot of the time he didn't know what to say ... he got nervous, and I said that he got nervous for no reason. I didn't hit him or do anything to

---

[14] "*A mi no me ha sucedido eso ... de halagarme en excesivo, no. Y yo creo que también depende de uno. Si uno se pone en la postura de ir a ser halagada, claro que va a ser halagada ... en cambio, si tú te plantas con una guitarra, y más, con un guitarrón todavía, y cantando contrapuntos en décima de igual a igual, eso choca o impresiona.*"

120   *Soundscapes from the Americas*

him. In one part he even messed up the rhyme, and I kept singing, and I didn't say anything so as to not make him feel any worse. And afterwards when I got offstage, don Arnoldo criticized me. He said, "when he makes a mistake, you have to let him know that very moment. You cannot allow him to step outside the meter, or mess up the rhyme. You have to educate the other *payador*; you have to teach him." ... I think he's right, but you have to critique with kindness. (Interview with author, 2008)[15]

As I described in the first part of this chapter, there is a legacy of musical and extra-musical modes of competition in *canto a lo poeta*: ways to boost one's reputation and tarnish another's. It could be argued that the staging of Myriam's duel against a fiery male opponent was a tactic through which a group of male poets succeeded in embarrassing a rival: in other words, that a woman's participation was simply a strategic element within a larger competition between men. While such an interpretation is viable, Myriam's personal reaction equally supports the case that her participation was intended to redefine for performers and audience alike the parameters of effective performance. A woman's style was presented by the male *payadores* of Pirque as the standard to follow, one in which steady musical technique and thematic depth are valued over provocative poetic fireworks. Furthermore, the encounter has also made Myriam aware of her own tendency to approach confrontation very gently, and has encouraged her to expand her stylistic boundaries with more direct, or even critical, poetic language.

While Myriam acknowledges the effect of a woman's presence on the *paya* stage, she does not feel that gender informs the thematic content of her improvisations:

I believe that each person has a perspective to bring to the *paya* ... in a woman's case, I would not say that just because I'm a woman I'm going to have special treatment on stage, but rather that if I do my role well, and I represent what my community really wants and needs, the goal is fulfilled, and that's the case whether you're a man or a woman. (Interview with author, 2008)[16]

---

[15] "... *esa vez en Pirque creo que los pircanos intencionalmente lo pusieron a él conmigo para darle una lección: de que como él payaba con otros payadores, diciendo ciertas cosas, de que eso no se debe hacer ... y después lo molestaban ... yo me daba cuenta de que él de repente no hallaba qué decir ... se puso nervioso, y yo dije que se puso nervioso sin necesidad, si yo no le pegué, no le hice nada. Incluso en una parte se equivocó y se pisó la rima, y yo seguí cantando y no le dije nada para no tirarlo más abajo a él. Y después cuando bajé del escenario, don Arnoldo me hizo una crítica a mi. Me dijo, 'cuando él se equivoca, usted tiene que hacerse lo saber en el momento. Usted no puede permitir que salga del octosílabo, que pise una rima. Usted tiene que educar al otro payador, tiene que enseñarle.' ... Le encontré la razón, pero hay que hacer la crítica con cariño.*"

[16] "*Yo creo que cado uno tiene una mirada que aportar en cuanto a lo que es la paya ... . Y en el caso de la mujer, yo diría que no por el hecho de ser mujer yo voy a tener*

Feminine Flowers among the Thistles

Angélica (Pepita) Muñoz also feels that a *payadora*'s duty is to be the voice of her community, but places more emphasis on unique performance opportunities related to her gender identity. Through performance she has crossed the gendered boundaries that divide the physical spaces of *canto* events. For more than a decade as the spouse of prominent *guitarronero* and *payador* Alfonso Rubio, Pepita has been a pillar in the organizational dimension of performance, assisting with publicity and preparation. At each *guitarrón* festival, she spends the entire evening cooking and attending to patrons at the food stand. In 2007 and 2008, however, she moved from behind the scenes to center stage and transformed before the community's eyes from Alfonso's wife to a *payadora* in her own right. As she described it to me in 2008, her first improvisation at the *guitarrón* festival brought on a feeling of emotional catharsis as she publicly shared her poetry. She sensed tremendous support from the audience that had previously known her only as a singer of popular folk songs:

> I felt like I was a point of connection between many women, and men too … it was my argument, my venting of my feelings, but the majority of the people took it as a release for themselves as well, besides the fact that they enjoyed it a lot, because it was very appreciated, a lot of laughter, a lot of applause, in a world where the *guitarrón* had only been used to showcase songs *a lo divino* and *a lo humano*, to see a woman arrive and speak her mind … .

> It's a form of social activism. It's a duty as a woman to represent the voices of other women. And perhaps I wouldn't feel so sure of this if it weren't for what people say to me each time I leave the stage.[17]

During the two years that she has performed actively as a *payadora*, Pepita has come to conceive of her performance as a form of social activism, crafting her improvisations to place utmost importance on engaging the audience:

> I've known of *payadores* that have felt so badly slighted in a *paya* that in the end they never look at each other again, or they never speak again … so, that's not

---

una preferencia dentro del escenario, sino que si yo hago bien ese rol, y representa lo que realmente necesita y quiere mi pueblo, ahí está el objetivo cumplido, y eso se da, sea hombre o sea mujer."

[17] "*Sentí como que fui un nexo entre muchas mujeres, y de hombres también … eran mis argumentos, era mi desahogo, pero también la gran mayoría de la gente lo tomó como un desahogo también para ellos. A parte de que la gente gozó mucho, porque fue muy gozado, mucha risa, mucho aplauso, en un mundo en que el guitarrón había sido empleado nada más en la muestra que se había hecho de las canciones a lo humano y a lo divino, llegar una mujer a ponerle una nota … . Es una labor social. Es un deber como mujer hablar por las voces de las otras mujeres. Y quizás no estaría tan segura de esto si no fuese por lo que me están diciendo cada vez que bajo del escenario.*"

the idea. The idea is to reach the audience and make the audience feel like part of what you are saying ... not just a *paya* in which I'm going to personally assault another, and the thread of the argument never reaches the public or makes the public the main actor.[18]

Pepita aims to transform perceptions of normative gender relations in her public performance, and in this regard, views her poetic style as more direct and more aggressive than that of most men. Both she and Myriam express a related notion that the presence of a confident woman on stage alters the performance dynamic, diverting the interaction from poetic frippery, excessive aggression, or personal slights. As Myriam expressed it to me,

> I think that whoever improvises against a woman has to be a good *payador*, because to fall into confrontation or profanity is very easy. It's an easy tool for a *payador* to latch onto. On the other hand, if he's going to improvise with a woman, he can't say those things. He has to talk about what's happening today, what's happening with the audience, with people, about some important issue. He can't just get up there and say any old thing.[19]

Although these artists maintain distinct views on their effect as *payadoras* within a primarily masculine community, they share a firm orientation towards a poetic style that draws the audience into their performance.

Conclusion

In terms of performer statistics, *canto a lo poeta* remains a masculine cultural domain, and in performance there are musical and poetic practices that distinguish masculine and feminine styles. Many female performers employ less confrontational poetic language than male *payadores* and *guitarroneros*, and their poetry is considered to occupy a "higher level," referring to bonds of affection as mother, wife, daughter, or open-hearted girl with "room in her heart for everyone."

---

[18] *"He tenido conocimiento de payadores que se han quedado tan mal herido en una paya que al final no se miran más, o no se hablan más ... entonces la idea no es ésa. La idea es llegar al público y que el público sea partícipe de lo que uno le está diciendo ... y no una paya en que yo simplemente yo vaya a agredir al otro como su persona, que no vaya ese hilo llegando al público, y poniendo al público como actor principal ... ."*

[19] *"Yo creo que quién va a payar contra una mujer tiene que ser un buen payador, porque caer en lo que es la confrontación, la grosería es muy fácil. Es un recurso fácil del cual se puede agarrar un payador. En cambio, si va a payar con una mujer, no puede decir esas cosas. Tiene que hablar de lo que está pasando en la actualidad, de que es lo que pasa con el público, con la gente, de algún tema importante. No puede llegar y decir cualquier cosa."*

Feminine Flowers among the Thistles 123

Most significantly, men wield the discursive freedom to comment on a woman's participation, defining her professionally, physically, and sexually. Also important is the fact that a woman's sexuality—or any sexual reference at all, for that matter—is a masculine discursive domain.

Particularly telling at the gathering in Codegua was a round of improvisation in which men declared their stance on divorce, birth control, and abortion, and the women in attendance remained silent. In this regard, discursive boundaries of performance in *canto a lo poeta* may reflect a trend that characterized public dialogue on gender in Chile in the late twentieth century. In 1997, the authors of *Discourse, Gender, and Power* affirmed that within dominant public discourse a woman's body is the ground on which the struggle for moral and social order is enacted. In this particular discursive battle, they argued, women in Chile have historically been silent (Grau, et al. 1997:213). The years since the mid-2000s have brought notable changes, however, from legislation legalizing divorce to the election of President Michelle Bachelet, who during her term promoted women's reproductive rights and denounced the patriarchal structures of Chilean politics in national and international forums.

In parallel with these political and social changes related to gender, prominent *payadoras* such as Myriam Arancibia, Cecilia Astorga, and Pepita Muñoz have carved a public space in which the possibility for reshaping perceptions of gender identity exists.[20] They express a desire to challenge the discursive framing that isolates them to a tangential, ornamental, or "special" position in the tradition. Furthermore, they seek to craft individual styles that transmit their unique visions of how feminine performance should be defined, taking into consideration the masculine structures of tradition as well as the most effective means of poetic confrontation that do not necessarily translate to direct, conflictive, or inflammatory language. While *canto a lo poeta* remains a musical realm in which many women feel more comfortable in the shadows than in the spotlight, leading *payadoras* are also constructing the poetic and musical means of diverting the public gaze from notions of women as delicate flowers, sexual objects, or special guests within the tradition.

---

[20] Since the conclusion of my research in 2008, Myriam Arancibia in particular has been working to create a national network of female singers. In addition to sponsoring informal gatherings where *payadoras* and *cantoras* share their experiences and concerns, she organized the first *encuentro* in Chile where all performers were women (Daniela Sepúlveda, Ana Irarrázabal, Soledad Menares, María Inés Donoso, and Ingrid Ortega).

PART III
Situated Events and Performance Politics: Fiesta, Festival, Stage, and Street

Chapter 6

The Way of Sorrows: Performance, Experience, and the Moral Society in Northern Ecuador[1]

Michelle Wibbelsman

Semana Santa: Performance Politics as Usual

In March 2001 quarreling broke out at a municipal meeting in the town of Cotacachi, Ecuador among members of the festival organizing committee for *Semana Santa*, or Holy Week. The argument revolved around the production of the Stations of the Cross, also known as the Via Dolorosa or Way of Sorrows—the Catholic dramatization that depicts Jesus' ascent to Golgotha to be crucified on Good Friday. Municipal interests focused on the Stations of the Cross as a major urban tourist event. Urban *mestizo* actors had traditionally performed the representation as part of the procession on Good Friday. In 2001, however, the director of the troupe of actors was sick and unable to assume the responsibility. This opened a window of opportunity for indigenous catechists to propose a performance of the *cuadros vivos*, the "living portraits" of the Via Dolorosa, for the general public with a script in Quichua, the language spoken by Otavalan indigenous people in the highlands of northern Ecuador. In response to municipal misgivings that this rendition would not appeal to tourist expectations, the catechists stated that for them this was an act of faith and not tourist production. Catholic priests were caught off guard by this moral conviction on the part of the indigenous catechists. Perhaps sensing a challenge to the Church's moral leadership, one priest went so far as to characterize the insertion of indigenous elements in the Catholic tradition as irreverent, and threatened to report the other priest to the archdiocese if he supported the catechists. The discussion came to an impasse.

In the weeks that followed, the director of the actor's group worsened and died. His widow petitioned municipal authorities to allow the *mestizo* troupe to perform the Stations of the Cross one last time as a tribute to her recently deceased husband. The *municipio* acceded to the request and the result was the performance of two different renditions of the living portraits—one staged by the *mestizo* actors in the city of Cotacachi as a dramatic presentation sanctioned by the *municipio* and

---

[1] An earlier version of this material was published originally as "Stations of the Cross: The Eternal Return to Existence and Hence to Suffering," in Wibbelsman 2009:139–54.

the Church, the other undertaken as a religious procession by indigenous devotees in the community of Arrayanes on the rural periphery of the canton. In this chapter I compare the urban *mestizo* and rural indigenous renditions of the ritual based on an analysis of performance aesthetics and ritual experience.

Given the racialized and racializing segregation of space in the context of Cotacachi's colonial legacy, which traditionally maps *mestizo* residents in urban centers and indigenous inhabitants in town peripheries and rural areas, one might easily conclude that the indigenous performance was banished to the outskirts of town as something which, from the urban *mestizo* perspective, did not belong in the city. This, however, was not the case. It was the catechists who *opted* not to compromise their understanding of the ritual by relocating the performance to the rural hamlet of Arrayanes. This concerted decision on their part ultimately supported a steadfast moral-political statement. This intersection of subaltern performance, politics, and religion provided a unique platform for cultural and political contention, and moral posturing. Moreover, it raises the broader question of what precisely is at stake in what Jean Comaroff (1985) refers to as the "unending struggle for the possession of the sign."

As historically marginalized indigenous peoples asserted control over the interpretation of the Catholic ritual and also its style of production, the procession in Arrayanes came to reflect a system of interpretation and experience that broke with both the hegemonic narrative and the dominant aesthetic of the ritual. The significance of this act lies in the alternative configurations of community and meaning-making it suggests. As communities defined by their cultural and political self-determination and their approach to adverse conditions "with transformative hope" (Whitten 2003), millennial identities come into sharp relief with powerful implications for collective action.

I argue elsewhere (see Wibbelsman 2009) that ritual practices operate as increasingly important settings for the formation and expression of new and emerging collective identities, especially in the context of diversifying ethnic experiences and lifestyles. Annual rituals offer spaces of encounter where, together, people periodically overcome their differences and affirm their inclusion as part of a single community. Communities, in other words, perform themselves into being on a regular basis (Barz 2003:6). The "wider set of 'possible' lives" (Appadurai 1991:198) produced by expanding experiences and expectations among these communities generates the multivocal discussions that are fundamental to a diversifying people's sense of participation and belonging, and to their evolving notion of who they are as *social persons* (Smith 1999:206). It is through this participation, argues Franca Tamisari (2005:56), that "it becomes possible to find the responsibility of our reciprocal historical and moral position. It is a participation in which questioning the other depends on being questioned; and affecting demands an openness to being affected, in a mechanism that allows us to recognize our history and act on it." As Gramsci (1971) points out, the community as a whole achieves empowerment once collective expression gives rise to culturally institutionalized forms of alternative moral articulation and

The Way of Sorrows   129

political action. Each successive ritual encounter, moreover, contributes to a sort of "cognitive scaffolding" (Bamberg 1983) that leads to an intensifying sense of inter-relatedness and shared understanding. In this context of transforming definitions and experiences of community, rituals function as dramatic attempts to present and shape particular social realities with a sense of plausibility and legitimacy (Moore 1975; Moore and Myerhoff 1977). Turino (2008:16–17), citing James Lea (2001), refers to this as the interplay between the Possible and the Actual, which, as Lea explains, is fundamental to all human experience.

In the Epilogue of *The Anthropology of Experience*, edited by Edward Bruner and the late Victor Turner, Clifford Geertz (1986:373) suggests that the job of the ethnographer is "all a matter of scratching surfaces." He endorses an approach to human experience as legible performance, text, and narrative. While this approach yields important insights, it also reveals a reluctance to explore questions of emotion and intuition that lie beyond the cognitive realm of representation. It seems to me that the thing to consider is not *that* we scratch at the surface of human experience, but *how* we scratch at it. Tamisari (2005:50) is correct in observing a "methodological tendency in anthropological studies of art and ritual to privilege structure over aesthetic experience, representation over expression, symbol over feeling, form over context" and a general scholarly concern with "the nature of knowledge and referential meaning rather than with the process of knowing." Scholars in the field of ethnomusicology have made productive inroads in going beyond representation and explaining experience as experience, not as text or definitional narrative. Among the most influential researchers in the discipline, Gerard Béhague stands out for his life-long dedication to performance as the primary object of ethnomusicological study and for his emphasis on the relation between performance, practice, and belief systems. Beyond his own research, Dr. Béhague mentored many generations of scholars who have not only provided theories that invite an exploration of performance as experience, but who have presented us with powerful methodologies for its analysis.

Semiotics, the study of sign systems, provides one such theory that scratches at the surface of affective human capacities and focuses an understanding of cultural performances not as reflections *about* or representations *of*, but as actual *processes of* lived experience (Turino 1999). Peircian semiotics, in particular, extends an understanding of signs beyond verbal language to include images, sounds, gestures, and objects, along with an appreciation for feelings, perceptions, and experience as tangible (and hence, "studiable") aspects of society (Hoopes 1991). As such, this paradigm is useful for analyzing richly layered ritual performances that appeal to all of the senses. Semiotic analysis, moreover, resonates with local emphases in Andean Ecuador on ritual as practice emergent from lived experience and as a transcendental affective encounter.

In this chapter I explore different conceptions of performance, memory, experience, and participation in the two distinct renditions of the living portraits of Christ, and I consider how they affect (or fail to affect) feelings of community and collective action. The production of the Stations of the Cross as tourist event

130 *Soundscapes from the Americas*

by the *mestizo* acting troupe in the city of Cotacachi ultimately circumscribed the religious drama as a professional performance tethered to public entertainment. This rendition was shaped by an aesthetic of expediency in a performance style insistent on narrative abbreviation, aural and visual editing, and dramatic impressionism. In contrast, the multivocality, overflowing detail, generalized participation, and sensual experience of the indigenous procession affirmed the Christian ritual not as dramatic representation but as lived experience. I argue that pronounced repetition, rhythmic movement, and collective prayer, along with extended temporal duration and spatial range, drew indigenous participants together in an empathetic community centered on an evolving moral claim as brothers with Christ in suffering. I turn at once to the details of the two renditions of the living portraits I documented in 2001.

Expediency and Performance in an Urban *Mestizo* Context

The performance in the city of Cotacachi was well rehearsed. The *mestizo* actors were trained to project their voices and exaggerate their gestures for dramatic effect. Roman soldiers escorting Jesus doubled as experts in crowd control for the rowdy urban audience, delimiting the performance area with a brightly colored rope. The troupe was photogenic, exhibiting well-crafted, matching costumes. Each scene, performed at street intersections or in doorways that served as improvised proscenium stages along the main avenue, was brief, lasting no more than five to ten minutes. The crowd would then move on for one block, stopping for the next dramatic frame. Prayers ("The Lord's Prayer," "Hail Mary," "Glory Be …") were only inserted during scenes where they complemented the dramatic narrative, at which points devotees among the crowd of locals and mostly national tourists would chime in. The performance relied on its visual impact and on its adherence to a minimalist version of the Bible story.

Jesus, the sizable cross he was carrying, and the torrent of people, actors, vendors, and raucous teenagers finally poured forth in chaotic fashion onto the main square. The crucifixion was to take place in front of the Church of La Matriz in the central plaza. This was to be the last portrait, abbreviating the stations to 12 instead of 14 for dramatic effect. The actor portraying Jesus was hastily stripped of his garments and tied to the cross. There were no accompanying thieves and no playing dice for Jesus' clothes—perhaps considered to be peripheral narrative threads that would detract from the main story. To my disbelief, when Jesus dropped his head, indicating his death and the end of the performance, people applauded.

Walking with Jesus

The all-indigenous troupe of performers in the rural community of Arrayanes was clearly amateur. Some had to be reminded of their lines; others mumbled shyly

The Way of Sorrows 131

into the microphone. Costumes were simple—mostly improvised except for the matching Roman capes and spray-painted cardboard helmets. One of the most striking aspects of the rendition was its duration. The indigenous depiction of the Via Dolorosa resisted abbreviation. Each stage of the procession was extended, fraught with repetition of gestures to convey the idea of temporal and spatial transition.

The crowd gathered at the schoolhouse in Arrayanes where the participants enacted at length the visit to Pontius Pilate and Herod, who try to condemn Jesus. The soldiers walked Jesus through the circle of observers and around the sizeable crowd not once but twice each time to convey the distance traveled and time elapsed. A choir of women sang in Quichua during this prolonged depiction. After this portrayal of the beginning scenes of the Stations of the Cross, the procession got under way. Jesus led the way, carrying an enormous cross mostly unassisted across difficult terrain. Participants, most of them indigenous, followed down the rugged dirt road, slowing down to chat along the way with people they knew from other communities. An ice-cream vendor wove through the crowd advertising multicolored popsicles and adding a festive (but by no means rowdy) element. Once we got to the highway, weekend traffic quickly backed up behind the procession—buses, cars, jeeps, and tour vans headed to the Cotacachi-Cayapas reserve and the crater lake, Cuicocha. The crowd would advance about one quarter of a mile and stop for each new station. In addition to the detailed enactment of the scenes, at each stop, everyone knelt on the asphalt and prayed. Not a single car honked or tried to bypass the procession as the chorus of voices rose in unison:

Padre Nuestro, que estás en los cielos; santificado sea tu nombre; venga tu reino; hágase tu voluntad en la tierra como en el cielo. Danos hoy nuestro pan de cada día; perdona nuestras ofensas como también nosotros perdonamos a los que nos ofenden; no nos dejes caer en tentación y líbranos del mal. Amén.

Dios te salve María, llena eres de gracia! El Señor es contigo; Bendita eres entre todas la mujeres y Bendito es el Fruto de tu vientre, Jesús. Santa María, Madre de Dios, ruega por nosotros pecadores, ahora y en la hora de nuestra muerte. Amén.

Gloria al Padre, Gloria al Hijo y Gloria al Espíritu Santo, como era en el principio, ahora y siempre, por los siglos de los siglos. Amén.

This collective prayer periodically drew the crowd together in a single, fervent voice, and in a single gesture of veneration as we knelt as one, hats off and hands clasped. Jovial interaction among the followers subsided at these moments as the repeated act of praying side by side punctuated the procession with solemnity and provided a discernible cadence for the ritual.

Upon reaching the place where the crucifixion was to take place, the Roman soldiers spent half an hour digging the holes needed to erect the three crosses. Jesus, who had been prematurely tied to his cross, just lay there uncomfortably

132 *Soundscapes from the Americas*

until they finished digging. Once the crosses were up, Jesus and the two thieves hung painfully from their arms. Coordinators rushed to borrow materials at a nearby house and eventually improvised a foot rung for the actors to stand on. No one seemed to mind these delays as performance and the practicalities of daily life intertwined in a single experience.

While the 12th station in Cotacachi was brief and highlighted an expeditious and dramatic death, here the soldiers, now more relaxed in their performance roles, played dice for Jesus' clothes and taunted his thirst with vinegar in an extended scene. Jesus died almost unnoticed while the soldiers gambled. Jesus was finally taken down from the cross and the body carried off by the women. There was no climactic finale and certainly no applause.

Whereas in Cotacachi the crowd simply dispersed at the end of the performance, in Arrayanes a respected community leader, former president of UNORCAC (Union of Peasant Organizations of Cotacachi) Alberto Anrango, approached the microphone. Jesus reemerged in full costume to walk and listen among the crowd—a seamless transition between performance and real life in a sort of resurrection that was entirely befitting of a fulfillment of the 14th station.[2] Anrango congratulated the community in Quichua for taking on the responsibility of the performance and for enacting the living portraits of Christ in accordance with indigenous traditions and in a language and interpretation of their own. He then reflected on the experience they had just been through:

> In the same way that Jesus fought against the Romans, we too, the poor of today, have to fight against the tyrants who harm us. They are the corrupt ones. The poor, not just indigenous, but also nonindigenous, white-*mestizos*, blacks, have to fight against those who have dominated this country for all times … .

This reflexive turn, along with Jesus' reemergence as part of the congregation, highlighted the shared nature of the procession and shifted the focus from Jesus *per se* to the poor who, like Jesus, had suffered unjustly.[3] This final confluence of events effectively transposed the biblical story into contemporary social context and political relevance.

---

[2] The 12th station presents the death of Jesus on the cross. In one version of the ritual representation, Jesus' body is removed from the cross in the 13th station, and in the 14th station he is laid in the tomb. In a different version, Jesus' body is removed from the cross and carried off for burial in the 13th station, and in the 14th station he rises from the dead.

[3] Orta (1990) observes a similar and consistent turn of phrase in a Via Crucis performance in a Nicaraguan *comunidad eclesial de base*. The repetition of "those who like Christ …" accentuates ongoing injustices, leading Orta to consider the Via Crucis a ritual of resistance. The ritual also involves asking for forgiveness, thus holding people accountable for "having allowed the injustice suffered by Jesus to continue today" (Orta 1990:81). Orta interprets the Via Crucis within a broader frame of Latin American liberation theology, whose followers see themselves at the vanguard of a transformative social movement.

Two Crucifixions in Juxtaposition

From its inception, the performance in town was planned as a tourist attraction. Eye-catching costumes and visual impressions achieved through snapshot-quality poses functioned as external anamnetic referents for recollecting the story of Christ's crucifixion. Dialogue was minimized, highlighting only the most recognizable phrases to carry the story. Suffering and sacrifice, central themes of the Stations of the Cross, were reduced to visual cues focusing on Christ's bloodstained clothes and face (Figure 6.1). The short distance traveled and the relative brevity of the event omitted any real, if only trivial, suffering either on the part of the performers or of the accompanying public.

Figure 6.1   Presentation of the Stations of the Cross in Cotacachi by a troupe of *mestizo* actors. Photograph by Michelle Wibbelsman, 2001

The final expression of applause upon the symbolic death of Jesus, aside from striking me as ironic, confirmed the spectacle-like aspect of the performance. Thomas Russell (1941) signals an important distinction among performance pieces that merit applause, noting that "pseudo-sacred" performances should appropriately be received in "dead silence." Although in many instances, applause can have a collectivizing effect among what would otherwise be a splintered crowd (Coyne 2009; Feldman 1995; Néda et al. 2000), in this case the clapping created a schism between audience and performers, and among the audience members themselves. Most significantly, the clapping put an abrupt end to the

134   *Soundscapes from the Americas*

sustained moment of the religious drama, creating a sonic rift that generated an anti-climax often associated with mistimed or inappropriate applause. Although the audience in Cotacachi was able to recognize and appreciate the performance aesthetically, their applause signaled an emotional dissociation from the suffering of Christ and from the numinous experience of the ritual. The abrupt end of the applause and the crowd's dispersal immediately after the performance suggested that the event had not brought onlookers together in contemplative dialogue as a community having passed through the intensity of a ritual process. Also significant, as one of the indigenous catechists who accompanied me in the city observed, was the fact that the procession of saints that followed the depiction of the living portraits in Cotacachi received virtually no attention.

It is not that the procession in Cotacachi somehow fell short of achieving an intended ritual transcendence, but rather that the event was consciously orchestrated to remain within tightly controlled limits of theatrical interpretation and experience. Feldman's (1995:461) insights into performances as contained "frames" that govern and distance the response of the audience speak to this point. My observation is that structuring rituals as secularized performances in the city revealed a reluctance on the part of local political entities, Church authorities, and the Cotacachi *mestizo*, middle-class urbanites to engage in a potentially transformative dramatic dialogue. Turner (1995:200) points out that, as a phase of indeterminacy or condition of reversal, ritual liminality for the strong represents weakness since it requires them to abandon the structured hierarchies they enjoy. This explanation would, in fact, account for the institutionalized approach in Cotacachi to the Stations of the Cross as an event of fixed interpretation, as opposed to a dynamic context of experience. This emphasis is reflected in the *Plan de Desarrollo del Cantón Cotacachi*, published by the *municipio* (n.d.:25, 33–6), wherein important religious festivals consistently appear with immutable labels and descriptions under systematized economic development policies for the promotion of tourism (see also Ortiz Crespo 2004:131).

The event in Arrayanes constituted a different experience altogether. Attention to detail manifested itself primarily in terms of practice and participation, and less as a factor of costume. Enacted segments marking transition were long, and spoken dialogue in Quichua by the actors was lengthy, requiring a narrator to assist them with their lines. The distance covered by the procession was substantial—about 5 kilometers—demanding exertion on the part of actors and public alike. The length of the walk and acts of talking casually along the way, sharing food, offering help, and praying together imbued the experience with pilgrimage-like overtones. It also blended everyday dispositions into the performance script. Among the cast of performers the physical sacrifice was quite real. Either by design or due to oversight by coordinators, the actors suffered through the performance, walking away in the end with some semblance of real experience encrusted under their toenails and splintered into their skin—the line between experience and representation suddenly less discernible (Figure 6.2).

Figure 6.2 Indigenous catechists perform the Living Portraits of Christ in Arrayanes. Photo by Michelle Wibbelsman, 2001

Signs of Feeling and Emotion

As basic human experiences that bridge sensation as well as emotional and evaluative registers, pain and discourses about suffering are pivotal in the recognition of a common humanity. Such emotional and visceral responses to a performance appeal to theories of embodiment and experience. Signs *of* feeling, namely semiotic icons and indices, can contribute significant depth to an analysis of performance as felt experience (Turino 1999:223–4). Semiotic indices and icons work at the level of emotion and are experienced as real or natural connections. Often operating in tandem, icons are based on resemblance, and indices derive from signifying relations that draw on co-occurrence in actual experience and on personal experience. Most significantly, the progressive nature of semiotic sign-object chains unfolds as a process that builds on cumulative and collective experience. And as Turino (2004:18) describes, in the context of collective rituals semiotics can provide us with a mechanism for understanding how people create a sense of collective unity through sounding and moving together, wherein acts like praying, walking, and suffering together are "not propositions *about* identity but rather are the very experience *of* similarity, *of* identity, each participant responding to and coordinating with the sounds and movements of others."

136   *Soundscapes from the Americas*

A third level of semiotic sign relations involves *rheme* and *dicent* signs, as Turino (1999) discusses in the context of Peircean semiotics. These add a qualitative dimension to the relation between sign and object, signaling whether a representation simply falls within the realm of the possible (in the case of *rheme*) or whether the representation carries a true/false judgment (as in the case of *dicent*). Body language such as facial expression, body position, and gesture are *dicent* signs interpreted as being the direct result of a person's actual attitude, and grasped as actually being affected by it. They are often bundled with indices to achieve more complex semiotic combinations in the dynamic interplay of sign-object relations, continually generating new interpretations and evolving processes of signification.

As the sequence of signification progresses, we can see in an application of these definitions to the description at hand that the cross, for instance, can symbolize Christianity or Christian redemption. At the level of iconicity, the cross evokes the crucified Christ. Similarly, based on the criterion of resemblance, the suffering Christ may be perceived as iconic of human suffering. An analysis of *dicent*-indices establishes a connection between the performance of agonized facial expressions and pain. In the case of the indigenous devotees, the experience of real suffering supports a *dicent*-index relation within the ritual act, rendering it a more powerful general icon of suffering in the evolving spiral of interpretative representations. As Vijay Iyer (2002:388) observes, we must take into consideration that embodied cognition (perception) and sensory and motor processes (action) evolve together and are fundamentally inseparable and mutually informative. Among those walking with Jesus, I saw bare feet, weathered and cracked, with toenails and soles encrusted with dirt that had become a permanent part of the skin. I saw torn *alpargates* [indigenous sandals] attempting to look their best for this occasion; baby feet, bare and already taking on the characteristics of those of their parents' and grandparents'. These were not acts of penance for Holy Week, but rather testaments to a lifetime of suffering and walking in sorrow.

In sharp contrast, the *mestizo* performers remained within the exclusive realm of symbolism and iconicity consistent with perception, but not with the sensory experience Iyer describes, which is integral to the third, interpretive point on the Peircean semiotic triangle. The trichotomy of sign relations in the indigenous representation draws out a powerful indexical correspondence between suffering and injustice, experienced as co-occurring phenomena both in historical perspective in the Christian story and in the personal experience of contemporary indigenous people. Indexicality renders these relations naturalized, casting them as inextricable causal dynamics in a way that one immediately calls forth the other. From a Catholic outlook, suffering and redemption may also work in the same way.

This semiotic process, which draws on personal experience, is what enables individual suffering to find resonance with Christ's suffering, and, through the equivalence, to become transformative, religious pain (Glucklich 2001:29). The impact of direct signs of feeling, moreover, is often harnessed through contextualizing symbols—hence the importance of Anrango's speech in its

The Way of Sorrows 137

ability to both articulate and demarcate the collective affective experience, and to synthesize the suffering of Christ and the poor. This intimate and now generalized identification with Christ through empathy and co-suffering supports indigenous ethnic claims as brothers with Christ, and not just in suffering, but, through suffering, in the redemptive cleansing of the world's sins. Beyond the assertion of a common humanity of shared pain, the transcendental character of religious pain acts as a socially and spiritually integrative force that defines a moral community (Glucklich 2001:34). Ultimately, the achievement of this moral community through the experience of transformative pain encircles the sufferers from both the past and the present in an all-embracing condition of interrelatedness—*communitas*—which Turner (1974:238) describes as "almost always thought of or portrayed by actors as a timeless condition, an eternal now."

Embodied Memory and Performance as Lived Experience

For Mircea Eliade (1963:107) religious ceremonies are "festivals of memory." Among Andean indigenous people, ancestors (as well as *wakas*—Andean ancestral deities and sacred objects—and Catholic saints) are traditionally brought into festive participation as embodied souls with material needs and tangible influences. The symbolic enactment of parity between the worlds of the living and the dead through the sharing of food and conversation generally observed on ritual occasions affirms this sustained relation. I build on Eliade's (1963:120) assertion that memory supports ongoing contact with the world of the dead, and suggest that it is more specifically empathetic memory rooted in experience and co-suffering that maintains this connection. In everyday life, the personal and vicarious experience of pain in its many forms—suffering, distress, sickness, grief, sorrow, hunger, agony—contributes to a moral community of charitable obligation among the living. This obligation extends to the dead through detailed remembrance of those who have passed away—their personalities, their favorite foods, anecdotes about celebrations and sorrows in their lives. Empathy in ritual context encircles people as well as animated landscapes and otherworldly beings from the past and the mythic past into this moral community, and holds this inclusive community together through experiences of both communion and commiseration as contemporaries in an eternal present.

The performance of detail provides the foundation for embodied memory and understanding. Repetition of motion is the principal technique in indigenous performances for evoking the past or depicting any given traditional activity. When I filmed such events, I was coached by indigenous participants and organizers not to abbreviate the recordings, and told that the repetitions were, in fact, especially important to document. I eventually came to understand that this was because detailed repetition is not gratuitous, but rather requires a high degree of attentiveness, meditation, and focus that leads to complete absorption in the task and allows one to "experience anew the emotions attached to the original event"

(Frank 2006:11). Frank (2006) discusses "sense memory" and "emotion memory" in the context of the sensual experience of the Chinese martial arts form *taijiquan*. He writes that in certain styles of the art repetition is emphasized as a means by which each movement receives concentrated attention, allowing for improvement of both the form and its understanding (Frank 2006:72). To a great extent this method of mindful, sensual, meaningful repetition intersects with Turino's (2008:4, 43) description of *flow* in music performance as a state of heightened concentration achieved through intense activity that is necessarily focused on what is going on at the moment. In a similar manner, indigenous performances aim to emulate life, to relive the past, and not just reference it. The best performances are considered to be those that capture, as one indigenous leader observed, "something real, not invented." Realistic portrayals of the way things used to be, achieved through intense concentration and empathy, effectively bring the past into the present in the context of performance, and, in a moment of suspended disbelief, render the present and the past concurrent rather than contiguous.

It bears mentioning that invoking the extended community through this type of embodied ritual remembrance ultimately tempts Andean millenarian myths—specifically, the Inkarrí myth of the resurrection of the last Inka and the religious revival of Taki Unquy. The myth of Inkarrí (or Inka Rey, spelled variously *incari*, *incarrí*, *inkari*) recounts a prophecy, which gained popularity in the eighteenth century, of the return of the last Inka. Jan Szemiński (1987:179) writes that the return of the Inka was associated with moral cleansing and the restoration of the world to its proper order. It called for the destruction of Spaniards and sinners in order to achieve this goal. During the European conquest, Atahualpa, the last Inka emperor, was decapitated by the Spaniards. His body was dismembered and the various body parts buried in different places throughout the empire. The Inkarrí legend relates that when the far-flung body parts of the Inka emperor come together as one again, the Inka will be resurrected and return to power against the oppressive system of the Spaniards, bringing colonial reign to an end. The rebellions of Tupac Amaru and Tupac Katari in the eighteenth century reflected the ongoing appeal of the prophecy. Szemiński (1987) further documents allusions to the millenarian myth in twentieth-century indigenous insurrections, which also resonate with contemporary Ecuadorian indigenous conceptions of the *pachakutik*, understood generally as an overturning of time and space that will bring about a new moral order. Michael Uzendoski (2005:23, 165) describes this powerful phenomenon among the Napo Runa of Amazonian Ecuador as an embodied subjectivity of transformation that inhabits each person and is expressed in the poetics of "destroying, recuperating, and transforming society and history" for the production of a better life. (See also Whitten 1988:283, 295 and 2003:x.)

Taki Unquy (also spelled Taki Onqoy, literally "dancing sickness") similarly calls for the return of the *wakas* [*huacas*, Andean ancestor gods] along with upheaval and renewal through the elimination of Spaniards (Stern 1993:51–5). Frank Salomon (1999:33) writes that Taki Unquy constitutes a "revolution in the uses of memory" that not only required followers to hark back to pre-Inka deities, but importantly,

The Way of Sorrows   139

caused them to begin thinking of the *wakas* as "emblems of a new macro-category—
the indigenous ... ." (See also Spalding 1999:955.) The movement was thus
grounded in moral principles of solidarity and resistance within the Andean world
(Stern 1993:56). Both myths evoke the powerful political implications of a moral
rhetoric inclusive of an extended community and articulated in ethnic terms.

The Moral Community

In the indigenous rendition of The Way of Sorrows in Arrayanes, resurrection of
the mythic and historical dead, embodied in Jesus and those like Jesus, as part of
an extended moral-political community was achieved through empathetic memory
and performance as embodied experience. We can appreciate the gravity of the
indigenous challenge to the rather narrow urban circumscription of the ritual when
we consider that in the evolving indigenous moral perspective, the only way the
"strong," in hegemonic terms, enter the moral community is through the forgiveness
of their sins via the sacrifice of others. Suffering is empowering, whether it is in the
form of endurance, individual and collective transformation toward a moral agency
and a sense of *communitas*, or transcendence in the form of religious sacrifice. The
collective self-determination derived from suffering for the expiation of the sins of
society, moreover, can easily be harnessed as impetus for other agendas. Rituals of
status reversal and symbolic inversion that project the poor as the redeemers of the
world have the potential to awaken an awareness about the "powers of the weak."
Alberto Anrango's call to action resonates with such an epiphany.

Asserting that the poor had paid long enough for the tyranny of the corrupt
bankers who have oppressed the country since the beginning of time, Anrango
called for people to rise up and fight against the modern tyrants the way that Christ
"fought" against the Romans. Although the concept of Christ rising up against
his assailants is nowhere to be found in the representation of the Stations of the
Cross, the semiotic chain reaction that enabled the original indexical connection
between suffering and injustice, and between suffering and redemption, overflows
the delimitations of the performance script, and in a creative indexical reshuffling
establishes a correspondence between suffering and retribution.

The ease of Anrango's transition from Christ-like to modern poor, and from
Romans to tyrants to corrupt bankers is predicated on the semiotic work already
under way prior to his political intervention.[4] Specifically, as old indexical

---

[4] Anrango's specific targeting of corrupt bankers refers to the collapse of several banks
beginning in March 1999, when the dollar fluctuated wildly above an unprecedented 20,000
sucres, causing spiraling devaluation, and resulting in a federally mandated national "bank
holiday" (*feriado bancario*). On Monday, March 8, 1999, personal checking and savings
accounts across the country were frozen and the banks closed to the public to prevent
withdrawals. This economic crisis was compounded by corruption and mismanagement.
Corruption scandals that reached to the highest levels of bank management remained

140   *Soundscapes from the Americas*

associations are layered and re-inscribed with new ones, "the condensing of a variety of meanings and emotions" leads to what Turino (2008:9) calls a "semantic snowballing" effect with powerful and unpredictable outcomes. In addition, Anrango's political reflection coincides with the relation Turner (1995:128) signals between *communitas*, poverty, marginality, and structural inferiority. Anrango's speech symbolically reformulates inclusion in the brotherhood of Christ more specifically as comprising the poor—an ethnically "open society" of indigenous, non indigenous, white-*mestizos*, and blacks. While the experience of hardship among minority and disadvantaged communities in Ecuador is quite real, Turner's (1974:165) clarification that liminal poverty need not be confused with real poverty (although they may overlap) re-centers an awareness of material differences on moral conviction. He writes that "liminal poverty, whether it is a process or a state, is both an expression and instrumentality of *communitas*" (Turner 1974:165). *Communitas* as conceived by Turner is a voluntarily egalitarian and nonmaterialist community. In other words, it is not a factor of circumstance but of choice in conformance with a moral economy of reciprocity that defines a leveling process that may impoverish economically, but empowers politically (Varese 1996:63). Anrango's carefully chosen words reflect a similar awareness, juxtaposing not poor and rich, but poor and corrupt in a contrastive conceptual pair that does not condemn financial achievement *per se* (and therefore does not preclude subaltern people from moving up the socio-economic ladder—an important distinction to make in an area and an era of economic success among groups that have been historically marginalized).

Although there were no explicit references to liberation theology in Anrango's speech, both his rhetoric and his message are pregnant with overtones of "a movement engaged in the overturning of 'institutional structures of sin,'" described by Orta (1990:80) as the aim of Latin American liberation theologians and practitioners. Both positions, furthermore, resonate with the call to restore the moral order of the world in Andean millenarian myths. The weight of Anrango's reflection rendered symbolically in words thus rests on an already familiar religious message and a broader political awareness in the Andes.

The Political Community

Ritual not only moves people to think reflexively, but can incite people to action (Turner 1995:129). In immediate context, Anrango seized the opportunity of a

---

unresolved and many bank clients were never refunded their money. In subsequent years, the government funneled significant federal funds to try to rescue some of the banks from bankruptcy. The crisis was experienced as all the more ruinous by middle- and lower-income Ecuadorians, given the simultaneous cuts in social programs and benefits for the poor due to lack of funding and International Monetary Fund (IMF) pressures for increased austerity measures.

captive audience to communicate, through a particularly effective metaphor, the national indigenous agenda to broaden the bases of support for political action. In *The Ritual Process* (1995) and *Dramas, Fields and Metaphors* (1974:270), however, Victor Turner draws a systematic correspondence between ritual, liminality, *communitas*, and the powers of the weak, linking ritual and politics in a structural (and not merely opportunistic) relation. Similarly, Tamisari (2005:49) insists on an analysis of performance that underscores the interweaving of the political, the religious, the aesthetic, and the affective, stating that "the political and the aesthetic are not only inseparable but mutually constitutive and productive." The vigorous contest over possession of the sign in local performances and experience unfolds in a strategy of symbolic and semiotic engagement, participation, and moral critique with stakes that are ultimately political in the sense that they call for profound social change.

The condition of heightened collective awareness and human interrelatedness achieved through ritual is often thought of as an ephemeral phenomenon. Nonetheless, the intensity of ritual activity and the emphasis on participation among indigenous people in northern Ecuador invokes this collective process of reflection, interpretation, and embodied experience with relative frequency. Turner (1995:132, 95) describes the people who consciously sustain a heightened sense of interrelatedness, who seize and prolong opportunities for advancing shared understanding, as liminal *personae* or "threshold people." The threshold marks a point of entry or beginning. As *limen*, it captures a moment of sufficient intensity to begin to produce an effect. Poised at an intersection of contested ways of living and understanding, the liminal poor—those eager to transform society and history for the production of a better life—come to embody this moment of transformation as points of passage, beginning, and *limen* at the heart of the moral and political society.

Chapter 7

Performing Indigeneity:
Poetics and Politics of Music Festivals
in Highland Bolivia

Thomas Solomon

It is an early evening in mid-June 1993 in the highland village of Irupata, in the eastern range of the Bolivian Andes that runs through the northern region of the department of Potosí. This rural community, home to Quechua-speaking peasant farmers, has been the host all day to a music festival in honor of the third anniversary of the radio station Mallku Kiririya, built by the Bolivian NGO Taypikala with financial support from French and German foundations. Since early afternoon, a series of musical groups representing different communities in the surrounding countryside has taken the stage inside the large hall built adjacent to the radio's control room and small studio, while hundreds of spectators, mostly people from the same communities, but also including invited dignitaries and politicians from urban centers in the region, crowd the hall to watch. Each performing group, consisting of troupes of adult men playing consorts of wind instruments such as panpipes or duct flutes, or mixed groups of teenage girls singing accompanied by boys playing stringed instruments, has given a display of colorful indigenous clothing and textiles while playing autochthonous musical instruments and singing songs in the Quechua or Aymara languages. All afternoon a group of judges consisting mostly of visiting dignitaries from outside the community has sat near the stage, carefully observing the performances and rating each performing group. Now in the early evening the winners are finally announced and the prizes of agricultural implements, rubber sandals made from discarded automobile tires, and bags of coca are distributed, and the winning groups are asked to return to the stage and spontaneously perform again, representing the best of local indigenous music and culture. The members of one of the winning groups have, however, subsequent to their performance earlier in the day, already changed out of their colorful "peasant" clothing back into their everyday clothes. Not having time to change back into their festive dress, the young men in the group take the stage to play their encore wearing blue jeans or slacks of synthetic cloth bought in stores in the nearby mining town of Llallagua, instead of the pants of black or white homespun with delicate embroidery around the cuffs, and without the many woven scarves, carrying cloths, belts, small pouches for carrying coca,

144   *Soundscapes from the Americas*

and other decorations they had worn during their competition performance. The young women singers in the group are similarly less adorned than in their earlier performance, their many decorative textiles having already been safely stowed away. While their clothes are now different, the group performs again one of the songs they presented earlier in the day. The song text includes the line in Quechua "*Ñawpa kulturasninchista ni qunqakusunchu*"—"Let's not forget our ancient cultures." No one seems to note the costume change; or if they have noticed it, no one openly comments on it.

Performance, Identity, Representation, Subjectivity

In a well-known discussion of cultural identity, Stuart Hall has argued that "Perhaps instead of thinking of identity as an already accomplished fact, which ... cultural practices then represent, we should think, instead, of identity as a 'production,' which is never complete, always in process, and always constituted within, not outside, *representation*" (1990:222, emphasis added). While the humanistic tradition of cultural studies within which Hall works has for the most part taken mass-mediated textual material as the point of departure for analysis of the poetics and politics of representational practices, anthropologists and ethnomusicologists have recognized that real-time, interactive performances are also key sites where identities are actively negotiated. *Performance* thus becomes an arena for experimenting with, trying out, and "trying on" new identities in situations where the social relations at stake in identity formation are made the center of attention. The close relationship between performance and *representation*, in the sense that Hall uses it, is perhaps suggested by the way that the Spanish word *representación* (like similar cognate terms in other Romance languages) is one of the possible translations of the English word *performance*. Following the implications of Hall's argument, performance is thus seen as a representation, not of a pre-existing cultural essence, but of an identity-in-process. Kathleen Stewart succinctly states the significance this approach has for the practice of ethnography: "Analytic practice shifts from defining given identities and their causes to tracking the operations by which identities are ascribed, negotiated, and performed" (1991:409).

Ethnographers are increasingly confronted with situations where people have become aware of the constructedness of their own identity discourses, and do not necessarily see (if indeed they ever did) traditional ways of constructing identity either as natural or the only way. Ethnographic description and analysis become further complicated when people, despite their awareness of the constructedness of traditional identity discourses, still find it to their advantage to deploy these discourses in self-conscious practices of strategic essentialism (Adams 1997; Fuss 1989; Spivak 1996). In situations like these, the reflexive "performance of identity" may be quite literal as people self-consciously engage

Performing Indigeneity: Poetics and Politics of Music Festivals   145

in role-playing, depending on the intended "audience." Understanding the relationship between performance and identity in situations like these requires the ethnographer to recognize the agency of social actors, audible and visible in their very acts of performance. Such performances should be understood as conscious representations of an identity—a momentary inhabiting of a subject position, and the creation of a subjectivity that can again be inhabited later by the same performers or by others who have witnessed the performance and found the subject positions it represents useful and meaningful to inhabit. But this is an *active* subjectivity that actors creatively engage with and reflect over, not one wholly determined by external discourses and representations over which the performing subject has no awareness or control, as postulated by the most extreme versions of the poststructuralist paradigm influenced by the work of Foucault and (especially) Lacan.

These issues become particularly salient for discussions of the politics of indigeneity and authenticity. In the case of the post-colonial Latin American states, as indigenous peoples become self-conscious of how their own indigeneity constitutes a kind of symbolic capital they can draw upon when maneuvering within the states in which they find themselves, the performance of their indigeneity can become a strategy for negotiating their relationships with the state (Bigenho 2002; Seeger 1994). Such performances can be read from various perspectives: as participation by the performers in their own co-optation by the state, or as the creation of a space in which to talk back to the state's folklorized representations of them—in short, as hegemonic or as counterhegemonic.

In this chapter I explore some of these issues through an analysis of ethnographic data on performances in highland Bolivia.[1] I examine music festivals in Norte Potosí as sites for working through and performing the contradictions of experience and identity, and thus consider these festivals as sites for constituting and performing an indigenous subjectivity in a particular regional context within a modern postcolonial state.[2] Counter to a reading of these festivals that would see them as vehicles for the commodification of indigenous cultural expression, I argue that the festivals provided performers and local spectators with a means for reflecting on and creatively constructing their own identity as indigenous people, explicitly in articulation with other social groups within the Bolivian state.

---

[1]   Field research in Bolivia during 1990 and 1993–94 was made possible by a grant from the Tinker Foundation and a Fulbright-Hays Dissertation Research Abroad Fellowship. Thanks to the many people who read and commented on various earlier versions of this material when it was part of my doctoral dissertation (Solomon 1997), especially Steven Feld, Richard Schaedel, and Margot Beyersdorff.

[2]   Space limitations prevent me from theorizing *indigeneity* as an analytical term here, so the meaning of this important term must, within the context of this chapter at least, unfortunately be taken as a given.

146   *Soundscapes from the Americas*

Setting

The province of Bustillo in the northern tip of the department of Potosí in the Bolivian highlands, the region known in Bolivia as Norte Potosí, contains nine indigenous groups that self-identify as *ayllus*. While the Quechua- and Aymara-language term *ayllu* has meant different things in different times and places throughout the central Andes (Castelli, et al. 1981; Godoy 1985, 1986), in the context of the *ayllus* of Bustillo Province it can be said to evoke a corporate identity based on four interrelated things: 1) common ancestry (whether real or imagined), 2) a territorial base, 3) a contemporary network of kin relations, and 4) a perceived shared way of life and set of cultural practices (Godoy 1985, 1986; Harris 2000:97–8). The majority of *ayllu* people live in dispersed rural communities where they engage in a mix of agriculture and pastoralism, although many also do seasonal work outside the community (Kraft 1995:55) or small-scale mining within their *ayllu*'s territory (Godoy 1990). The population of individual *ayllus* ranges from the approximately 10,500 members of Ayllu Chayantaka, who live in some 45 village communities, to the estimated 2,350 members of Ayllu Sikuya, distributed among about 20 communities (Mendoza et al. 1994). The twin towns of Chayanta and Aymaya, located in the center of the province where the territories of most of the *ayllus* come together like spokes at the center of a wheel, function as the *marka* or ceremonial center, being the site of several *fiestas* between *ayllus* throughout the year.

Overlaid on top of the indigenous socio-spatial system in the region, and articulating with it in a number of complex ways, is the society of *mestizos* [literally "mixed-blood"], including proletarianized full-time miners, shopkeepers, and professionals such as schoolteachers, lawyers, pharmacists, and workers in non-governmental organizations (NGOs). The *mestizo* population of the region is concentrated in towns such as Chayanta and mining centers such as the Llallagua-Siglo XX tin mine complex. The origins and current constitution of *mestizo* society is complex, ranging from *ayllu* members who have permanently migrated with their families to the city and become Hispanized (*cholos*), to families who have lived in the city for many generations and maintain little, if any, historical memory of their ancestors' origins in indigenous peasant communities. *Mestizo*, while ostensibly a racial category, is thus better understood as a social category based on social and cultural capital.

After the 1952 Bolivian revolution, intellectuals and politicians began to encourage the use of the Spanish term *campesino* ["peasant"] as a supposedly neutral substitute for the word *indio* ["Indian"], which carried negative connotations because of its frequent use as a racial epithet (Albó 1979:488–9). This change from a blatantly racial category to a category that is—at least in theory—solely economic was also ideologically consistent with the newly empowered professional middle class's project of eventually assimilating the indigenous peasantry into the rest of the population (*mestizaje* or *blanqueamiento*) and forging a modern Bolivian state (Rivera Cusicanqui 1987:83, 99, 1991:23n.26). In local practice, however,

Performing Indigeneity: Poetics and Politics of Music Festivals 147

the people of the *ayllus* use the Spanish term *campesino* as a de facto broad *ethnic* self-designation that crosscuts distinctions between individual *ayllus*.

Fiesta and *Festival* as Performance Occasions

During my fieldwork from January 1993 to January 1994, the members of the *ayllus* of Bustillo Province identified two very different kinds of musical occasions, which they respectively called *fiesta* and *festival*.[3, 4] They used different musical strategies in these two different kinds of musical occasions in order to accomplish different social purposes. These different musical strategies could be seen in how they chose which musical instruments to play, in the content of song texts they composed, and in various aspects of performance practice. They manipulated the musical forms of the *fiesta* in the comparatively newer musical context of the *festival*, whose terms were largely set by *mestizos*, in order to succeed in this musical moment of articulation between rural community-based *ayllu* members and the *mestizo* society of the towns. My discussion here of the differences between *fiesta* and *festival* is based on conversations with participants in these events, as well as observations of both, and some participation (discussed below) during my fieldwork.

Fiesta

What the *ayllu* members called *fiestas* were the traditional annual celebrations of the agricultural-religious calendar: Carnival, Easter, saints' feast days, and so

---

[3] In this and the following ethnographic sections, I use the past tense (rather than the ethnographic present) not necessarily to imply that the practices described have ceased, but to acknowledge that, since I have not returned to Bolivia since my fieldwork there ended in January 1994, I simply do not know how they have developed since then. The use of the past tense is also a way of stressing that I am concerned with specific *performances* by specific actors at specific moments in time, rather than with an ahistorical kind of *Performance* that is thought to encapsulate or symbolize an essential, timeless, unchanging culture. The latter notion is characteristic of Milton Singer's (1955) notion of *cultural performances*, which was highly influential in ethnomusicology during the 1970s and 1980s (see, e.g., Béhague, ed. 1984; Herndon and McLeod 1979; McLeod and Herndon 1980).

[4] Many writers on Andean festivities use the terms *fiesta* and *festival* interchangeably (cf. Baumann 1981; Crandon-Malamud 1993:591n.8; LaBarre 1948:187; Mangin 1961; Otter 1985:228; Rasnake 1988:173–209). Other writers use the two terms to distinguish between the fiestas of the religious-agricultural calendar and staged folkloric festivals (Buechler and Buechler 1971:87; Turino 1993:220, though Turino is not always consistent in his use of the terms). During my fieldwork in 1993, the indigenous peasants of Bustillo Province I spoke with consistently distinguished between these two terms in the latter way. To emphasize that I am discussing the way the people of the *ayllus* use the terms, in this chapter I italicize the two words throughout and use the Spanish plural *festivales* of the second, as they do.

148   *Soundscapes from the Americas*

forth. Rather than describe the details of any one specific *fiesta*, I will treat the concept of *fiesta* in more general terms, emphasizing the aspects that contrast it with *festival* as a separate category.[5]

Many *fiestas* were celebrated in the *ayllu* communities themselves. Each community had its own traditions about hosting particular *fiestas*, and not all *fiestas* were celebrated in every community. For example, one community was known for hosting the *fiesta* of *Navidad* [Christmas], another community was the site of a *fiesta* on *San Juán* [birth date of John the Baptist, June 24] every year, and yet another was known for its annual celebration of the *fiesta* of the Virgin of Copacabana (August 5). People from other communities traveled to the *fiestas* in these communities if they were not celebrating in their own community, especially if they had kin or close friends in the hosting community. Hosting a *fiesta* meant choosing *pasantes* [*fiesta* sponsors] from within the community every year; the *pasantes* (usually a married couple), relying on help from real and fictive kin, covered the costs of the *fiesta*, provided food and drink and contracted a musical group, often from within the community itself, to provide music for dancing. Musical groups usually played in the patio of the *pasantes'* house, where the food and drink were served. *Fiestas* were thus also important events in the social life of communities, as occasions in which *pasantes* articulated social networks of reciprocity and developed leadership skills. A man could not hold the position of *jilanq'u* [village headman] without having sponsored one or more *fiestas*.

Activities taking place during the course of *fiestas* were determined by community members, based on traditional practices. There was a certain flexibility in what happened during *fiestas*. While there was a general sense of what would go on, such as a shared meal, musical performance and dancing, the performance of certain rituals, and so on, there was not necessarily a sense of a strict schedule by which activities should be ordered. The organization of the *fiesta* was, rather, emergent in accordance with the specific occasion in which it was celebrated, the people who happened to be there at any given moment, and other factors unique to that time and place.

Other *fiestas* took place not in the peasant communities, but in centrally located towns within *ayllu* territory. These towns were nominally *mestizo*, but *ayllu* members also lived in them. *Fiestas* celebrated in the towns included the *Fiesta de la Cruz* [Feast of the Holy True Cross] (May 3) in Chayanta, *Exaltación* [Exaltation of the Cross] (September 14) in Phanakachi, and *Rosario* [Feast of the Holy Rosary] (in October) in Aymaya. During these *fiestas* people from communities of the surrounding *ayllus* all converged on the town in what amounted to a pilgrimage to a ceremonial center.

The many different kinds of musical instruments played in the region, including various sizes of guitar-like stringed instruments, panpipes, and vertical duct flutes with fingerholes, were roughly divided between instruments played during the rainy season, November to February or March (the exact date each year being determined by the moveable *fiesta* of *Karnawal* [Carnival]), and instruments

---

    [5]   Details about some specific *fiestas* are given in Solomon 1997 and 2000.

Performing Indigeneity: Poetics and Politics of Music Festivals   149

played during the dry season that begins on Easter Sunday, from March or April through October. For example, various kinds of panpipes (*julajulas, sikus, sikuras*) were played in the dry season, and duct flutes with fingerholes (*pinkillus*) were played during the rainy season. These rules were generally followed in *fiesta* performance, as it was conventionally said that their violation would cause climatological catastrophes such as hailstorms or early frosts that would destroy the crops still maturing in the fields.

Musical performance in *fiestas*, especially the playing of stringed instruments and singing, was primarily the activity of young unmarried boys and girls, mostly in their teens to early twenties. Since marriage followed a general rule of community exogamy, young people eagerly looked forward to *fiestas* since they were events in which people from different communities were all together in the same place: *fiestas* were excellent opportunities for meeting potential marriage partners and carrying on courtship activities (Solomon 2000:256). Musical performance during *fiestas*, with its gendered roles of male instrument player and female singer, gave young people from different communities the perfect opportunity to meet and mingle in a socially acceptable way. For young people especially, then, the most important identity affiliations in many *fiestas* were thus one's gender, marital status, and home community, since they were looking to meet people from other communities who might be prospective romantic partners or mates.

Musical performance in *fiestas* was geared toward maximizing participation and cooperation in creating a festive atmosphere. In addition to the musicians contracted by the *pasantes*, other performing groups or individuals might also play and sing. This informal music-making often filled up the time when the contracted group stopped playing to take a rest or quit for the day. Performers urged the people standing around watching (including the visiting ethnomusicologist) to join in the music making and dancing. When musicians from several communities were present at the same *fiesta*, there was also a general spirit of competition between the different communities, but the competition itself was emergent, not carefully organized. In cases when performing groups from different communities found themselves sharing the same space at the same time, they sometimes played different tunes simultaneously, each trying to drown out or play longer than the other, and girls from different communities sometimes spontaneously engaged in song dueling (Solomon 2000:271–2). Membership itself in groups of string players and singers was fluid. Young people came to the *fiesta* in community-based performing groups, but as the *fiesta* continued and they met members of the opposite sex from other communities, they might begin to leave their community groups to perform with people from other communities.

Festival

In contrast to the *fiesta*, the terms of the *festival* were largely defined by *mestizos*. These events were usually sponsored by NGOs such as development agencies and radio stations, and in Bustillo province the *festivales* I observed and heard about

150   *Soundscapes from the Americas*

but could not attend were generally held either out in the *ayllu* communities or in the mining centers of Llallagua-Siglo XX and Uncía. Examples of *festivales* that I observed during my fieldwork in 1993 include the annual anniversary *festival* of Radio Pío XII held in the mining center of Llallagua-Siglo XX; a one-time *festival* to inaugurate a literacy campaign sponsored by UNICEF-Pro Andes held in the community of Ñiq'ita; a *festival* to celebrate the third anniversary of the radio station Mallku Kiririya held in the community of Irupata, Ayllu Chayantaka (at which the events described in the opening vignette of this chapter took place); and the first *Festival de Canto y Sociodrama a la Salud* [Festival of Song and Socialdrama for Health] in the community of Jach'uxu, Ayllu Chullpa, sponsored by the Madre Obrera hospital of Llallagua.

The sponsoring organization coordinated all aspects of the *festival* and paid for most of the expenses. It could seek cosponsorship from other organizations or local businesses, asking them to donate prizes, provide a sound system, provide lodging for people coming from out of town, and so on. But for every bit for which the primary sponsoring organization solicited cosponsorship, it would also have to share credit. For image-conscious NGOs anxious to curry favor with rural communities, too many cosponsors could take too much of the limelight off them as the primary sponsor. Since there were no *pasantes* from the *ayllu* communities, *festivales* were not implicated in the social networks of reciprocity articulated by *fiesta* sponsorship.

The *festival* date might or might not coincide with a *fiesta* in the traditional calendar. The one main concession *festival* organizers made to the peasant calendar was that most *festivales* were scheduled during the dry season, which was the off-season for agricultural work. If an institution had attempted to convoke a *festival* during the rainy season, when planting, weeding, irrigating, and other agricultural chores occupied most of the peasants' time, it probably would have gotten little participation from the *ayllu* communities. Since most *festivales* were held outside in the open air, practical considerations also made it wiser to program *festivales* for the dry months. In *festivales* in rural *ayllu* communities, where there was no indoor hall and usually no electricity, *festival* organizers sometimes went to the community hours before the *festival* began (sometimes on the day before) to build a temporary outdoor wooden stage and set up a sound system with microphones, speakers, and a gasoline-powered generator to power the amplifier.

In *festivales* musicians performed on a stage in front of an audience. In the case of *festivales* held in the mining centers this audience consisted largely of urban *mestizos*; in *festivales* held in the *ayllu* communities, the audience consisted mostly of residents of the host community and surrounding communities within a few hours walk, plus members of the organizing institution and various invited *mestizo* dignitaries.

Sponsoring organizations carefully planned *festivales* to proceed according to a timetable with a specific sequence of events. They controlled who participated; for region-wide *festivales* they invited specific communities to send musical groups to participate, since it would have been impossible to accommodate all

Performing Indigeneity: Poetics and Politics of Music Festivals 151

the groups wishing to perform if entry were open to all comers. Groups were scheduled to play in a specific order; failure to be ready to take the stage when called could be grounds for disqualification. A master of ceremonies introduced each performing group by the name of its community and *ayllu*, and constantly mentioned the name of the sponsoring organization so that all in attendance would know of its beneficence. While members of performing groups from different communities could interact unofficially offstage, there was no onstage interaction between them, and groups were discouraged from continuing to play offstage within earshot of the *festival* site, since it interfered with the orderly progression of the *festival* and distracted attention from the groups still playing onstage.

In contrast to *fiestas*, where competition between performing groups was sporadic and emergent, *festivales* were explicit competitions with prizes awarded to named winners (usually first, second, and third place). The panel of judges (*jurado calificador*) was typically made up of a majority of non-*ayllu* members—usually people affiliated with the institution or organization that was sponsoring the *festival*, who were thought to be impartial—along with maybe one peasant from the area, such as a village headman (*jilanq'u*) or leader of a peasant union. Prizes typically included tools used in agriculture (e.g., hoes, pick-axes), bags of fertilizer, bags of coca, sandals, small transistor radios (a favorite prize for sponsoring radio stations to give[6]), and acrylic yarn used by peasants to knit caps, scarves, and belts.

To my chagrin, I was asked to be a judge at a *festival* in June 1993, after I had been in the field for about five months and people (both the *ayllu* members and the *mestizos* of the area) knew I was doing research on music. I was hesitant about accepting a role in which I could be perceived as favoring one community's musicians over another's, and I did not think I was really qualified to judge the competition. The *festival* organizer told me not to worry, that he was certain I knew enough about the local music to be a judge, and pleaded with me to accept, since one of the scheduled judges could not stay for the entire event. Since I was an outsider and recent arrival in the region, and so did not have especially close ties to any particular individuals or communities there, it was also assumed that I would be impartial. Despite my misgivings about being put in the position of being an "expert" on indigenous music, I accepted, justifying to myself that it would be a good ethnographic opportunity to see *festivales* from a new point of view as a participant observer, and that since I would be only one out of three judges, I would not be able to do too much damage if my decisions were inappropriate. I was given a list of all the groups scheduled to perform and told to give each group a ranking from 1 to 10 in each of three categories: *música* [music], *vestimenta* [traditional dress], and *alegría* [happiness].

---

[6] Ana María Gómez (personal communication 1993) recounted to me how the Catholic Church-operated radio station Radio Pío XII (named after Pope Pius XII) once distributed to the peasants of the *ayllus* transistor radios fixed so that the only station they could receive would be Radio Pío XII itself.

152 *Soundscapes from the Americas*

The use of the Spanish word *vestimenta* for the second category is significant. In contrast with the word *ropa*, which simply means "clothing," the connotation of *vestimenta* is "traditional clothing," or even "costume." The way *mestizos* used the term gave the implication that rustic peasants (read "Indians") have *vestimenta*, and Hispanicized urban-dwelling Bolivians have *ropa*. In many peasant communities that I visited, traditional clothing was in fact still used for everyday dress, and its only difference from festive dress was that the latter was generally the newest and cleanest clothing people had available. In other more acculturated communities, young people (especially young men) wore traditional clothing only to *fiestas* and *festivales*, and preferred Western clothing for everyday wear. Some young *ayllu* members seemed to have an especially ambivalent attitude toward traditional clothing. One young man from an indigenous community whom I knew, who usually wore Western-style clothing he bought in the market, asked me one day to take his picture "*como campesino*" [(dressed) like a peasant], and told me he would go dig out his peasant clothes from his things stored in his house and dress up especially for the photograph.

The last category for judging, *alegría*, was not explained to me, but I understood it to mean the general spirit with which the musicians performed and created a festive atmosphere, including specific things such as how the singers clapped their hands and danced during instrumental sections, how they interjected little shouts and exclamations into the performance, and their interaction with the audience—the kinds of things that might be referred to as "stage presence" in English. After the last group had performed, the other judges and I gave our rankings to one of the *festival* organizers, who then tabulated them to determine the winners. Many of the groups that I thought were the best were not among the winners later announced; I do not know if this was because the other two judges had preferred different groups, or if the *festival* organizers had also played a role in determining the winners, based on some other criteria I was not told about.

Musical Strategies for *Fiesta* and *Festival*

Fiestas and *festivales* were thus very different kinds of events. In *festivales* the usual local emphasis on maximizing participation in musical performance was replaced by a European-derived notion of the separation of the musical artist-specialist and the non-specialist general public, concretely constructed in the placement of performers on a stage physically separated from an audience that was supposed to politely watch the performances and applaud at the appropriate times. The local style of emergent, informal competition was also replaced by a European construct of how competition should be organized in rational, orderly terms.

Given the very different natures of the *fiesta* and *festival* as occasions for musical performance, it should come as no surprise that there were significant differences in form and content between the performance practices and musical sounds of these two kinds of events. The people of the *ayllus* had adapted *fiesta*

Figure 7.1   Performers from the community of Jant'a Pallqa at a music festival in the community of Irupata, June 1993. Photograph by the author

musical practice to the *festival*, developing new musical strategies for success in this relatively new kind of performance occasion.

In *festivales* musicians stood on a stage and had to perform for an audience, so instead of standing in the usual circular formation facing inward toward each other, they stood in a straight line or semicircle, facing outward toward the crowd (see Figure 7.1). While in *fiesta* performance musicians might play a single song or tune throughout the entire *fiesta*, playing without stopping for 30 minutes or more before taking a break, the *festival* format typically required performing groups to prepare two different pieces, each about four to five minutes long. Groups could be penalized if they only had one song or tune prepared. The apparent purpose of this rule was to require performing groups to show a breadth of repertoire or skill in composition. Since the site for *festival* performance was literally a stage toward which all attention was focused, in *festivales* each performing group tried to do things that would distinguish it from the rest. Different groups seemed to be jockeying for position within the *festival*, trying to second guess each other and do in their performance something unique that none of the other groups had thought of. Musicians thus developed new performance strategies so that their ensembles stood out from those of other communities.

One of these strategies was to violate the rules mentioned above about playing musical instruments only during their proper season. Intentional departure from the rainy season–dry season instrument scheme was a way of doing something different that would call attention to one's group, making it appear unique to the *festival*

154   *Soundscapes from the Americas*

judges. There is a certain irony here. *Festival* sponsors were often sympathetic *mestizos* who presented themselves as wanting to preserve "authentic" indigenous culture, and who saw the *festivales* they sponsored as fomenting traditional indigenous practices. Most of these *mestizos*, however, did not know the details of indigenous musical custom such as the rules about rainy season and dry season instruments. Musicians who took advantage of *mestizo* judges' ignorance about musical custom and engaged in innovative practices such as playing duct flutes out of their season were in fact doing something that would have been counter to the *mestizos'* wishes for authenticity, if they had known anything about "authentic" indigenous culture in the first place. But, if after a seemingly endless procession of panpipe ensembles a group took the stage performing on duct flutes, *mestizo* judges might well perk up their ears at the sheer sonic difference of the group and be more inclined to remember it when it came time to choose winners, never the wiser that the group's performance could be construed as "inauthentic" or a violation of traditional practices.

Mestizo sponsors of *festivales* thus prided themselves on the role which they perceived that they played in fomenting indigenous tradition. The peasants knew this, and they played up to *mestizos'* expectations. This often led to a self-presentation as a sort of hyper-Indian, "more Indian than Indian." An example of this could be seen in the way young people dressed for *festival* performance. They wore the same festive dress they would wear for a *fiesta*—for boys, their nicest pants woven from homespun and with brightly embroidered cuffs, and a *chakita*, a jacket with embroidery on the cuffs and along the front; for girls, an *aymilla*, a loose-fitting dress with embroidery on the sleeves and around the bottom and tied at the waist with a woven belt, or a skirt with similar embroidery around the bottom and a blouse. But on top of this basic clothing, for *festivales* both boys and girls also wore as many knitted pieces and weavings as they had available, in a manner that could be described as "piling it on." Girls wrapped around themselves and draped over their shoulders several *lliqllas* [woven carrying cloths] and brightly colored scarves. Boys hung down their backs or along the backs and sides of their legs as many as a half dozen woven scarves called *chupa* [literally "tail"], and hung just as many brightly colored *ch'uspas* [small knitted pouches for carrying coca] from cords around their necks. The performers knew that they were being judged in part on their "*vestimenta*," and so played up to the judges' expectation of a colorful display with this over-the-top presentation of indigenous weaving and knitting. This kind of self-presentation amounted to what I would call "strategic auto-essentialism," a kind of self-conscious acting out of the folkloric stereotypes *mestizos* had of indigenous culture, in order to succeed in this moment of articulation with the *mestizo* world. The peasants' self-presentation in *festivales* also calls to mind MacCannell's discussion of what he calls "staged authenticity," in which "mystification ... can be the conscious product of an individual effort to manipulate a social appearance" (1973:591).

Performing Indigeneity: Poetics and Politics of Music Festivals   155

The staged nature of this conscious self-presentation of "traditional" indigeneity through clothing was evident in the incident described at the beginning of this chapter. The group in question won a prize that was awarded to them in part for being authentically "indigenous" in dress, but then demonstrated in their encore performance that this authenticity had been staged and performed for the benefit of the audience and judges.

In *fiestas* young people did dress in nice clothes and show off their textiles, but not in such an over-the-top manner with so many scarves, carrying cloths, and woven bags that were not actually functional. To wear so many ornamental pieces on a daily basis or to a *fiesta* would simply not have been practical, as it would have required constant fussing with them as they shifted around whenever one moved, and these valued textiles would be in danger of being lost or ruined during a typical *fiesta* night of drinking and dancing.

The difference between *fiesta* and *festival* was also evident in the texts of songs people sang at these two kinds of events. The type of song most often performed at *festivales*, no matter what the season, was the rainy season song genre known locally as *Karnawal wayñu* [Carnival *wayñu*] or simply *wayñu*. The melodies of *wayñus* performed in *festivales* were the same as those performed in *fiestas*; it was in the texts that they differed. The verses of songs performed in *fiestas* were mostly about love and seduction. *Festival wayñus* could begin and end with the same formulaic verses sung during *fiestas*, in order to establish a festive frame. But they also included verses very different from those sung in *fiestas*. Performers usually composed new verses specifically for each *festival* they performed in. The girl singers might themselves compose verses, or the boys might compose verses and teach them to the girls prior to the *festival* performance.

To understand the differences between *fiesta* performance and *festival* performance, it is useful to look at how the same song was performed differently in each respective context by the same group of musicians. Below is a transcription of the song text "Alfa kanchita" [Alfalfa field], a *Karnawal wayñu*. This version was performed on February 24, 1993 by a group of musicians (three girl singers and three boys playing stringed instruments) from the community of Muramaya, Ayllu Chayantaka, upon a visit to the community of Irupata on *Miércoles de Cenizas* [Ash Wednesday] during the week-long *Karnawal fiesta*.

Quechua Text*	English Gloss
Takiysiway tusuysiway chulita	Let's sing, let's dance, Indian girl
Rimatusta churaysiway chulita	Let's make verses, Indian girl
Margarita	Margarita
Alfa kanchitayman, lirius	To my field of alfalfa, to my field of
kanchitayman	irises
Ñuqachá suwakusqayki chulita	Maybe I'll steal you away, Indian girl
Margarita	Margarita

Ribusachu castillachu chulita	Is it plain cloth or fine cloth? Indian girl
Ripusunchu manallachu chulita	Shall we go or not? Indian girl
Margarita	Margarita
Alfa kanchitayman, lirius kanchitayman	To my field of alfalfa, to my field of irises
Ñuqachá suwakusqayki chulita	Maybe I'll steal you away, Indian girl
Margarita	Margarita

Takiykamuy tusuykamuy chulita	Come sing, come dance, Indian girl
Rimatusta churaykamuy chulita	Come make verses, Indian girl
Margarita	Margarita
Alfa kanchitayman, lirius kanchitayman	To my field of alfalfa, to my field of irises
Ñuqachá suwakusqayki chulita	Maybe I'll steal you away, Indian girl
Margarita	Margarita

Takiysiway tusuysiway chulita	Let's sing, let's dance, Indian girl
Rimatusta churaysiway chulita	Let's make verses, Indian girl
Margarita	Margarita
Alfa kanchitayman, lirius kanchitayman	To my field of alfalfa, to my field of irises
Ñuqachá suwakusqayki chulita	Maybe I'll steal you away, Indian girl
Margarita	Margarita

*I have translated the Quechua word *chulita* (the diminutive of the Spanish word *chola*, pronounced according to Quechua phonology) as "Indian girl." In most contexts in Bolivia, a *chola* or *cholita* is understood to be not a rural Indian woman, but an urban *mestiza* woman who wears the large, pleated *pollera* skirt common in towns and cities in the central Andes. In the context of this song, however, the word was simply used to mean a local girl, the object of the song's narrator's affections, understood to be a girl from a rural *ayllu* community. In rainy season *Karnawal* songs from this region, while girls sang them, the texts were always from the point of view of a boy.

Several features mark this text as representative of *fiesta* performance. There is a limited number of verses, all from the standard repertoire of *wayñu* formulae. This use of common formulaic verses facilitated participation, since it was easy to remember the verses and anybody could join in the singing. There is extensive use of repetition and syntactic parallelism. The last verse is identical to the first; the third verse differs from these only by changing two syllables in the three imperative verbs: *takiysiway* becomes *takiykamuy*, *tusuysiway* becomes *tusuykamuy* and *churaysiway* becomes *churaykamuy*. All the verses refer to the familiar themes of love, seduction, and participation in the *fiesta* itself through singing and dancing. The same two-line refrain appears consistently after each two-line verse. This refrain alludes to the *suwakapuy*, the act of "stealing" a girl

Performing Indigeneity: Poetics and Politics of Music Festivals 157

away by bringing her home to one's own community to begin the marriage process with a period of living together.

This text contrasts sharply with the next example, the same song performed by mostly the same people from the community of Muramaya (two girl singers, three boys playing string instruments), at the *Tercer Festival de Música Chayantaka* [Third Festival of Chayantaka Music], held in Irupata about three weeks before the *fiesta* performance just discussed, on February 2, 1993. While the same young men were playing stringed instruments on both occasions, the tempo was slightly faster in the *festival* performance (134 bpm compared to the *fiesta* performance of 128 bpm), evidently to increase its rhythmic excitement.

Quechua Text	English Gloss
Takiysiway tusuysiway chulita	Let's sing, let's dance, Indian girl
Rimatusta churaysiway chulita Margarita	Let's make verses, Indian girl Margarita
Alfa kanchitayman, lirius	To my field of alfalfa, to my field of
kanchitayman	irises
Ñuqachá suwakusqayki chulita	Maybe I'll steal you away, Indian girl
Margarita	Margarita
Jamushayku chamushayku	We're coming, we're arriving,
chulita	Indian girl
Kay kinsa kaq fistiwalman chulita	To this third festival, Indian girl
Margarita	Margarita
Takiriq tusuriq ñuqayku jamuyku	We've come to sing and dance
Cantón de Irupataman chulita	To the canton of Irupata, Indian girl
Margarita	Margarita
[t'ajllaku]	[instrumental interlude with handclapping]
Irmanitus kampisinus chulita	Brother peasants, Indian girl
Ancha ñak'aripi kanchis chulita	We've got a lot of problems, Indian girl
Margarita	Margarita
Urkanisakusun kumunitatispi	Let's organize ourselves in the communities
Ñawpaqman jatarinapaq chulita	In order to move forward, Indian girl
Margarita	Margarita
Chhajrata tarpukusqanchispis chulita	The field that we've sown, Indian girl
Manaña allin puqunchu chulita	Doesn't produce well anymore, Indian girl
Margarita	Margarita
Qhasa qhasaykapun granisu	The freeze froze it all up, the hail took it
apapun	away
Watan watan ñak'aripi	Year after year we've got problems,
irmanitus kampisinus	brother peasants

[t'ajllaku]   [instrumental interlude with handclapping]

Kay Radyu Mallku Kiririyanchisqa   This Mallku Kiririya Radio of ours
Ñawpaman kallpacharisun   Let's strengthen it so it will move forward,
   irmanitus kampisinus   brother peasants
Jisq'untin ayllumanta Pruwinsia   From the nine ayllus of Bustillo
   Bustillumanta   Province
Astawan jatunyachisun   We're going to make it grow bigger,
   irmanitus kampisinus   brother peasants

Jamushayku chamushayku chulita   We're coming, we're arriving, Indian girl
Comunidad Muramaya chulita   The community of Muramaya, Indian girl
   Margarita   Margarita
Alfa kanchitayman lirius   To my field of alfalfa, to my field of
   kanchitayman   irises
Ñuqachá suwakusqayki chulita   Maybe I'll steal you away, Indian girl
   Margarita   Margarita

This *festival* version of "Alfa kanchita" began with the same formulaic opening verse inviting participation as the *fiesta* version. In the second verse the singers referred by name to the event in which they were performing (*kay kinsa kaq fistiwal*, "this third *festival*"), stating they were coming to the *festival* to sing and dance. This is not too different from *fiesta* texts, which also commonly referred to the performance context itself. But in this verse the singers departed from the format of two-line verse followed by two-line refrain. Instead of singing the refrain "*Alfa kanchitayman ... ,*" which would continue the allusions to seduction and the *suwakapuy*, they sang additional new text to the refrain melody, converting the verse format from two lines of verse text plus a two-line refrain into a four-line stanza without refrain. This allowed them to develop the themes of the text in more detail, which was desirable since maximizing the content of texts was more important in the *festival* context. This verse thus served as a transition from the first verse that evoked the participatory frame of *fiestas* to the next part of the song, in which the singers used the new four-line stanza form for three verses with overtly political content, very unlike *fiesta wayñu* performance.

The third verse uses the language of political oratory, exhorting the performers' "brother peasants" (*hermanos campesinos* in Spanish) at the *festival* to "get organized" (*urkanisakusun*) and "move forward" (*ñawpaqman*). The Quechua word *ñawpaqman* has a particular spatio-temporal significance, evoking the idea of moving forward in space while looking backward in time for precedents of behavior. This word figured prominently in the Quechua political oratory of the region. The fourth verse is a lament about the precarious position of the peasants: the crops they planted have been destroyed by a freeze and a hailstorm; the singers emphasize that year after year they are faced with these problems.

Performing Indigeneity: Poetics and Politics of Music Festivals 159

In the fifth verse the singers sang the praises of Mallku Kiririya Radio, the peasant-operated radio station at which the event was being held. This event was sponsored by Taypikala, an NGO (now defunct) that specialized in what it called "cultural development" (*desarrollo cultural*), fomenting indigenous cultural expression such as weaving and music. One of the main projects of this NGO had been obtaining grants from French and German foundations to build and maintain Mallku Kiririya Radio as a community-based mode of communication operated by and for the peasants, as opposed to the church-controlled Pius XII Radio in the mining center of Llallagua-Siglo XX or commercial radio stations in the region that played Spanish-language pop music or Bolivian urban folkloric music. To sing the praises of Mallku Kiririya Radio, while being in part a tribute to the role the radio was playing in fomenting *ayllu* culture and facilitating intra-*ayllu* communication, was thus also to praise the sponsoring NGO Taypikala, whose representatives were in attendance as *festival* sponsors and judges.

For the next and final verse of the song, the singers ended the middle section of the song and closed the performance by returning to a formulaic *wayñu* verse, here one in which they announced their identity as performers from the community of Muramaya. While this could be a verse for *fiesta* performance, here it also served to emphasize that it was they, members of a specific *ayllu* community, who had voiced the politically aware sentiments of the preceding three verses. Having completed the "wordy" part of the song, they also returned with this last verse to the original format of the two-line verse followed by a two-line refrain. The parallelism of form with the first verse brought closure to the performance, while also bracketing the verses with political content within the middle of the song, surrounding them with verses that evoked not politics but the traditional song themes of courtship and flirting. The verses were carefully chosen and sequenced, and the song performance was choreographed with interludes in which the singers rhythmically clapped hands and did a stomping dance after every two verses.

The singers thus used carefully planned textual strategies for this *festival* performance. They sang what they thought the *mestizo festival* sponsors expected to hear, combining "authentic" peasant custom with a demonstration of political awareness, and a validation of the development-oriented NGO's paternalistic stance that the peasants need help. The words of the song were thus a textual analog of the manner in which young people dressed up for *festivales*, as discussed above. The performers used the vocabulary of political oratory, addressing verses of the song to their "brother peasants" and invoking the idea of *ñawpaqman*, as much to please the left-leaning *mestizo* judges as to actually encourage the other peasants at the *festival* to organize. Similarly, the evocation of the hard life of the peasant whose crops are destroyed by frost and rain is what they have come to realize that paternalistic NGOs expect to hear: "The peasants are in a bad way and need help." While it is true they did have problems with droughts and other climatological disasters, the point here is that they generally did not sing about them during *fiesta* performance. This song was thus an example of a textual practice of strategic auto-

160　　　　　　　　　　*Soundscapes from the Americas*

essentialism; in performance the singers appeared to buy into the stereotypes that *mestizos*, in this case sympathetic but paternalistic NGOs, have of them.

The example discussed here illustrates how the people of the *ayllus* of Bustillo Province understood *festivales* to be moments of articulation between their rural communities and the *mestizo* world inhabited by NGOs and town dwellers. The *ayllu* members developed musical strategies for managing these moments and attaining success within a framework defined for them by *mestizos*. These strategies included playing up to *mestizo* stereotypes of indigenous culture and finding ways to make performing ensembles stand out in competition.

Folklorization and Musical Strategies

The people of the *ayllus* of Bustillo Province thus adapted the musical forms and performance practices of their *fiestas* to the *festival* context, musically performing an indigenous identity for *mestizo* audiences who, while sympathetic to indigenous culture in a paternalistic sort of way, ultimately identified not with peasant culture, but with town life and a regional identity more directly articulated to the Bolivian state. My discussion of how *fiesta* musical practice has been transformed for *festival* performance recalls Feld's discussion of "the process of hegemonic folkloricization: dominating outside parties legitimate condensed, simplified, or commodified displays, invoking, promoting, and cherishing them as official and authentic custom, while at the same time misunderstanding, ignoring, or suppressing the real creative forces and expressive meanings that animate them in the community" (1994:135–6). Feld argues that this kind of folklorization is particularly damaging for the Kaluli people of Papua New Guinea, where he did his research:

> [T]heir expressive style is clearly no longer the only natural model; increased confusion, struggle, alienation, and resistance may be around the corner, particularly as mission and government forces begin to give money prizes for performances and insist that Kaluli activities fit into other organizational frameworks to be valid. (1994:136)

Folklorization of indigenous cultural expression in the Andes can also be critiqued as a tool for establishing state hegemony over subaltern peoples. But I would suggest that for the members of the *ayllus* of Bustillo Province, participation in folklorized performance was much more complex than simple folklorization and cultural co-optation. While *festival* performance practice can be viewed as a folklorized version of *fiesta* musical practice, it is important not to see the *festival* as somehow replacing the *fiesta* in some kind of evolutionary progression. Rather, both sets of practices coexisted simultaneously; *ayllu* members made use of different musical practices as appropriate according to the occasion, and freely moved back and forth between the two kinds of occasions and sets of

Performing Indigeneity: Poetics and Politics of Music Festivals   161

practices. Musicians and singers performed with *fiesta* practices for themselves one weekend, and a week later performed with *festival* practices onstage before a crowd, and then a week or two later performed in yet another *fiesta* using *fiesta* practices again.

The *festival* thus had not replaced the *fiesta* as the context for musical performance. Rather, it existed simultaneously alongside and outside the *fiesta* system; the two coexisted as different kinds of occasions. The people of the *ayllus* did allow—even participated in—the folklorization of their musical expression, but only in certain contexts. They knew how to re-present their music and other expressive practices for a *mestizo* audience, but they still also maintained the original performance contexts with their different meanings and social agendas. This was a successful strategy for managing the *festival* as a moment of articulation with representatives of Bolivian society from outside the *ayllus*.

I do not mean to dismiss here the important issues of cultural co-optation and destructuration. I do suggest, however, that while we should recognize the hegemonic processes and potential for cultural destructuration inherent in folklorization of indigenous culture, we also need to ethnographically examine folklorization from the subaltern's perspective, and recognize that the people being, in Charles Keil's words, "folked over" (1978:264) are also actors in these scenarios. How do the participants understand "folk" events? What are their motivations for participating in them? How do they construct the relationship between "folk" versions of their practices and the ways they do these things back home in the community? Do they invent practices that subvert the folklorizing tendencies of "official" versions of their culture? Are practices for different kinds of occasions kept distinct, or do they begin to affect each other, creating newer hybrid practices and forms?

In the case of the *ayllus* of Bustillo Province, I would suggest that participation in *festivales* was only minimally about the status of individual performers and the prizes they might take home. As a whole the goal of musical groups was to draw attention not to individual performers, but rather to their home communities. Participation in NGO-sponsored *festivales* meant establishing their communities' interest in NGO projects such as the provision of potable water, literacy programs, health posts, food and seed potatoes during famines, and so on. (Interest in the latter may also account for the common practice in *festivales* of singing verses about low agricultural production, as in verse 4 of the *festival* song text discussed above.)

Performing Indigeneity: Subjectivity and Identity

Recently influential poststructuralist approaches to the constitution of subjectivity, following Lacan's famous aphorism "The subject is spoken rather than speaking" (1989:53), downplay the agency of social actors and see subjectivity as an effect created in the individual by symbolic systems of representation—especially language—which are always prior to and external to the subject him- or herself.

162 *Soundscapes from the Americas*

Such approaches to subjectivity should be distinguished from a conceptualization of identity as actively constructed through social interaction (Solomon 2012:96–8). In this chapter I have tried to show how *ayllu* members in Bustillo Province in 1993 were, through the vehicle of musical performance, active participants in the construction of themselves as "indigenous people."

This is not to say that such performances of indigeneity were constructed out of whole cloth. The people of the *ayllus* were very aware of the different ways Bolivian *mestizos* regarded them, both positive and negative. Their *festival* performances enacted, *pace* Taussig (1987:238), what "the Indians think *mestizos* are thinking about the Indians." The performances discussed here can thus be seen as a kind of mimesis, akin to Baudrillard's (2001) idea of the *simulacrum*—a copy of an original that never existed. Such mimesis is a creative act, constitutive of subjectivity itself. As Ricoeur argues, "[*M*]*imesis* does not mean the duplication of reality; *mimesis* is not a copy: *mimesis* is *poiesis*, that is, construction, creation" (1981:180, emphasis in the original). The people of the *ayllus* consciously manipulated *mestizo* representations of them, re-presenting themselves for *mestizo* audiences in the image they thought *mestizos* wanted to see, and creating thus an indigenous identity in and through performance.

But *mestizos* were not the only people in the audiences for these performances. The majority of the audience at most of the several festivals I observed actually consisted of members of the same *ayllu* communities as the performers themselves. In these performances of their identity, they thus also created a subject position as "indigenous person" that other *ayllu* members could also inhabit. These representations thus entered into the repertoire of re-presentations that could subsequently be incorporated into people's own reflective self-awareness. Representations like these, created through performance, are powerful because such performances offer what might be called a multimedia "subjectivity package," embodying identities not just in words, but in sights, sounds, and other feelingful sensations, creating a synesthetic experience that is powerful precisely because of the aesthetic appeal and pleasurable embodied experience they offer. Music is an important part of this package, organizing this multi-sensory experience as a process in and through time.

My approach here to performance and indigenous subjectivity parallels Judith Butler's (1988, 1993, 1999) theorization of how *performative acts* constitute gendered subjects. Butler privileges the performative nature of the mundane and everyday, and has clarified that her concept of *performativity* is not to be confused with *performance* (1993:169–85; see also Butler, et al. 1994). But it is clear that the social actions of the kinds of bounded and highlighted occasions that are more commonly understood as *performance* (including, of course, musical performance) can be understood in terms of the kinds of performative acts Butler discusses. This is true not least because of their iterative and citational nature—the way subsequent performances repeat and "cite" previous ones, reinscribing their categories and bodily modes of being, as well as opening up possibilities for challenging and changing their representational practices and the subjectivities they construct (a

Performing Indigeneity: Poetics and Politics of Music Festivals   163

topic which deserves further discussion, but which is beyond the limits of this short chapter). While Butler focuses on the performative constitution of gender, the relevance of Butler's theorization of performative acts for understanding the formation of indigenous subjectivity in the case study discussed here can be made clear by substituting "indigeneity" for "gender" and "indigenous" for "gendered" in Butler's discussion, as I do in the following quotation:

> [Indigeneity] is in no way a stable identity or locus of agency from which various acts proceede [*sic*]; rather, it is an identity tenuously constituted in time—an identity instituted through a *stylized repetition of acts*. Further, [indigeneity] is instituted through the stylization of the body and, hence, must be understood as the mundane way in which bodily gestures, movements, and enactments of various kinds constitute the illusion of an abiding [indigenous] self. (paraphrased from Butler 1988:519, emphasis in the original)

If, as Suzanne Cusick suggests with her pithy gloss on Butler, "gender is as gender does" (Cusick 1999:476), then one can similarly argue that "indigenous is as indigenous does," and indigeneity, like gender, is constituted through performative acts and has no essential existence outside of them. In short, indigeneity is a doing, not a being. My approach differs from Butler's, however, in also allowing much more space for a conscious, strategic agency in the construction, performance, and self-awareness of an indigenous subject position.[7]

I argue, then, that for the peasants of Bustillo Province in 1993, their own identity was emergent in the complex interplay of *fiesta* and *festival* expressive practices which provided a means for a self-awareness as *ayllu* members, a self-awareness of being "peasants," and a self-awareness of being "indigenous." *Festival* performance was thus not just a clear-cut participation in the commodification of their cultural expression, but rather a vehicle for reflecting on and strategically performing a version of their own identity, both for themselves and for outsiders, creatively articulating their communities with the world of *mestizo* politicians, townspeople, and NGOs.

---

[7] I should use the plural—indigenous *subject positions*—but, again, the short format of this chapter—as well as the limits of my ethnography—preclude me from pursuing that line of inquiry here.

References

Abrahams, Roger D. 1977. "Toward an Enactment-Centered Theory of Folklore." In *Frontiers of Folklore*, ed. William Bascom, 79–120. Boulder, CO: Westview Press.

Adams, Vincanne. 1997. "Dreams of a Final Sherpa." *American Anthropologist* 99(1): 85–98.

Albó, Xavier. 1979. "¿Khitipxtansa? ¿Quiénes somos? Identidad localista, étnica y clasista en los Aymaras de hoy." *América indígena* 39(3): 477–528.

Allen, Amy. 1998. "Power Trouble: Performativity as Critical Theory." *Constellations* 5(4): 456–71.

Alonso, Manuel A. 1986 [1849]. *El Jíbaro* [orig. *El Gibaro*]. San Juan, Puerto Rico: Cultural Puertorriqueña.

Anderson, Benedict. 1991. *Imagined Communities: Reflections on the Origin and Spread of Nationalism*. London: Verso.

Aparicio, Fraces. 1998. *Listening to Salsa: Gender, Latin Popular Music, and Puerto Rican Cultures*. Hanover: University Press of New England.

Appadurai, Arjun. 1991. "Global Ethnoscapes: Notes and Queries for a Transnational Anthropology." In *Recapturing Anthropology: Working in the Present*, ed. Richard G. Fox, 191–210. Santa Fe, NM: School of American Research Press.

Armstrong, Robert Plant. 1971. *The Affecting Presence: An Essay in Humanistic Anthropology*. Urbana: University of Illinois Press.

Asch, Michael I. 1982. Review of *The Ethnography of Musical Performance*, ed. Norma McLeod and Marcia Herndon (Norwood, PA: Norwood Editions, 1980). *Ethnomusicology* 26(2): 317–19.

Askew, Kelly M. 2002. *Performing the Nation: Swahili Music and Cultural Politics in Tanzania*. Chicago, IL: University of Chicago Press.

Atkinson, Paul. 2004. "Performing Ethnography and the Ethnography of Performance." Review of *Performance Ethnography: Critical Pedagogy and the Politics of Culture*, by Norman K. Denzin (Thousand Oaks, CA: Sage Publications, 2003). *British Journal of Sociology of Education* 25(1): 107–14.

Austin, J. L. 1962. *How to Do Things with Words*. Oxford: Oxford University Press.

Ayala Mora, Enrique. 2008. *Resumen de historia del Ecuador*. Quito: Corporación Editora Nacional.

Azadovskii, Mark. 1926. *A Siberian Taleteller*. English translation by James R. Dow. Austin: University of Texas Center for Intercultural Studies in Folklore and Oral History.

Babiracki, Carol. 1997. "What's the Difference? Reflections on Gender and Research in Village India." In *Shadows in the Field: New Perspectives for Fieldwork in Ethnomusicology*, ed. Gregory Barz and Tim Cooley, 121–38. New York: Oxford University Press.

Bamberg, Michael. 1983. "Metaphor and Play Interaction in Young Children." In *The World of Play: Proceedings of the 7th Annual Meeting of the Association of the Anthropological Study of Play*, ed. Frank E. Manning, 11–22. West Point, NY: Leisure Press.

Barros, Raquel and Manuel Dannemann. 1961. *El Guitarrón en el departamento de Puente Alto*. Instituto de Invesitgaciones Musicales, Universidad de Chile, Colección de Ensayos No. 12. Santiago de Chile: Editorial Universitaria.

Barthes, Roland. 1985 [1981]. *The Grain of the Voice: Interviews 1962–1980*. New York: Hill and Wang.

Bartra, Roger. 1992. *The Cage of Melancholy: Identity and Metamorphosis in the Mexican Character*, trans. Christopher J. Hall. New Brunswick, NJ: Rutgers University Press.

Barz, Gregory F. 2003. *Performing Religion: Negotiating Past and Present in Kwaya Music of Tanzania*. Amsterdam and New York: Rodopi.

Bateson, Gregory. 1972 [1955]. "A Theory of Play and Fantasy." In his *Steps to an Ecology of Mind*, 177–93. New York: Ballantine.

———. 1979. *Mind and Nature: A Necessary Unity*. New York: Bantam.

Batista, Gustavo. 1984. *Investigación preliminar relacionada con la bordonía, el cuatro y el tiple*. San Juan: Programa de Artes Populares, Instituto de Cultura Puertorriqueña.

Baudrillard, Jean. 2001 [1981]. "Simulacra and Simulations." In *Jean Baudrillard: Selected Writings*, 2nd edition, ed. Mark Poster, 169–77. Stanford, CA: Stanford University Press.

Bauman, Richard. 1975. "Verbal Art as Performance." *American Anthropologist* 77(2): 290–311.

———. 1977. *Verbal Art as Performance*. With supplementary essays by Barbara A. Babcock, Gary H. Gossen, Roger D. Abrahams, and Joel F. Sherzer. Prospect Heights, IL: Waveland Press.

———. 1992. "Performance." In *Folklore, Cultural Performances, and Popular Entertainments: A Communications-Centered Handbook*, ed. Richard Bauman, 41–9. New York: Oxford University Press.

———. 2002. "Disciplinarity, Reflexivity, and Power in *Verbal Art as Performance*: A Response." *Journal of American Folklore* 115(455): 92–8.

Bauman, Richard and Roger D. Abrahams. 1981. "Doing Folklore Texas-Style." In *"And Other Neighborly Names": Social Process and Cultural Image in Texas Folklore*, ed. Richard Bauman and Roger D. Abrahams, 3–7. Austin: University of Texas Press.

———. eds. 2011 [1981]. *"And Other Neighborly Names": Social Process and Cultural Image in Texas Folklore*. Austin: University of Texas Press.

Bauman, Richard and Charles. L. Briggs. 1990. "Poetics and Performance as Critical Perspectives on Language and Social Life." *Annual Review of Anthropology* 19: 59–88.

———. 2003. *Voices of Modernity: Language Ideologies and the Production of Social Inequality*. Cambridge: Cambridge University Press.

Bauman, Richard and Joel Sherzer, eds. 1974. *Explorations in the Ethnography of Speaking*. New York: Cambridge University Press.

———. 1975. "The Ethnography of Speaking." *Annual Review of Anthropology* 4: 95–119.

Baumann, Max Peter. 1981. "Music, Dance, and Song of the Chipayas (Bolivia)." *Latin American Music Review* 2(2): 171–222.

Béhague, Gerard. 1968. "Biblioteca da Ajuda (Lisbon) MSS 1595/1596: Two 18th-century Anonymous Collections of Modinhas." *Yearbook/Anuario* (Inter-American Institute for Musical Research, Tulane University) 4: 44–81.

———. 1979. *Music in Latin America: An Introduction*. Englewood Cliffs, NJ: Prentice-Hall.

———. 1982. "Ecuadorian, Peruvian, and Brazilian Ethnomusicology: A General View." *Latin American Music Review* 3(1): 17–35.

———. 1984a. "Introduction." In *Performance Practice: Ethnomusicological Perspectives*, ed. Gerard Béhague, 3–12. Westport, CT: Greenwood Press.

———. 1984b. "Patterns of *Candomblé* Music Performance: An Afro-Brazilian Religious Setting." In *Performance Practice: Ethnomusicological Perspectives*, ed. Gerard Béhague, 222–54. Westport, CT: Greenwood Press.

———. 1986. "La problemática de la investigación etnomusicológica en América Latina." *Revista de antropología* (Ecuador) 9: 192–206.

———. 1990. "Music in Latin America: Independence and Nationalism." In *The Early Romantic Era: Between Revolutions, 1789 and 1848*, ed. Alexander Ringer, 280–92. Englewood Cliffs, NJ: Prentice-Hall.

———. 1991. "Reflections on the Ideological History of Latin American Ethnomusicology." In *Comparative Musicology and Anthropology of Music*, ed. Bruno Nettl and Philip V. Bohlman, 56–68. Chicago, IL: University of Chicago Press.

———. 1992. "Music Performance." In *Folklore, Cultural Performances, and Popular Entertainments: A Communications-Centered Handbook*, ed. Richard Bauman, 172–8. New York: Oxford University Press.

———. 1997. "From Modinha to Aboio: The Luso-Brazilian Tradition in the Music of Bahia, Brazil." In *Portugal and the World: The Encounter of Cultures in Music*, ed. Salwa El-Shawan Castelo-Branco, 519–34. Lisbon: Dom Quixote.

———. 2006 [1997]. A Performance and Listener-Centered Approach to Musical Analysis: Some Theoretical and Methodological Factors." *Latin American Music Review* 27(1): 10–18.

———, ed. 1984. *Performance Practice: Ethnomusicological Perspectives*, Westport, CT: Greenwood Press.

Ben-Amos, Dan and Kenneth Goldstein, eds. 1975. *Folklore: Communication and Performance*. The Hague: Mouton.

Benson, B. E. 2003. *The Improvisation of Musical Dialogue: A Phenomenology of Music*. Cambridge: Cambridge University Press.

Berger, Harris M. 1999. *Metal, Rock, and Jazz: Perception and the Phenomenology of Musical Experience*. Hanover, NH: Wesleyan University Press.

Berger, Harris M. and G. P. Del Negro. 2002. "Bauman's Verbal Art and the Social Organization of Attention: The Role of Reflexivity in the Aesthetics of Performance." *Journal of American Folklore* 115(455): 62–91.

Berliner, Paul F. 1978. *The Soul of Mbira: Music and Traditions of the Shona People of Zimbabwe*. Berkeley: University of California Press

———. 1994. *Thinking in Jazz: The Infinite Art of Improvisation*. Chicago, IL: University of Chicago Press.

Bigenho, Michelle. 2002. *Sounding Indigenous: Authenticity in Bolivian Music Performance*. New York: Palgrave.

Blacking, John, ed. 1977. *The Anthropology of the Body*. London: Academic Press.

Blacking, John and Joann Kealiinohomoku, eds. 1979. *The Performing Arts: Music and Dance*. The Hague: Mouton.

Blumer, Herbert. 1969. *Symbolic Interactionism: Perspective and Method*. Englewood Cliffs, NJ: Prentice-Hall.

Bois, J. S. (1966) 1978. *The Art of Awareness*. Dubuque: Brown Company.

Borgo, David. 2006. "Sync or Swarm: Musical Improvisation and the Complex Dynamics of Group Creativity." Accessed March 15, 2009. http://musicweb. ucsd.edu/~dborgo/David_ Borgo/Writing.html.

Brace, Conor. 2009. Personal communication.

Briggs, Charles L. 1988. *Competence in Performance: The Creativity of Tradition in Mexicano Verbal Art*. Philadelphia: University of Pennsylvania Press.

Bright, William. 1963. "Language and Music: Areas for Cooperation." *Ethnomusicology* 7(1): 23–32.

Brown, D. P. 2006. *Noise Orders: Jazz, Improvisation, and Architecture*. Minneapolis: University of Minnesota Press.

Brown, Stuart. 2009. "Stuart Brown Says Play is More than Fun." In *TED: Ideas Worth Spreading*. Accessed March 25, 2009. www.ted.com/index.php/talks/ stuart_brown_ says_ play_is_more_than_fun_it_s_vital.html.

Buchanan, Donna A. 2006a. "Encomium for Gerard Béhague." *SEM Newsletter* 40(3): 6–7.

———. 2006b. *Performing Democracy: Bulgarian Music and Musicians in Transition*. Chicago, IL: University of Chicago Press.

Buechler, Hans C. and Judith-María Buechler. 1971. *The Bolivian Aymara*. New York: Holt, Rinehart and Winston.

Butler, Judith. 1988. "Performative Acts and Gender Constitution: An Essay in Phenomenology and Feminist Theory." *Theatre Journal* 40(4): 519–31.

———. 1993. *Bodies that Matter: On the Discursive Limits of "Sex."* New York: Routledge.

References

——. 1997. *Excitable Speech: A Politics of the Performative*. New York: Routledge.

——. 1999 [1990]. *Gender Trouble: Feminism and the Subversion of Identity*. New York: Routledge.

——. 2004. *Undoing Gender*. New York: Routledge.

Butler, Judith, Peter Osborne, and Lynne Segal. 1994. "Gender as Performance: An Interview with Judith Butler." *Radical Philosophy* 67: 32–9.

Carbonell, Walterio. 1961. *Crítica: Como surgió la cultural nacional*. Havana: s.p.

Carpentier, Alejo. 1946. *La música en Cuba*. Mexico City: Fondo de Cultura Económica.

Carrión, Benjamín. 2002 [1944]. *El cuento de la patria: Breve historia del Ecuador*. Quito: Casa de la Cultura Ecuatoriana.

Castelli, Amalia, Marcia Koth de Paredes, and Mariana Mould de Pease. 1981. *Etnohistoria y antropología andina*. Lima: n.p.

Centro de Investigaciones y Ediciones Musicales. 1981. *Instrumentos típicos Puertorriqueños*. San Juan: Instituto de Cultura Puertorriqueña.

Chambers, Ross. 1991. *Room for Maneuver: Reading (the) Oppositional (in) Narrative*. Chicago, IL: University of Chicago Press.

Chernoff, John Miller. 1979. *African Rhythm and African Sensibility: Aesthetics and Social Action in African Musical Idioms*. Chicago, IL: University of Chicago Press.

Chomsky, Noam. 1965. *Aspects of the Theory of Syntax*. Cambridge, MA: MIT Press.

Cohen, Joel and Herb Snitzer. 1985. *Reprise: The Extraordinary Revival of Early Music*. Boston, MA: Little & Brown.

Comaroff, Jean. 1985. *Body of Power, Spirit of Resistance*. Chicago, IL: University of Chicago Press.

Cook, Nicholas. 2003. "Music as Performance." In *The Cultural Study of Music: A Critical Introduction*, ed. Martin Clayton, T. Herbert, and R. Middleton, 204–214. New York: Routledge.

Cornell, Diane E. 2001. "The Performance of Gender: Five Comparative Biographies of Women Performers in Música Popular Chilena." Ph.D. dissertation, University of Illinois, Urbana-Champaign.

Coryell, L. 1998. *Jazz Guitar: Creative Comping, Soloing, and Improv*. San Francisco, CA: Miller Freeman Books.

Coyne, Richard. 2009. "Creativity and Sound: The Agony of the Senses." In *The Routledge Companion to Creativity*, ed. Tudor Rickards, Mark A. Runco, and Susan Meeger, 25–36. New York: Routledge.

Crandon-Malamud, Libbet. 1993. "Blessings of the Virgin in Capitalist Society: The Transformation of a Rural Bolivian Fiesta." *American Anthropologist* 95(3): 574–96.

Cruz, Mary. 1974. *Creto gangá*. Havana: Instituto Cubano del Libro.

Cusick, Suzanne G. 1999. "Gender, Musicology, and Feminism." In *Rethinking Music*, ed. Nicholas Cook and Mark Everist, 471–98. Oxford: Oxford University Press.

Danielson, Virginia. 1997. *The Voice of Egypt: Umm Kulthūm, Arabic Song, and Egyptian Society in the Twentieth Century*. Chicago, IL: University of Chicago Press.

Dannemann, Manuel. 2004. *Poetas populares en la sociedad chilena del siglo XIX*. Santiago de Chile: Archivo Central Andrés Bello, Universidad de Chile.

Davis, Miles. 1999. "Miles Davis Speaks His Mind." In *Keeping Time: Readings in Jazz History*, ed. Robert Walser, 365–76. Oxford: Oxford University Press.

Dawe, Kevin. 1996. "The Engendered *Lyra*: Music, Poetry and Manhood in Crete." *British Journal of Ethnomusicology* 5: 93–112.

Denzin, Norman. 2003. *Performance Ethnography: Critical Pedagogy and the Politics of Culture*. Thousand Oaks, CA: Sage Publications.

Deschamps Chapeaux, Pedro. 1970. *El negro en la economía habanera del siglo XIX*. Havana: UNEAC.

Dewey, J. 1958 [1934]. *Art as Experience*. New York: Capricorn Books.

Díaz Ayala, Cristóbal. 1981. *Música cubana del areyto a la nueva trova*. San Juan, Puerto Rico: Editorial Cubanacan.

Dreyfus, Laurence. 1983. "Early Music Defended Against Its Devotees: A Theory of Historical Performance in the Twentieth Century." *Musical Quarterly* 69: 297–322.

Duany, Jorge. 1994. "Ethnicity, Identity, and Music: An Anthropological Analysis of the Dominican Merengue." In *Music and Black Ethnicity: The Caribbean and South America*, ed. Gerard H. Béhague, 65–90. New Brunswick, NJ: Transaction Publishers.

Eliade, Mircea. 1963. *Myth and Reality*. Translated from the French by Willard R. Trask. World Perspectives 31. New York: Harper & Row.

Espinosa Apolo, Manuel. 2000. *Los mestizos ecuatorianos*. Quito: Tramasocial Editorial.

Feld, Steven. 1980. Review of *Music as Culture*, by Marcia Herndon and Norma McLeod (Norwood, PA: Norwood Editions, 1979). *Yearbook of the International Folk Music Council* 12: 91–3.

——. 1984. "Sound Structure as Social Structure." *Ethnomusicology* 28(3): 383–409.

——. 1994 [1988]. "Aesthetics as Iconicity of Sound (Uptown Title); or, (Downtown Title) 'Lift-up-over Sounding': Getting into the Kaluli Groove." In *Music Grooves: Essays and Dialogues*, by Charles Keil and Steven Feld, 109–50. Chicago, IL: University of Chicago Press.

Feld, Steven and Aaron A. Fox. 1994. "Music and Language." *Annual Review of Anthropology* 23: 25–53.

Feldman, Martha. 1995. "Magic Mirrors and the Seria Stage: Thoughts toward a Ritual View." *Journal of the American Musicological Society* (Special Issue: Music Anthropologies and Music Histories) 48(3): 423–84.

Fernández Vilarós, Francisco. 1868. *Los negros catedráticos: Absurdo cómico en un acto de costumbres cubanas en prosa y verso*. Havana: Impresa La Tropical.

Fingarette, H. 1972. *Confucius: The Secular as Sacred*. New York: Harper & Row.

Fischlin, D. and A. Heble. 2004. "The Other Side of Nowhere: Jazz, Improvisation, and Communities in Dialogue." In *The Other Side of Nowhere*, ed. D. Fischlin and A. Heble, 1–42. Middletown, CT: Wesleyan University Press.

Flores, Juan. 1993. "Cortijo's Revenge: New Mappings of Puerto Rican Culture." In his *Divided Borders: Essays on Puerto Rican Identity*, 92–107. Houston: Arte Público Press.

Foley, John Miles. 2002. *How to Read an Oral Poem*. Urbana: University of Illinois Press.

Fornet, Ambrosio. 1967. *En blanco y negro*. Havana: Instituto del Libro.

Fox, Aaron. 2004. *Real Country: Music and Language in a Working-Class Culture*. Durham, NC: Duke University Press.

Frank, Adam D. 2006. *Taijiquan and the Search for the Little Old Chinese Man: Understanding Identity through Martial Arts*. New York: Palgrave Macmillan.

Friedson, Steven M. 2009. *Remains of Ritual: Northern Gods in a Southern Land*. Chicago, IL: University of Chicago Press.

Frisbie, Charlotte J. 1976. Review of *Form in Performance: Hard-Core Ethnography*, ed. Marcia Herndon and Roger Brunyate (Austin: Office of the College of Fine Arts, University of Texas at Austin, 1976). *Yearbook of the International Folk Music Council* 8: 141–2.

———. 1980. "An Approach to the Ethnography of Navajo Ceremonial Performance." In *The Ethnography of Musical Performance*, ed. Norma McLeod and Marcia Herndon, 75–104. Norwood, PA: Norwood Editions.

Fuss, Diana. 1989. *Essentially Speaking: Feminism, Nature and Difference*. New York: Routledge.

Gadamer, H. 1989 [1960]. *Truth and Method*. 2nd revised edition. Translation revised by J. Weinsheimer and D. G. Marshall. New York: Crossroad.

García, Marina, ed. 1980. *Diccionario de la literatura cubana*, 2 vols. Havana: Editorial Letras Cubanas.

Geertz, Clifford. 1973. *The Interpretation of Cultures*. New York: Basic Books.

———. 1986. "Making Experience, Authoring Selves." In *The Anthropology of Experience*, ed. Victor W. Turner and Edward M. Bruner, 373–80. Urbana: University of Illinois Press.

Gefter, P. 2006. "Henry Wessel: Capturing the Image, Transcending the Subject." *New York Times*, May 21. Accessed June 20, 2009. www.nytimes.com/2006/05/21/arts/ design/21geft.html?_r=1.

Glasser, Ruth. 1995. *My Music is My Flag: Puerto Rican Musicians and Their New York Communities, 1917–1940*. Berkeley: University of California Press.

Glucklich, Ariel. 2001. *Sacred Pain: Hurting the Body for the Sake of the Soul*. Oxford: Oxford University Press.

Godoy, Ricardo. 1985. "State, *Ayllu*, and Ethnicity in Northern Potosí, Bolivia." *Anthropos* 80(1–3): 53–65.

172   *Soundscapes from the Americas*

——. 1986. "The Fiscal Role of the Andean *Ayllu*." *Man* 21(4): 723–41.
——. 1990. *Mining and Agriculture in Highland Bolivia: Ecology, History, and Commerce among the Juk'umanis*. Tucson: University of Arizona Press.
Goffman, Erving. 1959. *The Presentation of Self in Everyday Life*. New York: Anchor Books, Doubleday.
——. 1974. *Frame Analysis: An Essay in the Organization of Experience*. New York: Harper & Row.
Goguen, J. A. 2004. "Musical Qualia, Context, Time and Emotion." *Journal of Consciousness Studies* 11(3–4): 117–47.
Gramsci, Antonio. 1971. *Selections from the Prison Notebooks of Antonio Gramsci*, ed. and trans. Quintin Hoare and Geoffrey Nowell Smith. New York: International Publishers.
Grau, Olga, Riet Delsing, Eugenia Brito, and Alejandra Farías. 1997. *Discurso, género y poder: Discursos públicos: Chile 1978–1993*. Santiago de Chile: LOM Ediciones.
Grebe, María Ester. 1967. *The Chilean Verso: A Study in Musical Archaism*, trans. B. Hileman. Latin American Studies 9. Los Angeles: Latin American Center, UCLA.
Guerrero Gutiérrez, Pablo. 1997. *El pasillo ecuatoriano*. Quito: Conmúsica.
Guss, David M. 2000. *The Festive State: Race, Ethnicity, and Nationalism as Cultural Performance*. Berkeley: University of California Press.
Hall, D. L. and R. T. Ames. 1993. "Understanding Order: The Chinese Perspective." In *From Africa to Zen: An Invitation to World Philosophy*, ed. Robert C. Solomon and Kathleen M. Higgins, 1–23. Boston, MA: Rowman & Littlefield.
Hall, Edward T. 1981 [1976]. *Beyond Culture*. New York: Doubleday.
Hall, Stuart. 1990. "Cultural Identity and Diaspora." In *Identity: Community, Culture, Difference*, ed. Jonathan Rutherford, 222–37. London: Lawrence & Wishart.
Hallorans, A. O. 1882. *Guarachas cubanas: Curiosa recopilaciín desde las más antiguas hasta las más modernas*. 2nd edition. Madrid: Impresora de A. Pérez.
Hanna, Judith Lynne. 1979. *To Dance Is Human: A Theory of Nonverbal Communication*. Austin: University of Texas Press.
——. 1983. *The Performer-Audience Connection: Emotion to Metaphor in Dance and Society*. Austin: University of Texas Press.
Harris, Olivia. 2000. *To Make the Earth Bear Fruit: Ethnographic Essays on Fertility, Work and Gender in Highland Bolivia*. London: Institute of Latin American Studies.
Helg, Aline. 1990. "Race in Argentina and Cuba, 1880–1930: Theory, Policies, and Popular Reaction." In *The Idea of Race in Latin America*, ed. Richard Graham, 37–70. Austin: University of Texas Press.
Hellier-Tinoco, Ruth. 2011. *Embodying Mexico: Tourism, Nationalism & Performance*. New York: Oxford University Press.
Herndon, Marcia. 1971. "The Cherokee Ballgame Cycle: An Ethnomusicologist's View." *Ethnomusicology* 15(3): 339–52.

References

——. 1992. "Song." In *Folklore, Cultural Performances, and Popular Entertainments: A Communications-Centered Handbook*, ed. Richard Bauman, 159–66. New York: Oxford University Press.

Herndon, Marcia and Roger Brunyate, eds. 1975. *Proceedings of a Symposium on Form in Performance: Hard-Core Ethnography* (University of Texas at Austin, April 17–19). Austin: Office of the College of Fine Arts.

Herndon, Marcia and Norma McLeod. 1979. *Music as Culture*. Norwood, PA: Norwood Editions.

Hinojosa, Clarissa E. and Juan Carlos Rodríguez. n.d. "Paredes, Américo." *Handbook of Texas Online*. Denton: Texas State Historical Association. Accessed July 24, 2012. www.tshaonline.org/handbook/online/articles/fpa94.

Hockin, Nicholas. 2004. "Tradition: An Inquiry into its Meanings and Uses in Ethnomusicological Studies of African Music." Paper presented at the 49th annual meeting of the Society for Ethnomusicology, Tucson, AZ.

Hoopes, James, ed. 1991. *Peirce on Signs: Writings on Semiotic, by Charles Sanders Peirce*. Chapel Hill: University of North Carolina Press.

Hymes, Dell. 1962. "The Ethnography of Speaking." In *Anthropology and Human Behavior*, ed. T. Gladwin and W. C. Sturtevant, 13–53. Washington, DC: Anthropological Society of Washington.

——. 1964. "Toward Ethnographies of Communication." *American Anthropologist* 66(6): 1–34.

——. 1971. "The Contribution of Folklore to Sociolinguistic Research." *Journal of American Folklore* 84(331): 42–50.

——. 1972. "On Communicative Competence." In *Sociolinguistics: Selected Readings*, ed. J. B. Pride and Janet Holmes, 269–93. Harmondsworth: Penguin.

Ibarra, Hernán. 1998. *La otra cultura: Imaginarios, mestizaje y modernización*. Quito: Abya Yala.

Iyer, Vijay. 2002. "Embodied Mind, Situated Cognition, and Expressive Micro-timing in African-American Music." *Music Perception* 19(3): 387–414.

Jullien, F. 2004 [1996]. *A Treatise on Efficacy: Between Western and Chinese Thinking*, trans. Janet Lloyd. Honolulu: University of Hawaii Press.

Kapchan, Deborah. 1995. "Performance." *Journal of American Folklore* 108(430): 479–508.

——. 2007. *Traveling Spirit Masters: Moroccan Gnawa Trance and Music in the Global Marketplace*. Middletown, CT: Wesleyan University Press.

Keil, Charles. 1978. "Comment: Who Needs 'the Folk'?" *Journal of the Folklore Institute* 15(3): 263–5.

——. 1994. "Participatory Discrepancies and the Power of Music." In *Music Grooves: Essays and Dialogues*, by Charles Keil and Steven Feld, 96–108. Chicago, IL: University of Chicago Press.

Kenyon, N., ed. 1988. *Authenticity and Early Music: A Symposium*. London: Oxford University Press.

Kirshenblatt-Gimblett, Barbara. 1995. "Theorizing Heritage." *Ethnomusicology* 39(3): 367–80.

Kisliuk, Michelle. 1997. "(Un)doing Fieldwork: Sharing Songs, Sharing Lives." In *Shadows in the Field*, ed. Gregory Barz and Timothy Cooley, 23–44. New York: Oxford University Press.

——. 1998. *Seize the Dance! BaAka Musical Life and the Ethnography of Performance*. New York: Oxford University Press.

Klemperer, Paul. 2009. Personal communication.

Kligman, Gail. 1988. *The Wedding of the Dead: Ritual, Poetics, and Popular Culture in Transylvania*. Berkeley: University of California Press.

Koetting, James. 1970. "Analysis and Notation of West African Drum Ensemble Music." *Selected Reports in Ethnomusicology* 1(3): 115–46.

Korzybski, A. 1994 [1933]. *Science and Sanity: An Introduction to Non-Aristotelian Systems and General Semantics*. 5th edition. Englewood, NJ: Institute of General Semantics.

——. 2000. "Foreword." In *Music and Gender*, ed. Pirkko Moisala and Beverley Diamond, ix–xiii. Urbana: University of Illinois Press.

Kraft, Karen Elaine. 1995. "Andean Fields and Fallow Pastures: Communal Land Use Management under Pressures for Intensification." Ph.D. dissertation, University of Florida.

Krishnamurti, J. 1999. *This Light in Oneself: True Meditation*. Boston: Shambhala.

Kutzinski, Vera M. 1993. *Sugar's Secrets: Race and the Erotics of Cuban Nationalism*. Charlottesville: University Press of Virginia.

LaBarre, Weston. 1948. *The Aymara Indians of the Lake Titicaca Plateau, Bolivia*. Memoir Series of the American Anthropological Association 68. Menasha, WI: American Anthropological Association.

Lacan, Jacques. 1989. "The Function and Field of Speech and Language in Psychoanalysis." In his *Écrits*, 23–86. London: Routledge.

Lane, Jill. 2005. *Blackface Cuba, 1840–1895*. Philadelphia: University of Pennsylvania Press.

Largey, Michael. 1994. "Composing a Haitian Cultural Identity: Haitian Elites, African Ancestry, and Musical Discourse." *Black Music Research Journal* 14(2): 99–117.

Lea, James T. 2001. "Charles Sanders Peirce, the Extraordinary Moment, and Musical Affect." DMA thesis, University of Illinois, Urbana-Champaign.

Leach, Edmund. 1954. *The Political Systems of Highland Burma*. Cambridge, MA: Harvard University Press.

Leal, Rine, ed. 1975. *Teatro bufo siglo XIX*. 2 vols. Havana: Editorial Arte y Cultura.

——, ed. 1989a. *Antología de teatro cubano*. Havana: Editorial Pueblo y Educación.

——. 1989b. "Estudio preliminary para el teatro bufo." In *Antología de teatro cubano*, ed. Rine Leal, vol. III: 157–79. Havana: Editorial Pueblo y Educación.

Lenz, Rodolfo. 1919. "Sobre la poesía popular impresa de Santiago de Chile." *Anales de la Universidad de Chile* 9: 511–622.

References

Levine, Lawrence. 1988. *Highbrow Lowbrow: The Emergence of Culture Hierarchy in America*. Cambridge, MA: Harvard University Press.

Lewis, Gordon K. 1963. *Puerto Rico: Freedom and Power in the Caribbean*. New York: Monthly Review Press.

Limón, Jose. 1991. "Representation, Ethnicity, and the Precursory Ethnography: Notes of a Native Anthropologist." In *Recapturing Anthropology: Working in the Present*, ed. Richard G. Fox, 115–36. Santa Fe, NM: School of American Research Press.

———. 1994. *Dancing with the Devil: Society and Cultural Poetics in Mexican-American South Texas*. Madison: University of Wisconsin Press.

List, George. 1963. "The Boundaries of Speech and Song." *Ethnomusicology* 7(1): 1–16.

Lizana, Desiderio. 1912. *Como se canta la poesía popular*. Santiago de Chile: Imprenta Universitaria.

Lockwood, Lewis. 1991. "Performance and 'Authenticity.'" *Early Music* 19(4): 501–12.

Lomax, Alan. 1993 [1950]. *Mister Jelly Roll: The Fortunes of Jelly Roll Morton, New Orleans Creole and "Inventor of Jazz."* New York: Pantheon Books.

López, Álvaro. 1979. "Estudio complementario." In *Teatro Alhambra: Antología*, ed. Eduardo Robreño, 651–702. Havana: Letras Cubanas.

Lord, Albert B. 1960. *The Singer of Tales*. Cambridge, MA: Harvard University Press.

MacAloon, John J. 1984. "Introduction: Cultural Performances, Culture Theory." In *Rite, Drama, Festival, Spectacle: Rehearsals toward a Theory of Cultural Performance*, ed. John J. MacAloon, 1–15. Philadelphia, PA: Institute for the Study of Human Issues.

MacCannell, Dean. 1973. "Staged Authenticity: Arrangements of Social Space in Tourist Settings." *American Journal of Sociology* 79(3): 589–603.

Madrid, Alejandro L., ed. 2011. *Transnational Encounters: Music and Performance at the U.S.-Mexico Border*. New York: Oxford University Press.

Maitland, Jeffrey. 1980. "Creative Performance: The Art of Life." *Research in Phenomenology* 10(1): 278–303.

Mallon, Florencia. 1995. *Peasants and Nation: The Making of Postcolonial Mexico and Peru*. Berkeley: University of California Press.

Mangin, William. 1961. "Fiestas in an Indian Community in Peru." In *Symposium: Patterns of Land Utilization and Other Papers. Proceedings of the 1961 Annual Spring Meeting of the American Ethnological Society*, ed. Viola E. Garfield, 84–92. Seattle, WA: American Ethnological Society.

Manuel, Peter. 1985. "The Anticipated Bass in Cuban Popular Music." *Latin American Music Review* 6(2): 249–61.

McLeod, Norma. 1957. "The Social Context of Music in a Polynesian Community." Unpublished MA thesis, London School of Economics.

———. 1964. "The Status of Musical Specialists in Madagascar." *Ethnomusicology* 8(3): 278–89.

176   *Soundscapes from the Americas*

——. 1966. "Some Techniques of Analysis for Non-Western Music." Ph.D. dissertation, Northwestern University.

——. 1975. "Keynote Address." *Proceedings of a Symposium on Form in Performance: Hard-Core Ethnography* (University of Texas at Austin, April 17–19), ed. Marcia Herndon and Roger Brunyate, 1–17. Austin, TX: Office of the College of Fine Arts.

McLeod, Norma and Marcia Herndon, comp. 1980. *The Ethnography of Musical Performance.* Norwood, PA: Norwood Editions.

Mendoza, Fernando, Willer Flores, and Catherine Letourneux. 1994. *Atlas de los ayllus de Chayanta. Vol. I: Territorios del suni.* Potosí: Programa de Autodesarrollo Campesino, Fase de Consolidación.

Merleau-Ponty, M. 1989 [1945]. *Phenomenology of Perception,* trans. Colin Smith. London: Routledge.

Merriam, Alan P. 1964. *The Anthropology of Music.* Evanston, IL: Northwestern University Press.

Miller, Geoffrey. 1984. "Are You All Unhappy at a Twenty Dollar Bill? Text, Tune and Context at Antique Auctions." *Ethnomusicology* 28(2): 187–208.

Mitchell, Frank. 1978. *Navajo Blessingway Singer: The Autobiography of Frank Mitchell, 1881–1967,* ed. Charlotte J. Frisbie and David P. McAllester. Tucson: University of Arizona Press.

Mitchell, Stephen, ed. and trans. 1982. *The Selected Poetry of Rainer Maria Rilke.* New York: Random House.

Moisala, Pirkko and Beverley Diamond, eds. 2000. *Music and Gender.* Urbana: University of Illinois Press.

Monson, Ingrid. 1996. *Saying Something: Jazz Improvisation and Interaction.* Chicago, IL: University of Chicago Press.

Moore, Robin. 1995. "The Commercial Rumba: Afrocuban Arts as International Popular Culture. *Latin American Music Review* 16(2): 165–98.

——. 1997. *Nationalizing Blackness: Afrocubanismo and Artistic Revolution in Havana, 1920–1940.* Pittsburgh, PA: University of Pittsburgh Press.

——. 2006. "Editor's Note: A Selection of the Works of Gerard Béhague." Special Memorial Issue: Gerard Béhague, 1937–2005. *Latin American Music Review* 27(1): 1–9.

Moore, Sally F. 1975. "Epilogue: Uncertainty in Situations: Indeterminacies in Culture." In *Symbol and Politics in Communal Ideology: Cases and Questions,* ed. Sally F. Moore and Barbara Myerhoff, 109–43. Ithaca, NY: Cornell University Press.

Moore, Sally F. and Barbara G. Meyerhoff. 1977. "Introduction: Secular Ritual: Forms and Meanings." In *Secular Ritual,* ed. Sally Moore and Barbara Meyerhoff, 3–24. New Haven, CT: Van Gorcum, Assen.

Municipio de Cotacachi. n.d. *Plan de Desarrollo del Cantón Cotacachi.* Cotacachi: Municipio de Cotacachi.

Nachmanovitch, Stephen. 1990. *Free Play: Improvisation in Life and Art.* New York: Tarcher/Putnam.

Napoli, David, Alma M. Whiteley, and Kathrine S. Johansen. 2005. *Organizational Jazz: Extraordinary Performance through Extraordinary Leadership*. Sydney: eContent Management P/L.

Navarrete, Micaela, ed. 1998. *Aunque no soy literaria: Rosa Araneda en la poesía popular del siglo XIX*. Santiago de Chile: Ediciones de la Dirección de Bibliotecas, Archivos y Museos.

Néda, Z., E. Ravasz, Y. Brechet, T. Vicsek, and A.-L. Barabási. 2000. "The Sound of Many Hands Clapping." *Nature* 403 (24 February): 849–50.

Nelson, Kristina. 1982. "Reciter and Listener: Some Factors Shaping the *Mujawwad* Style of Qur'anic Reciting." *Ethnomusicology* 26(1): 41–8.

———. 2001 [1985]. *The Art of Reciting the Qur'an*. Cairo: AUC Press.

Nettl, Bruno. 2002. *Encounters in Ethnomusicology: A Memoir*. Warren, MI: Harmonie Park Press.

Norgaard, M. 2008. "Descriptions of Improvisational Thinking by Artist-Level Jazz Musicians." Ph.D. dissertation, University of Texas at Austin.

Orta, Andrew. 1990. "Iconoclasm and History: Remembering the Via Crucis in a Nicaraguan comunidad eclesial de base." *Nexus* 7 (Supplement): 79–140.

Ortiz, Fernando. 1906. *Hampa afro-cubana: Los negros brujos. Apuntes para un estudio de etnología criminal*. Madrid: Librería de F. Fé.

Ortiz Crespo, Santiago. 2004. *Cotacachi: Una apuesta por la democracia participative*. Quito: FLACSO, Sede Académica de Ecuador.

Otter, Elizabeth den. 1985. *Music and Dance of Indians and Mestizos in an Andean Valley of Perú*. Delft: Eburon.

Paquette, Robert L. 1988. *Sugar Is Made with Blood: The Conspiracy of La Escalera and the Conflict between Empires over Slavery in Cuba*. Middletown, CT: Wesleyan University Press.

Paredes, Américo. 1971 [1958]. *"With His Pistol in His Hand": A Border Ballad and Its Hero*. Austin: University of Texas Press.

Parra, Violeta. 1979. *Cantos folklóricos chilenos*. Santiago de Chile: Editorial Nascimento.

Peacock, James. 1968. *Rites of Modernization: Symbolic and Social Aspects of Indonesian Proletarian Drama*. Chicago, IL: University of Chicago Press.

Peña, Manuel H. 1983. "From *Ranchero* to *Jaitón*: Ethnicity and Class in Texas Mexican Music (Two Styles in the Form of a Pair)." *Ethnomusicology* 29(1): 29–55.

———. 1985. *The Texas-Mexican Conjunto: History of a Working Class Music*. Austin: University of Texas Press.

Pérez de Arce, José. 2002. "El guitarrón chileno y su armonía tímbrica." Unpublished manuscript. Facultad de Artes de la Pontificia Universidad Católica de Chile.

Phelan, Peggy. 1993. *Unmarked: The Politics of Performance*. London and New York: Routledge.

Pinkerton, Emily. 2007. "The Chilean *Guitarrón*: The Social, Political and Gendered Life of a Folk Instrument." Ph.D. dissertation, University of Texas at Austin.

Ponce, David. 2007. "Paya de verdad, de mujer y a dos razones." *Mus.cl* 55. Accessed March 7, 2007. www.mus.cl/entrevista.php?fId=55.

Propp, Vladimir. 1968. *Morphology of the Folktale.* 2nd edition. Austin: University of Texas Press.

Qureshi, Regula. 1987a. "Music Sound and Contextual Input: A Performance Model for Musical Analysis." *Ethnomusicology* 31(1): 56–86.

——. 1987b. "*Qawwali*: Making the Music Happen in the Sufi Assembly." *Asian Music* 28(2): 118–57.

——. 1995 [1986]. *Sufi Music of India and Pakistan: Sound, Context and Meaning in Qawwali.* Chicago, IL: University of Chicago Press.

——. 1997. "The Indian *Sarangi*: Sound of Affect, Site of Contest." *Yearbook for Traditional Music* 29: 1–38.

Rasnake, Roger Neil. 1988. *Domination and Cultural Resistance: Authority and Power among an Andean People.* Durham, NC: Duke University Press.

Rice, Timothy. 1994. *May it Fill Your Soul: Experiencing Bulgarian Music.* Chicago, IL: University of Chicago Press.

——. 1995. "Understanding and Producing the Variability of Oral Tradition: Learning from a Bulgarian Bagpiper." *Journal of American Folklore* 108(429): 266–76.

——. 2003. "Time, Place, and Metaphor in Musical Experience and Ethnography." *Ethnomusicology* 47(2): 151–79.

Ricoeur, Paul. 1981. *Hermeneutics and the Human Sciences: Essays on Language, Action, and Interpretation*, ed. and trans. John B. Thompson. Cambridge: Cambridge University Press.

Rivera Cusicanqui, Silvia. 1987. *Oppressed but not Defeated: Peasant Struggles Among the Aymara and Qhechwa in Bolivia, 1900–1980.* Geneva: United Nations Research Institute for Social Development.

——. 1991. *Pachakuti: Los Aymara de Bolivia frente a medio milenio de colonialismo.* La Paz: Taller de Historia Oral Andina.

Roach, Joseph. 1996. *Cities of the Dead: Circum-Atlantic Performance.* New York: Columbia University Press.

Roberts, John Storm. 1979. *The Latin Tinge.* New York: Original Music.

Robreño, Eduardo. 1961. *Historia del teatro popular cubano.* Havana: Oficina del Historiador de la Ciudad.

——, ed. 1979. *Teatro Alhambra: Antología.* Havana: Letras Cubanas.

Romero, Raul. 2001. *Debating the Past: Music, Memory, and Identity in the Andes.* Oxford: Oxford University Press.

Rosaldo, Renato. 1993 [1989]. *Culture & Truth: The Remaking of Social Analysis.* Revised edition, with a new introduction. Boston, MA: Beacon Press.

Roseman, Marina. 1984. "The Social Structuring of Sound: The Temiar of Peninsular Malaysia." *Ethnomusicology* 28(3): 411–45.

Ruskin, Jesse D. and Timothy Rice. 2012. "The Individual in Musical Ethnography." *Ethnomusicology* 56(2): 299–327.

Russell, Thomas. 1941. "On Audiences." *The Musical Times* 82(1176): 54–6.

Sahlins, Marshall. 1981. *Historical Metaphors and Mythical Realities*. Ann Arbor: University of Michigan Press.

———. 1987. *Islands of History*. Chicago, IL: University of Chicago Press.

Salomon, Frank. 1999. "Testimonies: The Making and Reading of Native South American Historical Sources." In *The Cambridge History of the Native Peoples of the Americas, Volume III: South America, Part I*, ed. Frank Salmon and Stuart B. Schwartz, 19–95. Cambridge: Cambridge University Press.

Samson, Jim. 2008. "A View from Musicology." In *The New (Ethno)musicologies*, ed. Henry Stobart, 23–7. Lanham, MD: Scarerow Press.

Sánchez, Luis Rafael. 1987. "The Flying Bus," trans. Elpidio Laguna-Díaz. In *Images and Identities: The Puerto Rican in Two World Contexts*, ed. Asela Rodríguez de Laguna, 17–25. New Brunswick, NJ: Transaction Books.

Sawin, Patricia E. 1984. "M.A. and Ph.D. Programs in Folklore at the University of Texas at Austin. Information Compiled by Patricia E. Sawin." Accessed July 13, 2013. https://scholarworks.iu.edu/dspace/bitstream/handle/2022/1922/18(1)%2069-76.pdf?sequence=1.

———. 2002. "Performance at the Nexus of Gender, Power, and Desire: Reconsidering Bauman's Verbal Art from the Perspective of Gendered Subjectivity as Performance." *Journal of American Folklore* 115(455): 28–61.

Sawyer, R. K. 2000. "Improvisational Cultures: Collaborative Emergence and Creativity in Improvisation." *Mind, Culture, and Activity* 7(3): 180–85.

Saxton, Alexander. 1975. "Blackface Minstrelsy and Jacksonian Ideology." *American Quarterly* 29 (March): 3–28.

Schechner, Richard. 1985. *Between Theater and Anthropology*. Philadelphia: University of Pennsylvania Press.

———. 1987. "Victor Turner's Last Adventure." In *The Anthropology of Performance*, by Victor Turner, 7–20. New York: PAJ Publications.

———. 1998. *Performance Theory*. Revised edition. New York: Routledge.

———. 2006. *Performance Studies: An Introduction*. 2nd edition. New York: Routledge.

Schechter, John M. 2005. "A Tribute to Gerard Béhague." *Latin American Music Review* 26(2): 143–57.

Schieffelin, Edward L. 1998. "Problematizing Performance." In *Ritual, Performance, Media*, ed. Felicia Hughes-Freeland, 194–207. London: Routledge.

Seeger, Anthony. 1980. "Sing for Your Sister: The Structure and Performance of Suyá Akia." In *The Ethnography of Musical Performance*, comp. Norma McLeod and Marcia Herndon, 7–43. Norwood, PA: Norwood Editions.

———. 1994. "Whoever We Are Today, We Can Sing You a Song About It." In *Music and Black Ethnicity: The Caribbean and South America*, ed. Gerard H. Béhague, 1–15. New Brunswick, NJ: Transaction Publishers.

180   *Soundscapes from the Americas*

———. 2004 [1987]. *Why Suyá Sing: A Musical Anthropology of an Amazonian People.* Urbana: University of Illinois Press.

Sewell, William. 2005. *Logics of History: Social Theory and Social Transformation.* Chicago, IL: University of Chicago Press.

Silva, Erika. 2004. *Identidad nacional y poder.* Quito: Abya Yala.

Silverman, Carol. 2012. *Romani Routes: Cultural Politics and Balkan Music in Diaspora.* New York: Oxford University Press.

Singer, Milton. 1955. "The Cultural Pattern of Indian Civilization: A Preliminary Report of a Methodological Field Study." *The Far Eastern Quarterly* 15(1): 23–36.

———. 1972. *When a Great Tradition Modernizes: An Anthropological Approach to an Indian Civilization.* New York: Praeger Publishers.

Slawek, Stephen M., Elliott M. Antokoletz, and Hunter C. March. 2006. "In Memoriam: Gerard H. Béhague." Documents of the General Faculty, University of Texas at Austin, "Memorials." Accessed July 6, 2012. www.utexas.edu/faculty/council, D 4325–6.

Smith, Gavin. 1999. *Confronting the Present: Toward a Politically Engaged Anthropology.* Oxford: Berg.

Snow, M. 2004. "A Composition on Improvisation." In *The Other Side of Nowhere*, ed. D. Fischlin and A. Heble, 45–9. Middletown, CT: Wesleyan University Press.

Solís, Ted. 1995. "Jíbaro Image and the Ecology of Hawai'i Puerto Rican Musical Instruments." *Latin American Music Review* 16(2): 123–53.

———. 2001. "'Let's Play One *Seis Caliente*': Coalescence and Selective Adaptation in a Diasporic Puerto Rican Musical Style." In *Essays on Music and Culture in Honor of Herbert Kellman*, ed. Barbara Haggh, 549–66. Tours: Klincksieck.

———. 2005. "'You Shake Your Hips Too Much': Diasporic Values and Hawai'i Puerto Rican Dance Culture." *Ethnomusicology* 49(1): 75–119.

———, ed. 2004. *Performing Ethnomusicology: Teaching and Representation in World Music Ensembles.* Berkeley: University of California Press.

Solomon, Thomas James. 1997. "Mountains of Song: Musical Constructions of Ecology, Place, and Identity in the Bolivian Andes." Ph.D. dissertation, University of Texas at Austin.

———. 2000. "Dueling Landscapes: Singing Places and Identities in Highland Bolivia." *Ethnomusicology* 44(2): 257–80.

———. 2012. "Theory and Method in Popular Music Analysis: Text and Meaning." *Studia Musicologica Norvegica* 38: 86–108.

Spalding, Karen. 1999. "The Crises and Transformations of Invaded Societies: Andean Area (1500–1580)." In *The Cambridge History of the Native Peoples of the Americas, Volume III: South America, Part I*, ed. Frank Salomon and Stuart B. Schwartz, 904–72. Cambridge: Cambridge University Press.

Spivak, Gayatri. 1996 [1985]. "Subaltern Studies: Deconstructing Historiography." In *The Spivak Reader: Selected Works of Gayatri Chakravorty Spivak*, ed. Donna Landry and Gerald MacLean, 203–36. New York: Routledge.

Stern, Steve J. 1993 [1982]. *Peru's Indian Peoples and the Challenge of the Spanish Conquest: Huamanga to 1640*. 2nd edition. Madison: University of Wisconsin Press.

Stewart, Kathleen. 1991. "On the Politics of Cultural Theory: A Case for 'Contaminated' Cultural Critique." *Social Research* 58(2): 395–412.

Stone, Ruth M. 1982. *Let the Inside Be Sweet: The Interpretation of Music Event among the Kpelle of Liberia*. Bloomington: Indiana University Press.

Strogatz, Steven. 2008. "Steven Strogatz on Sync." In *TED: Ideas Worth Spreading*. Accessed March 7, 2009. www.ted.com/index.php/talks/steven_ strogatz_on_sync.html.

Stutzman, Ronald. 1981. "*El Mestizaje*: An All-Inclusive Ideology of Exclusion." In *Cultural Transformations and Ethnicity in Modern Ecuador*, ed. Norman E. Whitten, Jr., 45–94. Urbana and Chicago: University of Illinois Press.

Sugarman, Jane C. 1997. *Engendering Song: Singing & Subjectivity at Prespa Albanian Weddings*. Chicago, IL: University of Chicago Press.

Sullivan, Lawrence E. 1986. "Sound and Senses: Toward a Hermeneutics of Performance." *History of Religions* 26(1): 1–33.

Szemiński, Jan. 1987. "Why Kill the Spaniard: New Perspectives on Andean Insurrectionary Ideology in the 18th Century." In *Resistance, Rebellion, and Consciousness in the Andean Peasant World, 18th to 20th Centuries*, ed. Steve J. Stern, 166–92. Madison: University of Wisconsin Press.

Tamisari, Franca. 2005. "The Responsibility of Performance: The Interweaving of Politics and Aesthetics in Intercultural Contexts." *Visual Anthropology Review* 21(1–2): 47–63.

Taruskin, Richard. 1992. "Tradition and Authority." *Early Music* 20(2): 311–25.

Taussig, Michael T. 1987. *Shamanism, Colonialism, and the Wild Man: A Study in Terror and Healing*. Chicago, IL: University of Chicago Press.

Titon, Jeff Todd. 1988. *Powerhouse for God: Speech, Chant, and Song in an Appalachian Baptist Church*. Austin: University of Texas Press.

Trouillot, Michel-Rolph. 1995. *Silencing the Past: Power and the Production of History*. Boston, MA: Beacon Press.

Tsitsishvili, Nino. 2006. "'A Man Can Sing and Play Better than a Woman': Singing and Patriarchy at the Georgian *Supra* Feast." *Ethnomusicology* 50(3): 452–93.

Turino, Thomas. 1990. "*Somos el Perú* [We are Peru]: 'Cumbia Andina' and the Children of Andean Migrants in Lima." *Studies in Latin American Popular Culture* 9: 15–31.

——. 1993. *Moving Away from Silence: Music of the Peruvian Altiplano and the Experience of Urban Migration*. Chicago, IL: University of Chicago Press.

——. 1999. "Signs of Imagination, Identity, and Experience: A Peircian Semiotic Theory for Music." *Ethnomusicology* 43(2): 221–55.

——. 2000. *Nationalists, Cosmopolitans, and Popular Music in Zimbabwe*. Chicago, IL: University of Chicago Press.

———. 2003. "Nationalism and Latin American Music: Selected Case Studies and Theoretical Considerations." *Latin American Music Review* 24(2): 169–209.

———. 2004. "Introduction: Identity and the Arts in Diaspora Communities." In *Identity and the Arts in Diaspora Communities*, ed. Thomas Turino and James Lea, 3–20. Warren, MI: Harmonie Park Press.

———. 2005. "Obituaries: Gerard Béhague (1937–2005)." *SEM Newsletter* 39(4): 12–13.

———. 2008. *Music as Social Life: The Politics of Participation.* Chicago, IL: University of Chicago Press.

Turner, Victor. 1974. *Dramas, Fields and Metaphors: Symbolic Action in Human Society.* Ithaca, NY: Cornell University Press.

———. 1982a. "Introduction." In his *Celebration: Studies in Festivity and Ritual*, 11–30. Washington, DC: Smithsonian Institution Press.

———. 1982b. *From Ritual to Theatre: The Human Seriousness of Play.* New York: PAJ Publications.

———. 1987. *The Anthropology of Performance.* New York: PAJ Publications.

———.1995 [1969]. *The Ritual Process: Structure and Anti-Structure.* Hawthorne, NY: Aldine de Gruyter.

Unión de Poetas y Cantores Populares de Chile. 1954. "Primer congreso nacional de poetas y cantores populares de Chile." *Anales de la Universidad de Chile* 93: 5–79.

Uribe Echevarría, Juan. 1962. *Cantos a lo divino y a lo humano en Aculeo: Folklore de la provincia de Santiago.* Santiago de Chile: Editorial Universitaria, S.A.

Urrutia y Blanco, Carlos, ed. 1882. *Los criminals de Cuba y D. José Trujillo.* Barcelona: Giró Press.

Uzendoski, Michael. 2005. *The Napo Runa of Amazonian Ecuador.* Urbana: University of Illinois Press.

Valdano, Juan. 2007. *Identidad y formas de lo ecuatoriano.* Prole del Vendaval 1. Quito: Eskeletra Editorial.

Vander, Judith. 1996. *Songprints: The Musical Experience of Five Shoshone Women.* Urbana: University of Illinois Press.

Varela, Francisco J., Evan Thompson, and Eleanor Rosch. 1991. *The Embodied Mind: Cognitive Science and Human Experience.* Cambridge, MA: MIT Press.

Varese, Stefano. 1996. "The Ethnopolitics of Indian Resistance in Latin America." In *Ethnicity and Class in Latin America*, ed. Michael Kearney and Rodolfo Stavenhagen, 58–71. Thousand Oaks, CA: Sage, 1996.

Wade, Peter. 2000. *Music, Race, and Nation: Música Tropical in Colombia.* Chicago, IL: University of Chicago Press.

Waxer, Lise A. 2002. *The City of Musical Memory: Salsa, Recorded Grooves, and Popular Culture in Cali, Colombia.* Middletown, CT: Wesleyan University Press.

Whitten, Norman, Jr. 1981. *Cultural Transformations and Ethnicity in Modern Ecuador.* Urbana: University of Illinois Press.

References 183

———. 1988. "Commentary: Historical and Mythic Evocations of Chthonic Power in South America." In *Rethinking History and Myth: Indigenous South American Perspectives on the Past*, ed. Jonathan D. Hill, 282–306. Urbana: University of Illinois Press.

———. 2003. "Preface." In *Millennial Ecuador: Critical Essays in Cultural Transformations and Social Dynamics*, ed. Norman E. Whitten, Jr., ix–xvii. Iowa City: University of Iowa Press.

Wibbelsman, Michelle. 2009. *Ritual Encounters: Otavalan Modern and Mythic Community*. Urbana: University of Illinois Press.

Wong, Deborah. 2001. *Sounding the Center: History and Aesthetics in Thai Buddhist Performance*. Chicago, IL: University of Chicago Press.

———. 2008. "Moving from Performance to Performative Ethnography and Back Again." In *Shadows in the Field: New Perspectives for Fieldwork in Ethnomusicology*, ed. Gregory Barz and Timothy J. Cooley, 76–89. New York: Oxford University Press.

Wong, Ketty. 2007. "*La Música Nacional*: Changing Perceptions of the Ecuadorian National Identity in the Aftermath of the Rural Migration of the 1970s and the International Migration of the Late 1990s." Ph.D. dissertation, University of Texas at Austin.

Yamashita, K. 1999. "Ferociously Harmonizing with Reality." In *Keeping Time: Readings in Jazz History*, ed. Robert Walser, 410–415. Oxford: Oxford University Press.

Zea, Leopoldo. 1986. "Negritude e indigenismo." *Ideas en torno a Latinoamérica*, vol. II, 1341–55. Mexico: Universided Nacional Autónima de México.

Discography and Videography

Contra-punto de Tahuada con Don Javier de la Rosa. 1969. *Antología del folklore musical chileno, quinto fasciculo*. LP. Santiago de Chile: Universidad de Chile.

Espígul, Ramón. 1916. "El Ford." *Diálogo y canto*, performed by Ramón Espígul and Lola Mayorga. RCA Victor '78 #72650-a.

Monteagudo, H. 1924. "El melonero." *Diálogo y pregón*, performed by Arquímedes Pous and Conchita Llauradó. Columbia '78 C-4153 (93207).

Solís, Ted. 1989. *Puerto Rican Music in Hawaii: Kachi-Kachi*. Notes by Ted Solís. Smithsonian/Folkways CD SF 40014.

———. 1994. *Puerto Rico in Polynesia: Jíbaro Traditional Music on Hawaiian Plantations*. Notes by Ted Solís. Original Music OMCD 020.

Index

Abrahams, Roger D. xiii, 2–3, 7–9
accompaniment 18, 32–3, 50–52, 55, 56n, 62, 69, 70n, 72–3, 83, 102–3, 106, 108–9
aesthetics 2–3, 12–13, 19, 45, 55, 83, 128
affect; *see* emotion
Africanisms 65
agency 2, 12–13, 14n, 20, 97–8, 139, 145, 161, 163
aguinaldo 62, 72
albazo(s) 44, 48, 50, 52–3, 58–9
Almacenes Feraud Guzmán **47**
amateur, non-specialist 49, 130, 152
Amazon 44n, 52, 138
Anderson, Benedict 43
Andes 45, 104, 140, 143, 146, 150, 156, 160
Anrango, Alberto 132, 136, 139–40
anthropology 4, 6, 8, 11, 26
Apolo, Espinosa 46, 48
applause 113, 115, 121, 132–4
Arancibia, Myriam 102, 107–9, 113–20, 122–3
Araneda, Rosa 115–16
Arrayanes, Ecuador 128, 130–32, 134–5, 139
Asch, Michael 10
Asia/Asians 65, 68, 83
Askew, Kelly 6n, 12n, 13n, 14
Astorga, Cecilia 123, 113–17
Astorga, Francisco 114, 118
audience 1, 7–8, 10, 11n, 16, 20, 27, 33–4, 37, 44, 52–4, 63, 91, 94, 103–4, 107, 110–13, 120–22, 130, 133–4, 141, 145, 150, 152–3, 155, 160–62
Austin, J. L. 6–13
Austin, Texas xiii, xiv, 4, 17–18, 44, 90
autoethnographic 11n
ayllu(s) 20–21, 55–6, 58–63, 146–8, 150–52
Aymara language 20, 143, 146

Babcock, Barbara 3n, 6
bandurria 32
banquillo 104, 112–13
bass 61, 81–3, 109
  acoustic 82
  anticipated 82–4
  double 81n, 82
  electric 57, 62, 71n, 75, 79, 81–2, 84
  running bass line 82
Bateson, Gregory 6, 9, 11, 92, 94, 96, 98
Batista, Gustavo 70n, 81–2
Baudrillard, Jean 162
Bauman, Richard 1–3, 5–9, 12, 147n
Béhague, Gerard Henri xiii, xiv, 1–5, 7–9, 14–15, 25, 44, 63–4, 90, 95, 129, 147n
behavior 1–2, 4, 7–9, 12–14, 19n, 25, 28, 39, 41, 44, 89, 92, 100, 117, 158
Berger, Harris M. 89–90, 94, 97–9
Berliner, Paul 8, 74, 89, 92n
blackface 15–16, 25–9, 32–7, 40–41
  character types 26–7, 33–4, 36, 38–9
    gallego 38–40
    mulatas 35, 39–40
    mulatas de rumbo 39
    ñáñigo 35, 38–9
    negrito 27–9, 33, 36, 38–41
    negro bozal 29
    negro catedrático(s) 26, 36
    Zip Coon 27, 36
Blacking, John 14
blanco(s) 32, 40, 45–6
blanqueamiento 46
body 14, 37, 93, 100, 123, 132, 136, 138, 163
bolero(s) 52, 54, 69, 73, 76, 82–3
Bolivia 15, 19–20, 143, 145–7, 152, 156, 159–62
bombo 32
bongós 62, 75–**7**, 79, 84

186   *Soundscapes from the Americas*

bordonua 70n, 71n, 81
Boy and His Family Troubadours **77**
bozal(es) 26–7, 29–34, 36, 38, 40–41
Briggs, Charles 9, 12
Buddhism 18, 89
Bustillo Province, Bolivia 20, 146–7, 149,
    158, 160–63
Butler, Judith 12–13, 162–3

cambujá 32
campesino 57, 101, 146–7, 152, 158
candomblé 5, 15, 64
canto(s) 103–4, 108, 117, 119, 121, 123
    canto a lo divino 18, 102–4, 108, 113,
        115
    canto a lo humano 18, 102–3, 115
    canto a lo poeta 17–19, 101–4, 109,
        112–14, 116–20, 122–3
    vigilias 103
cantores/as 117, 123n
Carbonell, Walterio 29
Caribbean 5, 15, 28, 57, 61–6, 67n, 70,
    72–3, 79, 82
Carnival (Carnaval, Karnawal) 31,
    147–8, 155–6
Carpentier, Alejo 29, 36–7, 39–40
Carrión, Benjamín 49
Castañeda, Miguel Luis 101
catechists 19–20, 127–8, 134–**5**
Catholic, Catholicism 19, 34, 43, 65, 68n,
    103–4, 127–8, 136–7, 151n
Caucasian 63, 65
Cedeño, Elías 51
censorship 16, 33, 104
ceremonies 137, 151; *see also* ritual;
    festivals
Céspedes, Carlos Manuel de 33, 37
chachachá 73
Chambers, Ross 43
charango 106
Chernoff, John Miller 8
chichera 44, 48, 56–8
Chile 15, 17–19, 101–5, 107, 111–14,
    118–19, 123
China, Chinese 18, 39, 63, 65, 89–90,
    96–8, 100, 138
cholos 45, 49, 146
Chomsky, Noam 9

choreography 17; *see also* dance
Chota Valley 43
Christianity 19–20, 32, 130, 136
Civil War (U.S.) 26, 36
claves 75–7, 83
clothing, dress 20, 36, 39, 44, 46 143,
    151–2, 154–5, 159
    costumes 57, 78, 83, 130–31, 133,
        134, 144, 152
Codegua, Chile 114, 116, 123
"cognitive scaffolding" 129
colonial, colonization 27–8, 33, 37, 39, 41,
    46, 73, 85, 105n, 128, 138, 145; *see*
    also postcolonialism
Comaroff, Jean 128
communication 1–2, 6, 10, 13n, 17, 21,
    63–4, 80, 159
"communicative competence" 9
communion 18, 89, 98–100, 137
communitas 137, 139–41
community 3, 17–20, 25, 28, 35, 40, 44,
    63, 67, 68n, 74–5, 77, 79, 93, 96,
    100, 103–4, 108, 117, 120–22,
    130, 132, 134, 140, 143, 146–53,
    155–61
    definition of 128–9
    experience 128–9
    extended 138–9
    "imagined community" 43
    inclusive 137
    moral 137, 139
    political 139–40
competition 18, 20, 43, 102–4, 120, 144,
    419, 151–2, 160
concursos de trovadores 62
Confucian, Confucius 18, 89, 97–9
congas 62, 75–7, 79, 84
"contexting" 94–6
contrapunto 114–15, 118–19
contredanse, contradanza 34, 73
cornet 32
corridos 47
corruption 139n
costumbrismo, costumbrista 28, 30
Cotacachi, Ecuador 19, 127–8, 130–4
courtship 31, 36, 149, 157, 159; *see also*
    marriage
crank organ 32

Index

187

creativity 93, 95–6, 103
Creole 28, 45, 47, 62, 65–6, 70n
Crespo y Borbón, Bartolomé "Creto Gangá" 27, 31–2, 38
criollos 45
cuartetas 102, 110
cuatro 61–2, 67n, 69–71, 73–5, 79–81, 83
  keyhole 70, **71**, 75, 80, 84
  modern **70**, 71, 75, 79–81
Cuba, Cubanization 15–17, 25–36, 38–41, 66n, 69, 72–4, 76, 78–9, 82–4
cultural destructuration 161
"cultural performance" xiv, 6n, 7, 8, 8n, 11, 15, 26, 63, 129, 147n
cumbia andina 56
Cusick, Suzanne 163

dance 14n, 15, 17, 29, 32, 34–5, 38–41, 48–50, 52, 55–7, 59, 61–3, 65–9, 72–3, 75–9, 81, 83–4, 152, 155–9; *see also* specific dance types; choreography
danza(s) 72–3, 76, 81n, 82
danza Puertorriqueña 73
danzantes 44, 48
danzón 34, 40, 73, 76
décimas 31, 102–4, 112, 114, 116, 119
  décima espinela 62
Denzin, Norman 2, 10–11, 13n
diablitos 106–7
disco 52, 61
discourse 3n, 5, 12–19, 27, 29, 32, 38–9, 43, 45, 49, 75, 116, 123, 135, 144–5
divergence 18, 92–3
Dobie, J. Frank 3
Dominican Republic 66n
dramatis personae 63, 68n, 74
duct flute (*pinkillus*) 143, 148–9, 154
Dúo Ecuador 51
dynamic contexting 95

Easter 103, 147, 149
Echevarría, Juan 103
economy, economics 7, 45, 49, 56, 65, 140
Ecuador 15–17, 19, 43
"Ecuadorianness" 49–50
Eliade, Mircea 137

embodied experience 2, 21, 139, 141, 162
emotion(al) 17, 28, 63–4, 94–5, 115, 121, 129, 134–5, 137, 140
encuentros de payadores 103–4
encuentro de poesía 114
  contrapunto en décimas 114
  canto a lo poeta; *see cantos*
Encuentro Nacional de Guitarroneros 119
ensemble, musical 4–5, 10, 19n, 20, 50n, 53, 62, 67–9, 75–9, 81–4, 89, 153–4, 160
  estudiantinas 50
  HPR ensemble 67, 76
  Jazz combo 89
  mariachi 5, 47
  Neo-Cuban 76–9, 77
  Otavalan pan-Andean ensembles 56
  plantation trio 75, 84
entonaciones 103–4, 107–8
  la común 102, 106–7, 109
entrainment 92
Espígul, Ramón 33
ethnography xiv, 4, 6–7, 11–12, 14n, 21, 114, 163n
ethnography of performance 1, 3n, 5–12, 14n, 15, 25–6, 63
ethnomusicology xiii, 3n, 4–5, 7–10, 12, 68, 90, 129, 147
ethnonyms
  Afro-Caribbean 65, 67n
  Afro-Cuban 15, 17, 27–9, 32–5, 38, 64, 67, 78, 82
  Afro-Ecuadorian 16, 43–6, 59
  Afro-Latin 61, 66
  Afro-Puerto Rican 64–5, 67
  Amerindian 64, 66
  black American 15–16, 26–30, 32, 34, 36–41, 66, 83, 143
  Caribbean Hispanic 73
  Chinese 39, 63, 65, 90n, 96–8, 100, 138
  Euro-Cuban 34
  Filipino 63, 65
  Hawaiian Puerto Rican (HPR) 17, 64–9, 71–85
  Hispanic 5, 73, 752
  Iberian 17, 62n, 64–6, 73, 74n, 83–4
  Iberian-African 65

Jíbaro 15, 17, 62–7, 69, 70n, 73–6, 78–81, 83–4
Korean 63, 65
Nuyorican 64, 68
Polynesian 63, 65, 83
Spanish, Spaniard 15–16, 26–7, 29–34, 37–41, 43–6, 48, 55, 61, 65–6, 68–70, 72–3, 75–6, 78, 81, 83, 138, 144, 146–7, 152, 156, 158–9
Taino Caribbean Amerindian 66
Quechua, Quichua 19–20, 55, 131–2, 134, 127, 143–4, 146, 155–8
ethnopoetics 10
European musical aesthetic 5, 108
experience, experiential 2, 8, 11–12, 14, 18–21, 53–4, 57, 64–5, 84, 89–93, 96–100, 102, 123, 127–30, 132, 134–7, 139–41, 145, 162

feeling, *see* emotion
Feld, Steven 8–9, 10n, 90, 93, 145n, 160
Feldman, Martha 133–4
female 18, 38, 50, 101–102, 106, 109–110, 113, 116–19, 122, 123n, 149; *see also* feminine; woman
feminine 111
performance, tuning 106–7, 113–19, 122–3
festival 6n, 9, 18–20, 52, 62, 102, 119, 121, 127, 134, 137, 143, 145, 162; *see also festival*
festival(es) (Spanish) 20, 147–55, **153**, 157–63
Fiallos, Nicolás 53
fiesta 9, 19–20; *see also fiesta*
fiesta (Spanish) 146–61, 163
flow 9, 18, 90–91, 94n, 97, 99–100, 138
interrelated flows 91
folk 18, 32, 34, 38, 62, 66, 73, 81–2, 102, 104, 108, 121
folklore, folklorists, folkloric xiii, 1–3, 5–6, 11n, 14, 19–20, 29, 32, 55–6, 62, 66n, 68n, 69, 103, 145, 147, 154, 159
folklorization 19, 160–61
Fornet, Ambrosio 28–9

frame 9, 11, 63, 100, 110, 130, 132n, 134, 155, 158
Frank, Adam D. 137–8
Friedson, Steven 12n, 21
Frisbie, Charlotte 7–8, 10

Gadamer, Hans Georg 96, 98
Garzón, Guillermo 55
Geertz, Clifford 41, 129
gender 2, 3n, 4, 17–18, 26, 61, 101–2, 107, 109, 111, 114, 118, 120–23, 149
gender studies 11, 13, 111–2, 123, 162–3
globalization 11
González, Hugo 67, 114
Gramsci, Antonio 128–9
"Gran nación pequeña" 49
"Grandes Compositores Ecuatorianos" 52
guaracha(s) 28, 31, 33–5, 72–4, 82
Guayaquil, Ecuador 45, 47, 48n, 50n, 53n
güiro 62, 67n, 69–73, **70**, 75–7, 79, 83–4
guitar 16, 32–3, 36, 50–52, 55, 61, 71–3, 75–7, 79, 81–4, 97, 102–3, 105–6, 108, 119, 148
acoustic 53, 62
Creole; *see cuatro*
electric 72, **77**
Martin tenor guitar 80
Rickenbacker steel guitar 80
Rickenbacker tenor guitar **77**, 80
six-string Spanish guitar 69–**70**, 72, 83
tenor guitar 70, 75–6, 79–80, 84
guitarrón(es) 18, 102–19, **105**, 121–2

habanao 76
Hall, Stuart 144
haole 63, 65
Haiti 35, 66n
Hawai'i 15, 17, 61–5, 67, 70–71, 73, 77–82
healing 49, 100
self-healing 92–3
hegemonic, hegemony xiii, 5, 16, 43–5, 48, 59, 62, 128, 139, 145, 160–61
Hellier-Tinoco, Ruth 4n, 19n
heritage 11n, 15–17, 28, 45–6, 64, 66
Herndon, Marcia xiii, 3n, 6–8, 9n, 10n, 63, 147n
Herrera, Francisco Paredes 51

Index 189

"Hispanization" 46
Hockin, Nicholas 75
Hollywood 76–8, 83–4
  films 78, 83
  Latin music 76–7
  musicals 78, 84
homogenization 64–5, 83
huacas; *see wakas*
huayno; *see wayñu*
Hymes, Dell 3n, 5–6n, 9

identity xiv, 4, 15, 17, 83, 102–3, 105n,
    113, 119, 135, 144–6, 149,
    159–63
  collective 2
  ethnic 46
  gender 121, 123
  musical 65
  national 19n, 43–5, 59
  political 17, 63
  sexual 110–11, 113
  social 6n
imagination 104
imagined nation 45
immigrant(s) 26n, 30, 39–40, 64–5, 66n,
    68–71, 75, 81
improvisation 9, 18, 62, 64, 66, 78, 83,
    108, 111, 114, 116–17, 120–23
  jazz 17–18, 89–97, 99–100
  montuno(s) 74, 78, 83
indeterminacy 18, 91–2, 134
Indian 45, 66n, 146, 152, 154–58, 162
"Indianness" 46, 58
indigenous, indigeneity 5, 14, 16, 19–21,
    28, 37, 43–6, 48–9, 53, 55–9,
    105n, 127–8, 130–32, 134, 136–41,
    143, 145–6, 147n, 151–2,
    154–5, 159–63
indigenous performance 20, 128, 137–8
indio 49, 66n, 146
industrialization 52, 65
Infante, Carlos Rubira 56
Inka 138
Inkarrí (Inka Rey, incari, inkari) 138
instruments, musical
  keyboard
    crank organ 32
    sinfonía button accordion 69

percussion
  bombo 32
  bongós 62, 75–7, 79, 84
  claves 75–7, 83
  congas 62, 75–7, 79, 84
  güiro 62, 67n, 69–73, **70**, 75–7,
    79, 83–4
  maracas 69, 75–**7**, 79, 84
  marímbula lamellophone 76–**7**,
    82
stringed
  bandurria 32
  bass; *see* individual entry
  bordonua 70n, 71n, 81
  cuatro 61–2, 67n, 69–71, 73–5,
    79–81, 83; *see also* individual
    entry
  guitar 32–3, 36, 50–2, 55, 61,
    71–3, 75–**7**, 79, 81–4, 97,
    102–3, 105–6, 108, 119, 148;
    see also individual entry
  guitarrón 18, 102–19, **105**,
    121–2
  requinto 50, 52, 55, 70n, 81
  tiple(s) 70n, 81
  ukelele(s) 80
wind
  cornet 32
  duct flute (*pinkillus*) 143, 148–9,
    154
  panpipes (*julajulas, sikus, sikuras*)
    143, 148–9
  septeto-style trumpet 79
"interactional synchrony" 92
Irupata, Bolivia 143, 150, 153, 155, 157
Iyer, Vijay 136

Jakobson, Roman 6
jazz 17–18, 62, 78, 89, 91–3, 96–100
Jíbaro 15, 17, 62–7, 69, 70n, 73–6, 78–81,
    83–4
Jim Crow 26, 29

Kapchan, Deborah 2, 11n, 12n, 14
Keil, Charles 92, 161
Kisliuk, Michelle 11, 112
Koetting, James 72
Konitz, Lee 74

Lacan, Jacques 145, 161
Landaluze, Víctor Patricio, *The Kiss* (Museo Nacional de Bellas Artes, Havana, Cuba) **30**
Lane, Jill 28–9, 33–4, 36, 39, 41
language, and music 1, 9–10, 13, 18–19, 26, 37, 46, 53, 55, 64, 68n, 76, 100, 102, 114–15, 119–20, 122–3, 127, 129, 132, 136, 143–4, 146, 158–9, 161
Latin America 4–5, 14–16, 25–6, 28, 34, 47, 62n, 66, 76, 104, 132n, 140, 145
Lea, James 129
Leal, Rine 27, 33–8, 41
Liberal Revolution of 1895 45, 49
limen, liminal, liminality 79, 134, 140–41
liminal *personae* 141
Limón, José E. 3n, 4n
linguistics 6
Living Portraits of Christ; *see Via Dolorosa*
Lomax family (John, Alan, and Bess) 3, 66
López, Álvaro 38–9
Los Conquistadores 57–**8**

MacCannell, Dean 154
Madariaga, Arnoldo 114–16
male 18, 39, 102, 106–11, **109**, 114–17, 119–20, 122, 149
man, men 34, 36, 39, 61, 78, 101, 104, 107, 109–11, 113, 117–18, 120–23, 143, 148, 152, 157
Mallku Kiririya Radio, Bolivia 143, 150, 158–9
Mallon, Florencia 43
mambo 73, 78
Manuel, Peter 82
"*mapolca*" 72
maracas 69, 75–7, 79, 84
mariachi 5, 47
marímbula lamellophone 76–**7**, 82
marriage, wedding; *see also* courtship 31, 36, 56, 68, 149, 157
masculinity 102; *see also* male, man
mazurca 72, 78
McLeod, Norma xiv, 3n, 7n, 8, 63
memory 25, 66, 69n, 71–2, 75, 129, 137–9, 146

memorial, commemoration xiii, 4n, 103
merengue 61, 67, 73
mestiza/o 16, 20, 43–6, 48–9, 55–9, 105n, 127–8, 130, 132–4, **133**, 136, 140, 146–52, 154, 156, 159–63
mestizaje 39, 45–6, 59, 146
metaphor 16, 33, 43–4, 50–1, 53, 68n, 92n, 110–11, 113, 119, 143
migration 4, 15, 17, 53, 57, 64–5, 70, 73, 83–4
mimesis 21, 162
mind 64, 93, 98
minstrelsy; *see* blackface
models 10, 41, 52, 68 78, 89–90, 160
Monson, Ingrid 95
moral, morality 11n, 19–20, 28, 34–5, 39–40, 123, 127–8, 130, 138–41
moral community 137, 139
Morton, Jelly Roll 66
movement, physical 14n, 15, 61, 83, 96–7, 135, 138, 163; *see also* dance; choreography
demographic 38, 75, 83
harmonic 106–7
rhythmic 20, 130
sociopolitical 25, 30, 33, 40, 43, 101, 104, 132n, 139–40
Mukařovský, Jan 6
mulata(s) 33, 35, 38–40; *see also* blackface character types
Muñoz, Angélica (Pepita) 119, 121, 123
Muramaya, Allu Chayantaka, Bolivia 155, 157–9
music; *see* dance; instruments; ensemble; rhythm; song; and names of specific musical genres
"music event" 8; *see also* musical occasion; performance occasion
música mexicana 47
música nacional 15–16, 43–50, 52–9
música nacional antigua 59
"musical anthropology" 9
musical nationalism 43; *see also* nationalism
musical occasion 7–9, 15n, 147; *see also* performance occasion

Index

191

musical space 18, 102
myth(ic), mythology 40, 137–40

"*nación criolla*" 49
nacional bailable 59
Napo Runa 138
narrative 11, 39, 64–5, 69, 72, 74, 109,
128–30
nationalism 2, 3n, 4, 15–16, 43
Nelson, Kristina 10
Nettl, Bruno 65
New York 51, 65, 66n, 68, 78, 80
NGO 143, 146, 149–50, 159–61, 163
Taypikala 143, 159
Nicaragua 132n
norteño 47

"objective reality" 95
occasion; *see* musical occasion;
performance occasion
Oller, Francisco, "El velorio" 70
"open society" 140
ontology 14, 17–18, 21
orality, and music 9; *see also* verbal art
Orta, Andrew 132n, 140
Ortega, Ingrid 110, 113, 123n

panpipes (*julajulas*, *sikus*, *sikuras*) 143,
148–9
Paredes, Américo xiii, 3, 4n
Parra, Violeta 103
participant observer 20, 151
participation 1–2, 17–20, 43, 101–2, 110,
116, 120, 123, 128–30, 134, 137
participatory performance 8, 20, 141,
145, 147, 149–50, 152, 156, 158,
160–61, 163
pasacalle 44, 48, 50, 52–3, 56, 58–9
pasillo 15–16, 44–7, 50–54, 56, 59
canciones de maldición 50
elite 46, 49–54, 56, 58
working class 53–4, 56
pasodoble 48
"pathoscape" 64
patterns 2, 8, 18, 79, 82–3, 93–100, 108
paya 18, 101–2, 104, 108–9, 111, 113–14,
117–22
payador/a/es 18, 102–4, 109–14, 116–23

perception 8, 16, 20, 43–4, 54, 57, 59,
91, 94–5, 98, 109, 117, 122–3,
129, 136
performance xiii, xiv, 1–15, 17–21, 25–6,
34, 44–5, 52–4, 57, 63, 96, 98,
100, 102–3, 106–11, 113–14,
116–23, 127–30, 132–9, 141,
143–5, 147–9, 152–63; *see also*
types of performance and names of
performances
performance occasion 1, 4, 6, 8n, 19–20,
44, 63, 136–7, 147–8, 153, 160–62
"performance of identity" 144–5
performance participation 8, 10, 19, 104,
141, 145, 147, 149–50, 152, 156,
158, 160–61, 163
performance practice xiv, 1, 5–6, 10, 17,
20–21, 44, 62–5, 67, 74–5, 77, 79,
81, 83–5, 118, 129, 147, 152, 160
performance space, venue 6, 18–20, 26,
33, 38–41, 50, 54, 56, 61–2, 75,
83, 89, 91, 96, 99, 103–4, 108,
112, 114, 117–22, 130, 133, 143,
150–54
performance studies 2–15, 17–21
performative acts 162–3
"performative utterance" 13
performativity 6, 11n, 12–14, 17, 20–21,
162
"performism" 19n
Peru 49, 57
philosophy
Buddhist 18, 89
Confucian 18, 89, 98–9
ontology 14, 17–18, 21
phenomenology 14, 18, 89–90
Pirque, Chile 102, 105n, 119–20
place xiv, 4, 21, 91–2, 107, 148–49; *see*
also space
plantation 17, 26–7, 29, 32–3, 63–5, 67–9,
72–5, 79, 81, 83–4
play 11, 94, 96–7, 100
plena 67
poesis 12
poetics 6, 17, 21, 138, 143–4
poetry 16–18, 21, 40, 46, 51, 53, 62,
67, 101–2, 111, 114, 116–17,
121–2

192   *Soundscapes from the Americas*

polca, polka 48, 72, 78
polca-ranchera 72
political community 139–41
politics, political activism xiii, xiv, 2–3, 6,
    11–12, 14–17, 19, 26–28, 31, 33,
    39, 41, 43, 45, 63, 104, 113n, 123,
    127–9, 132, 134, 139–41, 143–5,
    158–9
Ponce, David 116–7
popular music 5, 14–15, 25, 33, 39, 48–9,
    52, 53n, 55–6, 59, 82
populism, populist 34, 40–41, 101
postcolonialism 11
poststructuralism 11
Potosí, Bolivia 20, 143, 145–6
Pous, Arquímedes 33
power 3–4, 6, 12, 13n, 14–15, 18, 20–21,
    26, 36, 43, 45, 48, 54, 81, 97, 98,
    103, 123, 128–9, 136, 138–41,
    150, 162
Prague School of Linguistics 6
Proaño, Ana Lucía 53
professional, specialist 12, 18, 20, 40, 49,
    63, 69, 72, 102, 108, 110–11, 130,
    146, 152
professional performance 130; *see also*
    performance
Puente Alto, Chile 105n, 112
Puerto Rico 15, 17, 62, 64–5, 67–70,
    72–5, 79–84

Quechua, Quichua 19–20, 55, 127, 131–2,
    134, 143–4, 146, 155–58
Quito, Ecuador 45, 48n, 53–4, 56, 59

race 15–16, 27–8, 31, 34–5, 38–41, 46, 66
radio 50, 52, 57, 104, 143, 149, 151, 159
    Mallku Kiririya Radio 143, 150,
        158–9
    Radio Pío XII 150, 151n, 159
"Ramito" 67, 80
range, musical 80, 81n, 82, 91–2, 106–9
record labels
    Original Music 68
    Smithsonian 68
religion 5, 64, 128; *see also* names of
    specific faiths; philosophy

repetition, reiteration, redundancy 2, 13n,
    20, 37, 74n, 91, 97, 130–31, 132n,
    137–8, 156, 163
representation 3n, 4, 12, 16, 19n, 20,
    27–30, 32, 41, 45, 127, 129–30,
    132n, 134, 136, 139, 144–5, 161–2
requinto(s) 50, 52, 55, 70n, 81
rhumba; *see rumba*
rhythm 16, 20, 33, 44, 46, 49–50, 56–7,
    61, 72, 74, 77–9, 82–4, 91–2, 102,
    108, 130, 157, 159
rhythmic patterns
    anticipated bass 76, 79, 82–4
    Caribbean triplet 76
    son clave rhythm 82
    tresillo 33, 76, 82, 84
Ricoeur, Paul 21, 162
ritual, rite xiv, 3n, 4, 6, 8n, 9, 11, 13–15,
    19–20, 55, 128–31, 132n, 134–41,
    148
Roberts, John Storm 68, 78
rock 52, 61, 81–2, 97
rocolera 44, 48, 53–4, 56–8
Rodrigues, Eva the "Rhumba Queen" 76,
    82
Rodrigues, Miguel 70–**71**
Rubio, Alfonso 106, 112, 121
Rubio, Santos 108–9, 119
rumba/rhumba 34–5, 39, 69, 76–8, 84
rural 18, 38, 53, 73, 101–4, 105n, 108, 128,
    130, 143, 146–7, 150, 156, 160
Russell, Thomas 133

sainete rioplatense 26, 29, 38–9
Salas, Miguel 33–4, 38
Salomon, Frank 138–9
salsa 52, 61–2, 66–7, 74
Samson, Jim 79
San Juan festivities 55, 62, 48
sanjuanito(s) 15–16, 44–6, 48, 54–9
Santiago, Chile 18, 102, 108
Sarrachaga, Ignacio 27, 35, 39
Schechner, Richard 1, 6n, 10–13, 69
Schieffelin, Edward 14
seis 61–2, 66, 72–4, 82
Semana Santa (Holy Week) 19, 127, 136
"semantic snowballing" 54, 140

Index

semantics 18, 89
semiotics 129, 135
 Peircean 54, 129, 136
senses, sensory 12, 21, 129, 136, 162
septeto-style trumpet 79
Sewell, William 25
sexuality 18, 111, 123
 double entendres 56–7
"shared experiences" 99
Sherzer, Joel 3n, 6n
simulacrum 162
sinfonía button accordion 69
Singer, Milton xiv, 6–7, 147n
situated practice 18, 91
slavery, slave trade 16, 26–8, 38, 41
Slawek, Stephen 4, 90
social activism 11, 121; *see also* agency
social class, hierarchy 27, 34, 38, 40–41,
 43–8, 50, 53–4, 57–9, 65, 101n, 108
social theory 11
"socioesthetics" 11
song 2, 7n, 9, 10n, 14–15, 18, 20, 26,
 31–3, 35, 37, 39, 40, 44, 46, 48–55,
 57–9, 72–3, 102–3, 105, 117, 121,
 143–4, 147, 149–50, 153, 155–59,
 161; *see also cantos*; names of
 song genres
songbooks 45, 52
space xiii, 2, 3n, 74, 83, 91, 93–4, 100,
 103, 128, 138, 145, 149, 158, 163;
 see also place
 cultural 118
 musical 18, 102
 physical 93, 121
 public 123
Spain 16, 26, 29, 33, 35, 38, 104
spectacle 6, 9, 19–20, 78, 133
spiritual 99–100, 137
"staged authenticity" 154
Stations of the Cross 19–20, 127, 129,
 131, **133**–4, 139; *see also Via
 Dolorosa* or Way of Sorrows
stereotyping 20, 26n, 48, 58, 74, 154,
 160
Stewart, Kathleen 144
stochastic systems 91
Stoeltje, Beverly 3n
Stone, Ruth 8, 10

"strategic essentialism" 144; *see also*
 agency
"strategic auto-essentialism" 20, 154
structure, structural 2, 6, 7n, 8n, 9, 13n,
 38, 73–4, 80, 82, 91, 93–6, 100,
 103, 105n, 118, 123, 129, 134,
 140–41
 class 16, 65; *see also* social class,
 hierarchy
 event 18
 musical 17
 power 13n, 36, 43, 55
 social 9
Stutzman, Ronald 43, 46
subaltern, subalterity 4, 11, 20, 128, 140,
 160–61
subjectivity 13–14, 17, 20–21, 138, 144–5,
 161–3
"subjectivity package" 21, 162
synchronization 93, 100
Szemiński, Jan 138

Taki Unquy (*Taki Onqoy*) 138
Tamisari, Franca 138–9, 141
Teatro Alhambra 33
teatro bufo
 character types in; *see* blackface
 character types
 defined 15–16, 26–7, 40–41
 early era (1810–1867) 29–33
 early revolutionary period 33–8
 late nineteenth century 38–40
 racial relationships 28–9
Teatro de Villanueva 37
"technologies of Othering" 58
tecnocumbia 56–9
temporal, temporality xiv, 6, 13, 17, 20,
 90, 130–31, 158
Ten Years War 33
Tercer Festival de Música Chayantaka 157
textual object xiii, 5
theater 6, 10–11, 15, 18, 25–6, 28–9,
 33–41, 54, 73; *see also* blackface
"thick present" 90, 100
timbre 16, 46, 53, 62, 84, 93n, 103, 105n,
 107, 109
tiple(s) 70n, 81
tonadilla 29, 39

194   *Soundscapes from the Americas*

toquíos 106, 109
Toro, "Yomo" 80
tourism 11n, 15n, 19–20, 127, 129–30,
    133–4
tradition 2, 5, 14, 18–19, 26, 41, 46, 48,
    55, 62n, 63–5, 67–9, 71n, 72–6, 78,
    81, 84, 89, 91, 93n, 95–8, 100–104,
    105n, 108, 113–16, 123, 127–8,
    132, 137, 144, 147–8, 150–52,
    154–5, 159
transformation, transformative 13–14, 16,
    18, 20, 29n, 43, 89, 94, 98–100,
    128, 132n, 134, 136–9, 141
tres 70, 108n
tresillo 33, 76, 82–4
Trío Los Brillantes 52
Trouillot, Michel-Rolph 48
tuning 81, 106–7
Turino, Thomas 2n, 3n, 4n, 6n, 12n, 28,
    44n, 54, 56, 129, 135–6, 138, 140,
    147n
"turn to performance" 5
Turner, Victor 1, 6, 10–11, 129, 134, 137,
    140–41

ukelele(s) 80
Ulloa, Osvaldo 103
Union of Peasant Organizations of
    Cotacachi (UNORCAC) 132
United States 26–9, 36, 41, 112
unity 48, 57, 93, 98–100, 135
University of Texas at Austin xiii, 4, 90
urban, urbanization 5, 17, 19–20, 26–7,
    34, 36, 38, 44, 48–9, 52–3, 55–6,
    64–5, 69, 75, 81n, 83, 101, 104,

    105n, 108, 127–8, 130, 134, 139,
    143, 150, 152, 156, 159
Urban, Greg 3n
Uzendoski, Michael 138

Valdano, Juan 49
Valdés, Jacinto 33, 37
vals(es) 54, 72, 73n
vals criollo 47
verbal art xiii, 1, 5, 7
versos 101, 103, 112
Via Crucis 132n
Via Dolorosa (Way of Sorrows) 19, 127,
    131, 139
    cuadros vivos (living portraits of) 127,
        129–30, 132, 134, **135**
vigilia; *see cantos*
Vilarós, Francisco Fernández 35–6

wakas, huacas 137–9
Waxer, Lise 69
Way of Sorrows; *see Via Dolorosa*
wayñu, huayno 47, 155–6, 158–9
"web of action" 18, 191
Whitten, Jr., Norman 46, 128, 138
woman, women 18, 30, 34–5, 39, 50, 54,
    78, 101–2, 106, 108–23, 131–2,
    144, 156; *see also* female
World War II 76–7, 82, 84

yaravíes 48

Zamorano, Águeda 101
zarzuela 35, 40
Zea, Leopoldo 28